CORPORATE
CONTROL AND BUSINESS BEHAVIOR

CORPORATE
CONTROL AND

an inquiry into the effects of

PRENTICE HALL, INC., Englewood Cliffs, New Jersey

Oliver E. Williamson
University of Pennsylvania

BUSINESS BEHAVIOR

organization form on enterprise behavior

CORPORATE CONTROL AND BUSINESS BEHAVIOR
Oliver E. Williamson

© 1970 by Prentice-Hall, Inc., Englewood Cliffs, New Jersey

13-173203-**X**
Library of Congress Catalog Card Number: 72-117527

Current printing (last digit)

10 9 8 7 6 5 4 3 2 1

Printed in the United States of America

Prentice-Hall International, Inc., *London*
Prentice-Hall of Australia, Pty. Ltd. *Sydney*
Prentice-Hall of Canada, Ltd., *Toronto*
Prentice-Hall of India (Private) Ltd., *New Delhi*
Prentice-Hall of Japan, Inc., *Tokyo*

to my father

preface

Although few would dispute the claim that the modern corporation is a remarkable institution, there is less general agreement over the factors that are responsible for this condition. A proposition advanced here is that its vitality is attributable in large part to organizational innovations that have permitted the corporation to limit the degree of control loss and subgoal pursuit that, without innovation, were predictable consequences of large size. Rather than be overcome by what otherwise would have been serious bureaucratic disabilities, the corporation has responded with a demonstrated capacity for self-renewal. One of the purposes of this book is to examine whether and for what reasons these changes have transformed the large corporation from its antecedents of some thirty or more years ago.

The analysis is in two parts. The first part, which pulls together several of my earlier pieces, is concerned with the phenomenon of managerial discretion: What is responsible for it, what limits does it experience, and what are its consequences? This is all conducted in the context of what will be referred to as the "traditional" or unitary form of organization. The second part considers organizational innovation and its influence on goal pursuit and internal efficiency. The organization form treated there will be referred to as the "modern" or multidivision structure.

Although the transformation of the large corporation from the unitary to the multidivision form has not gone undetected, its significance for the theory of the firm and as a manifestation of capitalist dynamics has been largely undeveloped. In particular, essential connections between organizational innovation and corporate control have been neglected. One of the reasons for this, probably, is the general reluctance among economists to concede that a corporate control problem has ever existed. Among those who take "managerialist" theories of the firm at all seriously, however, concern over the disposition of discretionary opportunities is a matter of genuine importance. The organization form analysis developed here is directly concerned with the consequences of internal organization as they relate to corporate control and, hence, to managerial discretion.

Most previous treatments of corporate control, including my own, have focused mainly on *external control* forces. What I regard as distinctive about the present theory is that it examines how, through changes in organization form, the corporation has been able to mobilize the much more powerful forces of *internal control* to shrink opportunities for discretion. Enterprise behavior emerges that conforms (more nearly than would otherwise have obtained) to that which is imputed to the firm under the neoclassical profit maximization hypothesis.

Some will regard as paradoxical the fact that that support for the neoclassical hypothesis should result from a study that has managerialist origins. I do not really regard this as paradoxical myself. For one thing, the neoclassical result has always been a special case of the managerialist models. Organization form analysis does not upset this general proposition but merely makes evident the circumstances under which the special case may become prevailing. In addition, the managerialist literature has generally emphasized the important connections between rudimentary organization theory and economic theory, while the neoclassical literature has rather neglected these relations. If anything, therefore, it would be more paradoxical if an approach to firm behavior that did not regard internal organization as a relevant dimension were to discover that internal control had "solved" the discretionary dilemma.

I have occasionally been asked by those who read early versions of the manuscript what it was that was responsible for my "vision on the road to Damascus." There is no single answer. Among the factors that contributed to it are the following: (1) a continuing desire to explain in a systematic way the variety and vitality of observed business behavior; (2) a year spent with the Antitrust Division of the Department of Justice during which, among other things, the need to understand the conglomerate phenomenon became particularly apparent; (3) a reading of the superlative historical survey of 20th century corporate organization by Alfred D. Chandler, Jr.; (4) fascination with competition in the capital market arguments. Collectively, I would judge, these are the most important influences that have contributed to the outcome.

In a book that traces its origins back to my dissertation, it is appropriate that I begin my acknowledgments by recalling those at Carnegie who were most responsible for my interest in the firm as an object of analysis: R. M. Cyert and Herbert Simon. A group brought together by Armen Alchian and Roland McKean to study aspects of the "economics of property rights" at UCLA one summer also provided stimulation. At Pennsylvania I have had the frequent counsel of D. W. Conrath and Almarin Phillips. Reviews of the manuscript by William Comanor, Joseph McGuire, Lee Preston, and James Mckie helped me to put the argument in sharper perspective. Finally, my lawyer friends from the Department of Justice (many of whom are now engaged in practice or academic pursuits) will detect that aspects of our numerous controversies have found their way into these pages. To each I express my appreciation.

I wish also to thank the following journals and publishers for permission to borrow freely from earlier published materials: the *American Economic Review*, the *Journal of Political Economy*, the American Enterprise Institute, the Markham Publishing Company, and the University of Pennsylvania Press. Mrs. Ella Schmid typed much of the manuscript, some of it under conditions that must be regarded as trying. Her cheerful response to my "demands" has been greatly appreciated.

I have been fortunate to receive research support from the National Science Foundation over most of the period during which various pieces of the manuscript were originally developed. Initial work on the material appearing in Chapters 7 to 10 was supported by the Harvard University Program on Technology and Society under a long-term grant from the International Business Machines Corporation. Research support from The Brookings Institution has permitted me to put the final version in order. I am grateful to each.

Finally, I should like to express my particular gratitude to my wife and children for what, in many respects, must be regarded as a uniquely stimulating research atmosphere—complete with essential diversions as well as opportunities for retreat. The individual assistance that each has rendered in his special way is deeply appreciated; the cooperative aspects of this endeavor have been manifold.

OLIVER E. WILLIAMSON

contents

PART I
THE UNITARY FORM ORGANIZATION

1
introduction   3

2
rationale for the multifunction firm   14

3
subgoal pursuit and the managerial discretion phenomenon   41

4
managerial discretion in the unitary from corporation:
static aspects   54

xi

5
managerial discretion in the unitary form corporation:
dynamic aspects   *74*

6
competition in the capital market in relation to
unitary form behavior   *89*

PART II
THE MULTIDIVISION FORM ORGANIZATION

7
the multidivision form innovation   *109*

8
properties of the multidivision form   *120*

9
applications of the multidivision form hypothesis   *136*

10
qualifications to the multidivision form hypothesis   *154*

11
concluding remarks   *168*

index   *192*

THE
UNITARY
FORM
ORGANIZATION

1

introduction

It is the purpose of this book to offer some new perspectives regarding the behavior of the modern corporation. The book is concerned to a large extent with aspects of hierarchical decision-making and control. This emphasis on hierarchy is only incidentally a matter of who reports to whom in the chain of command; it is mainly concerned with the important and pervasive effects of organization structure on goal formation and internal efficiency. This focus on internal organization places the study on more of a micro-level than is characteristic of traditional treatments of the theory of the firm. At the same time, its organization theory inputs must be regarded as being relatively gross and rudimentary. Falling, as it does, between the level of aggregation employed by traditional economic treatments of the firm and that of modern organization theory, the analysis might be said to be intermediate level in its emphasis. The intent is to be sensitive to, without being swamped by, institutional detail.

3

1
THE CORPORATE CONTROL
DILEMMA

Corporate control has been regarded as a serious social problem at least since Adolph A. Berle, Jr. and Gardiner Means exposed it as such in the early 1930s [31]. However, many who have studied the corporation carefully have been struck by what, given the apparent latitude for misdemeaning behavior that the corporation sometimes enjoys, often appears to be quite remarkable performance. Edward S. Mason, for one, has expressed puzzlement over this condition [112, p. 4]:

> It is . . . generally recognized that, in the United States, the large corporation undertakes a substantial part of total economic activity, however measured; that the power of corporations to act is by no means so thoroughly circumscribed by the market as was generally thought to be true of nineteenth-century enterprise; and that, in addition to market power, the large corporation exercises a considerable degree of control over nonmarket activities of various sorts. What all this seems to add up to is the existence of important centers of private power in the hands of men whose authority is real but whose responsibilities are vague. . . .
>
> All this is very interesting but very unsatisfactory, particularly to the intellectual who is bothered by apparent missing links in the chain of authority and by a seeming equilibrium of forces that by every right should be disequilibrating. The nineteenth century produced a social doctrine that not only explained but justified. But the functioning of the corporate system has not to date been adequately explained, or, if certain explanations are accepted as adequate, it seems difficult to justify.

Although I do not pretend to have disposed of these troublesome issues here, it is intended that the argument have some bearing on them. Of special importance are the unsuspected equilibrating tendencies of organizational innovations and of the processes of internal control that have been developed over the past fifty years.

2
QUANTITATIVE SUBSTANTIALITY

A. S. Miller takes the position that "America is a society that gets its tone from and whose economy is dominated by a rather small number of giant enterprises. Not more than four of five hundred corporations, to take *Fortune* magazine's annual listing, are the economic entities that set the pace for the remainder of the economy"

[**116**, p. 7]. Miller's view is shared by other social critics in the United States [**32**] [**64**]. Unfortunately, despite its importance, social domination is not a very precise notion; its defining characteristics and consequences tend often to be ill-specified. But the quantitative substantiality of the modern, large corporation is easy to establish.

Manufacturing, mining, and the regulated industries (transportation, communication, and public utilities) accounted for 30.6 percent, 1.1 percent, and 8.1 percent, respectively, of net national income in 1965. The figures for employment compensation for these three sectors were roughly the same. Although other indices could be worked up, it is doubtful that aggregate measures having general economic significance would show the combined activity of these sectors to differ greatly from 40 percent of the total. While the 1965 figures are somewhat lower than those for 1954, these combined sectors, at present and for the foreseeable future, account for a substantial share of the national product. A detailed breakdown by sector is given in Table 1-1.

TABLE 1-1

Percent of Net National Income and Employment Compensation, by Economic Sector, 1954 and 1965

Sector	1954		1965	
	NNI	Employment Compensation	NNI	Employment Compensation
Manufacturing	31.2	34.3	30.6	33.1
Mining	1.7	1.8	1.1	1.2
Transportation, communication, public utilities	8.4	9.1	8.1	7.8
Agriculture, forestry, fisheries	5.4	1.7	3.7	0.9
Wholesale and retail trade	15.9	17.4	14.9	16.1
Contract Construction	5.1	5.7	5.2	5.9
Services	9.2	8.8	11.4	11.1
Finance, insurance, real estate	10.5	4.2	11.0	4.7
Government	11.9	17.0	13.3	19.1
Other	0.5	—	0.7	—

Sources: Column 1: *Survey of Current Business*, July, 1968, p. 23; column 2: *ibid.*, p. 41; column 3: *ibid.*, August, 1965, p. 44; column 4: *ibid.*, July, 1955, p. 14.

TABLE 1-2

**Percent of Business Receipts Accounted for by
Corporate Form of Organization, by Economic
Sector, 1954 and 1965**

Sector	1954	1965
Manufacturing	94.5	97.5
Mining	81.2	87.1
Transportation, communication, public utilities	91.2	92.7
Agriculture, forestry, fisheries	8.1	16.3
Wholesale and retail trade	56.6	73.4
Contract Construction	47.2	68.1
Services	35.0	46.5
Finance, insurance, real estate	66.3	81.6
Government	N.A.	N.A.
Other	13.6	U.

"N.A." denotes that the classification is "not applicable" to this category; "U." that the data is "unavailable."

Source: Derived from *Statistics of Income*, Corporate Tax Returns and Business Tax Returns. The data are complied on a fiscal-year basis.

Enterprises organized under the corporate form accounted for 97.5 percent of total business receipts in manufacturing, 87.1 percent in mining, and 92.7 percent in regulated industry in 1965—an increase in each instance over the corresponding 1954 figure. While corporate enterprise is less dominant in other sectors (see Table 1-2), these three industrialized sectors are the ones of principal interest to us here: manufacturing, mining, and regulated industry, accounting for about 40 percent of the total economic product of the nation and within which the corporate form is predominant, constitute the subset of the economy to which our analysis is addressed.

Among the corporations in these three sectors, interest will be directed especially toward the larger firms. The 100, 200, and 500 largest industrials accounted for 36, 45, and 56 percent respectively of business receipts in the manufacturing and mining sectors.[1] Inspection of Table 1-3 reveals that the corresponding figures for employment were roughly identical; asset concentration ran higher; value added was somewhat lower. An increase over the corresponding 1954 percentages occured in every category. Table 1-4 reveals even greater dominance by the largest firms in public utilities (which here includes communications) and transportation.

TABLE 1-3

**Percent of Sales, Employment, Assets, and Value Added
by Largest Corporations in Manufacturing and Mining,
1954 and 1965**

Largest Firms	Fortune Industrials				Manufacturing			
	Sales		Employment		Assets		Value Added	
	1954*	1965	1954*	1965	1955	1965	1954	1963
5	8	10	8	9				
10	11	14	10	12				
25	17	21	16	19				
50	23	28	22	27			23	25
100	29	36	29	36	44	46	30	33
200	36	45	36	46	46	56	37	41
500	45	56	47	59				

* Ford Motor Company not included in 1954 data on largest industrials.

Sources: Fortune Industrial Series: July 1955 Supplement and July 15, 1966 *Fortune.*
Manufacturing Assets: Staff Studies, *Cabinet Committee on Price Stability,*
Washington, D.C. 1969, p. 92.
Value Added: Bureau of the Census, *Concentration Ratios in Manufacturing
Industry,* 1963, Washington, D.C., 1966, p. 2.

TABLE 1-4

**Percent of Operating Revenues Accounted for by
the Largest Firms in Utilities and Transportation, 1965**

Largest firms	Utilities	Transportation
5	29.2*	9.3
10	34.7	16.4
25	45.4	27.1
50	56.3	33.9

* Over 80 percent of the operating revenues of the 5 largest utilities are accounted for
by AT&T.

Source: Derived from *Fortune, 500 Largest Industrials,* July 15, 1966. (Corporations
ranked by assets.)

Although interest in the corporate control question need not be
limited exclusively to these large firms, much of it properly is. Within
this large-firm universe, it will occasionally be useful to distinguish
a giant-firm subset. Arbitrarily, this will be taken to be the 25 largest
industrials, the 10 largest utilities, and the 10 largest transportation
firms—which corresponds, approximately, to the subset of firms in

these three sectors with assets in 1967 in excess of $2 billion. Of the large-firm universe (500 industrials, 50 utilities, and 50 transportation companies) the giants account for roughly 40 percent of the business receipts in the industrial sector, 60 percent in utilities and 50 percent in transportation. Thus, of the 40 percent of national income and employment attributable to manufacturing, mining, transportation, and public utilities, large firms in these sectors account for somewhat over one-half, and the giant-sized subset for almost one-fourth, of the total.

Although these are not trivial proportions, they do not clearly constitute dominance.[2] Even allowing for significant "leadership" by the large-firm core, so that activity initiated there has, through imitation or market processes, substantial spillover (both on smaller firms in the industrialized sectors and on firms and other economic organizations outside), it is presumptuous to suggest that an analysis which focuses on these large firms is addressed to *most* of what is relevant in the American economy. To claim that it is concerned with *much* of what is relevant is, however, sufficient for our purposes.

3
ALTERNATIVE APPROACHES
TO THE CORPORATE CONTROL ISSUE

Three approaches to the corporate control issue will be distinguished. The first two, which will be dealt with briefly here, can be characterized as the traditional approaches and recent alternatives. The third approach, which is discussed in the next section and occupies our attention throughout much of the book, is internal or self-regulatory control.

Competition in the product market and/or competition in the capital market are the usual bases upon which a priori standing for the profit maximization hypothesis is established [4] [5]. The latter is a back-up argument and is invoked when, for whatever reason, competition in the product market is weak or lacking. Although widely embraced, the competition in the capital market argument is less well developed. An evaluation of its adequacy, in both old and new forms, will be deferred to Chapters 6 and 9. Provisionally, it will be assumed that competition in the capital market provides a partial but incomplete substitute for intensive product market competition.

A permissive product market is usually attributable to market structure conditions—mainly, high concentration in combination with barriers to entry, which may include franchise limitations of regulatory agencies. But it can also be due, as Kenneth Arrow has pointed out [11], to temporary (but not necessarily short) periods of excess demand. Collusion provides still a third, if somewhat more tenuous, basis. Relief from the pressures of competition in the product market for any of these reasons provides the firm with a nontrivial opportunity set upon which to operate, where by "opportunity set" is meant the region of nonnegative profits.

The quantitative significance of the structural conditions which commonly result in the attenuation of product market competition of the first type has been characterized by Carl Kaysen as follows [83, pp. 45–46]:

> Not all industries which have oligopolistic structures depart significantly from competitive behavior; but in the absence of detailed study of particular markets, the existence of oligopoly structures at least raises the question. Besides the oligopolistic markets in mining and manufacturing, we should take into account transportation and public utilities. These are regulated industries, but the regulatory constraints are often loose, or even perverse; typical firms are large, and "natural" market structures in them are oligopolistic or even monopolistic. Together, these sectors and the oligopolistic sectors in mining and manufacturing produce at least 20% and probably more like 25% of the national income. . . . We can certainly say the broad picture is not that of an episodic or negligible phenomenon.

The intersection of this oligopolistic and regulated group of industries with the large-firm universe constitutes, for the most part, the policy-relevant subset of interest to us here.

Among the administrative or regulatory alternatives to product and capital market competition that have been considered from time to time as means of controlling the exercise of managerial discretion are more extensive accounting discloure, the professionalization of management, "jawbone" control, and more vigorous antitrust enforcement. These are even less well developed arguments than that of competition in the capital market. No attempt will be made to evaluate them here other than to express general skepticism that disclosure and jawbone control are apt to have really pervasive consequences,[3] while antitrust experiences formidable political obstacles,[4] and professionalization can perhaps best be treated in the context of organization form analysis.

4
THE PROPOSED APPROACH

That the corporation might, through appropriate restructuring, overcome discretionary tendencies by invoking internal control processes has, for the most part, gone unexplored. The issue can be posed as follows: How does organization form influence goal formation and the efficacy of various internal control devices? The goal formation aspect of the argument is not even meaningfully posed within the neoclassical framework; goals other than profit maximization are usually disallowed from the outset.[5] Neoclassical analysis likewise finesses the question of internal control techniques by assuming, implicitly, that the firm is appropriately adapted in this respect—which can hardly be said to face the issue. To hold otherwise, however, is to challenge foundations. It is not accidental that an examination of the efficiency of internal controls in general, much less in relation to organization form, has typically been ignored in the traditional literature.

The managerialist approaches, by contrast, begin by focusing explicitly on discretionary conditions. An advance commitment to the profit maximization assumption is thereby avoided. Despite being freed up in this respect, however, this literature has likewise neglected the importance of organization form differences. Usually, the organization form implicit in the analysis has been the functional or unitary form of organization. Here the principal operating parts are functional divisions (manufacturing, marketing, finance, etc.), each of which has parochial interests. For the reasons given in Chapter 3, enterprise behavior typically emerges in a way that gives effect to these underlying functional considerations.

Of the variety of alternative organization structures, the most important, and the one which the analysis here addresses, is the multidivision form.[6] The principal operating parts of this organization form are semiautonomous operating divisions, each of which is subsequently organized along functional lines. These operating divisions report to a general office that is at least formally responsible for overall enterprise activity and is assisted by an elite staff. Among the principal questions to be investigated is how and for what reasons a simple shift of a large unitary form organization to a multidivision structure influences goal formation and internal efficiency.

5
ORGANIZATION
OF THE ANALYSIS

The rationale for the multifunction firm, the process of firm growth, and limitations to firm size are examined in Chapter 2. The unitary form structure is assumed to prevail here and throughout the next five chapters. The effects of bounded rationality on firm size are manifested in what will be referred to as the "control loss" phenomenon. Costs of this sort must be set off against the integrative shortcomings that the market experiences (commonly referred to as market "failures") in determining the overall configuration of the firm.

Chapter 3 is concerned with the emergence, under the unitary form of organization, of the managerial discretion phenomenon. Discretionary opportunities in the unitary form enterprise will be assumed to vary directly with the degree to which product market competition has been attenuated and with firm size. Large size is necessary for the effects of bounded rationality on strategic decision-making (and hence goal pursuit) to be significant, and for the control loss experience cumulatively to become great.

Chapters 4 and 5 are an effort to model the discretionary behavior which Chapter 3 describes. Static aspects of this behavior, using both variable and fixed proportions models, are examined in Chapter 4. Dynamic-stochastic aspects are considered in Chapter 5. Chapter 4 includes a special application of the argument to the behavior of public utilities, while Chapter 5 considers the implications of the argument for business pricing decisions.

The ways in which competition in the capital market influences behavior in the unitary form enterprise are examined in Chapter 6. The treatment examines the conventional arguments in conventional terms—in other words, the relation of organization form to capital market competition is not treated here; the unitary form is assumed everywhere to prevail. Within this paradigm, the capital market arguments are found to be less than wholly efficacious in producing the intended effects.

A summary of the properties of the unitary form organization is provided in Chapter 7. This sets the stage for the analysis of the multidivision form as an organizational alternative. The circumstances that led to this innovation are then briefly examined. The structural characteristics of the multidivision form, including an examination of its strategic decision-making and internal control properties, are developed in Chapter 8. The superior goal pursuit and internal efficiency consequences of this organization form are shown to be a natural result of these design changes.

A series of implications and qualifications to the multidivision form hypothesis are given in Chapters 9 and 10. Shifting from a firm to a systems context permits its product and capital market impact to be assessed. Among the more important implications are the significance of this organization form for the vitality of capitalism. The potential economies attributable to "conglomerate" organization are also noted. Among the more important qualifications are the bounds on firm size that this organization form experiences and its limitations with respect to technical innovation.

A brief recapitulation of the elementary organizational inputs to the argument is provided in Chapter 11, which concludes with a sketch of certain policy implications.

The mathematical modeling effort, such as it is, is concentrated in the early chapters of the book where the focus is mainly on managerial models. Some may regard this effort as disproportionately distributed. With respect to the book itself, this may be true. Viewed more broadly, however, in the context of the literature on the theory of the firm, it is less clear that a misallocation is involved. For one thing, the argument in the later chapters supports (up to a first approximation at least) more general use of the neoclassical profit maximization hypothesis. The conventional economics and management science models that rely on this assumption are already well developed. Managerial models, by contrast, have been much less thoroughly explored in the standard literature. In addition, the neoclassical assumption can be regarded as a special case of the utility-maximizing hypothesis, and thus can be subsumed within managerial discretion analysis by characterizing the utility function appropriately. Finally, to the extent that the multidivision form enterprise permits opportunities for discretion to pass by default to the operating divisions, with subsequent discretionary consequences, the managerial behavior observed is apt to be of the sort described in the earlier chapters. Thus, although the wholly "new" parts of the argument (insofar as my contributions to this literature are concerned) are mainly in the later chapters, the mathematical modeling is concentrated in the forward parts.

It is relevant to note in this regard that the policy implications of the multidivision form innovation are a relatively neglected aspect of this development. The internal pricing rules for the divisionalized structure are, by comparison, well worked out (as illustrated, for example, by [25] [44]). But, as perhaps should be expected of any significant organizational change, the economic impact of this innovation greatly transcends its immediate efficiency consequences. The present study, therefore, shifts the analytical emphasis to address problems more commonly of interest to industrial organization specialists. A distribution of effort emerges that is different from that characteristic of the management science literature. Among the extra-technical issues that the present analysis raises and, in varying degrees, attempts to assess are the following: the influence of role design on corporate goal pursuit; the similarities and distinctive differences between internal and external controls, with special attention to the ways by which internal control techniques in the multidivision enterprise permit certain capital market failures substantially to be overcome; the symbiotic relations that, in a systems sense, develop between internal and external controls; the significance of organizational innovation to the evolution of capitalism and to the enforcement of antitrust. Thus the focus is on policy matters that fall outside the usual purview of management science but that, nevertheless, have a vital bearing on an evaluation of the performance of an enterprise system.

FOOTNOTES

[1] Total business receipts in manufacturing and mining (as reported to the Internal Revenue Service) constitute the base in computing the percentage of sales accounted for by the largest industrial firms in the *Fortune* 500 series. Variations in accounting practices may result in slight discrepancies between sales and business receipts; also, the business activities of industrial firms in the *Fortune* 500 series may sometimes include sales and employment in sectors other than manufacturing and mining. The basic argument is unaffected, however, by a correction of a few percentage points either way.

[2] In part the growth of these largest industrials may be attributed to diversification into other sectors, especially services, during the 1954–65 interval. But much of it has remained within, as is evidenced by the fact that the percentage value added by manufacture attributable to the 50, 100, and 200 largest manufacturing companies in 1963 was uniformly greater than the corresponding percentages in 1954. (See Table 1-3.)

[3] For a brief (and inconclusive) discussion of each of these, see [165, pp. 330–34].

[4] As every Assistant Attorney General for Antitrust has quickly come to appreciate, activating antitrust is more easily said than done. Vigorous enforcement of antimerger legislation can be important in this connection, but attacking established enterprise presents quite another problem. For a recent admission of these difficulties by a chief of the Antitrust Division, see [60, p. 23].

[5] The economic natural selection support for the neoclassical hypothesis relies more on a process than on behavioral assumptions [4] [61]. This makes this approach more appealing in many respects, but leaves the argument vulnerable when product market competition is attenuated [160, pp. 19–21].

[6] Another form of organization believed to have desirable characteristics in firms involved in a number of relatively small, short-duration projects (and also used extensively for aerospace contracting) is the "matrix" structure. This involves superimposing a project management structure on a functional or unitary form organization, "creating a 'matrix' of vertical and horizontal relationships. Under such an organizational arrangement, personnel from the various functional departments (e.g., research scientists, engineers, machinists, etc.) are assigned to projects on a temporary basis as their particular skills are required. These personnel remain permanently assigned to their functional departments, however, and effectively work for both the project manager and the functional manager." (D. W. Conrath and W. F. Hamilton, "The Economics of Manpower Pooling," Working Paper No. 101, Department of Industry, Wharton School of Finance and Commerce, 1969.)

2

internal organization
and limits
to firm size[*]

The multiperson, multifunction enterprise is so commonplace that to imagine that productive activity might be organized in any other way requires genuine effort. It will nevertheless be useful, for purposes of understanding internal organization and the control of enterprise behavior, to begin with an examination of the rudimentary reasons for the multifunction firm. The process of expanding firm size is considered next. Two alternative expansion processes are described: amplification and multidivisionalization. The focus in this chapter is on the former. The amplification of a functionally organized firm is shown to experience control losses which cumulatively are responsible for a limitation to firm size.

*Portions of this chapter have been reprinted from O.E. Williamson, "Hierarchical Control and Optimum Firm Size," *Journal of Political Economy*, 75, April, 1967, 123–38.

1
RATIONALE FOR THE
MULTIFUNCTION FIRM

Suppose that a task is broken down into a series of elementary operations. The differential distribution of talents and the acquisition of skill through drill are sufficient to explain why it may be advantageous to have some of these operations performed by distinct individuals rather than to have each bring the task to completion by himself. If, however, no stage experiences indivisibilities, each step might be performed by a single individual with market transactions mediating the exchanges between stages.

Invoking claims of indivisibilities may make it attractive to bring several individuals together to perform a single stage, and on this account intrastage coordination might be provided by an administrator. But this is administrative coordination of a most limited variety —of the sort that Frank Knight characterized as routine [**87**, p. 268]. Moreover, all that is involved is the multiperson operation of a single stage; the multifunction firm, which combines several separable stages, is not justified on these grounds.[1] What explains this phenomenon?

This question has already been raised by Ronald Coase in his classic discussion of the issue: Why, since the price mechanism has integrating properties that permit decentralized decision-making, does one also observe centralized (administrative) decision-making being used to perform this integrating function across several technically separable activities [**45**, p. 344]?

Actually, although this is perhaps the usual way for economists to consider the matter of integration, there is an alternative way to view it. After all, administrative coordination antedates market exchange. Why has market exchange displaced it?

Whichever way the question is put, it is obvious that neither administrative nor market exchange integration has completely prevailed. Each, presumably, has characteristic strengths and weaknesses. It will be our purpose in this section to consider some of the limits that market mediation experiences. Administrative weaknesses will be examined subsequently.

Three reasons will be offered to explain the multifunction, administratively coordinated enterprise: incomplete information regarding the present state of the world, transaction costs, and uncertainty with respect to the future. Although these are sometimes regarded as sources of market "failure," they are at the same time elementary properties of the system rather than aberrations thereof. Much of what is considered interesting economic behavior dissolves if these conditions are removed.

Supplanting the price mechanism of course becomes attractive in relation to the costs experienced in using it [**45**, p. 336]. Information is incomplete if all of the relevant prices are not continuously known to all of the potential transactors. The opportunity costs of expending the effort or resources necessary to become informed thus constitutes one of the costs of using the price system. In addition, there are costs of negotiating contracts once prices are known. Although costs of both types would, over time, asymptotically approach zero in a perfectly static world, this is not an especially interesting condition. It does not correspond to the universe with which we mean to deal.

The existence of such costs naturally provides an incentive to explore devices for circumventing the market. The entrepreneur can be regarded as an individual who brings together several related processes and internalizes what would otherwise be a series of market transactions. This continues until the administrative expense of bringing the incremental unit under common control is just equal to the cost of using the market for this purpose.

Among the costs that may be overcome in this way are those that are commonly referred to as externalities. With perfect information and zero transaction costs, bargaining can be relied on to drive the system to an allocatively efficient result [**46**] [**54**]. In the absence of these conditions, however, incomplete adaptation to externalities can be expected to obtain. Given the incorrect signals that the price system affords in these circumstances, an incentive exists to combine the interacting parts and substitute an administrative solution for the defective market solution. Such an adaptation to an externality problem is referred to as internalizing the externality [**51**].

Uncertainty affords still another reason for the multifunction firm to emerge. Two elements have been adduced to explain the development of the firm on this account: the "moral" factor and the differential capacity to bear risk. Only the former would appear to have true multifunction consequences; the differential capacity to bear risk, which Frank Knight regards as the distinguishing characteristic of entrepreneurship and as being responsible for the enterprise system as we know it, might support greater size but does not clearly require multifunction operations. As Knight points out, in the absence of uncertainty there is no occasion for entrepreneurship to develop. The introduction of uncertainty, however, makes it attractive to organize in such a way as to permit "the confident and venturesome [to] 'assume the risk' or 'insure' the doubtful and timid by guaranteeing to the latter a specified income in return for an assignment of the actual results" [**87**, pp. 269–70]. He goes on to observe that the "result of this manifold specialization function is *enterprise and the wage system of industry*" [**87**, p. 271]. Yet if by the enterprise system he means to include the multifunction firm, the argument is overextended. Entrepreneurship might, because of intrinsic indivisibilities connected with the supply of this factor, give rise to larger single-function organizations than would otherwise result. Multifunction operations, however, need not obtain on this account.

The "moral" factor is referred to in the insurance literature as a condition which, by dulling the incentives of the insured, affects the terms on which insurance will be offered [**14**] [**12**, pp. 612–14]. A fire insurance policy, for example, weakens the incentive to protect against fire. This is a particular example of a more general phenomenon that Kenneth Arrow refers to as the confounding of risks and decisions: "In general, any system which, in effect, insures against adverse final outcomes automatically reduces the incentives to good decision making" [**14**, p. 55]. Thus, consider the problem of contracting for an item the final cost and/or performance of which are subject to considerable uncertainty. Someone has to bear the risk. One possibility is for the seller to bear it. But he will undertake a fixed price contract to deliver a specified result the costs of which are highly uncertain only after attaching a large risk premium to the price. Alternatively, the buyer may bear the risk by offering a cost-plus contract. But this impairs the incentives of the seller to achieve least-cost performance. A mixture of intermediate risk-sharing arrangements is possible [**161**]. One outcome with especially attractive properties is vertical integration; a cost-plus equivalent is in this way arranged which overcomes (internalizes) the moral hazard. A multifunction enterprise thereby results.

A variety of market failure that has both uncertainty and transaction cost aspects is haggling. This can be illustrated by considering again the problem of adapting appropriately to externalities. Suppose that the marginal private net benefits of an activity are a decreasing function of output. Assume also that the activity generates external costs that are an increasing function of output. In the absence of either a rule that external costs be reimbursed, or of negotiation between the parties, the agent generating the external costs will operate at the point where marginal private net benefits are equated to zero. This, however, is an excessive output from the standpoint of both parties; overall gains would be maximized by equating marginal private net benefits to marginal external costs.

As Coase points out, there are incentives for the two parties to arrange a bargain that will bring output into adjustment in this way [**46**]. But the terms of the bargain are not determinate; a range of possible outcomes is possible. Thus haggling over the terms of the bargain can be expected. Although this haggling will have no direct effect on volume produced, it does represent a real resource drain. Each agent will be prepared to invest in bargaining until the marginal expected net pecuniary gain from haggling is driven to zero. Perhaps, in a perfectly static environment, the parties might recognize this waste and eliminate it through agreement, but this may be much less easy to arrange when markets are subject to random or other disturbances. Thus, rather than haggle repeatedly, the parties might integrate instead and eliminate these bargaining costs in the process.

While it has been convenient to illustrate the argument by reference to externalities, the latter is by no means essential. An incentive to extinguish bargaining costs through internalizing transactions exists for any market situation where, because of the ill-specified nature of the exchange, haggling can be anticipated. Uncertainty in the nature of the product or service that makes it difficult or costly to specify contractual terms unambiguously, presumably contributes to this result.

2
EXPANSION OF THE FIRM
AND HIERARCHICAL STRUCTURE

Assume, for any or all of the reasons given above, that a multi-function enterprise has been established. To facilitate the exposition, assume that it has the following properties: (1) there are two functions (e.g., manufacturing and distribution); (2) indivisibilities or specialization of labor requires that two operating employees be hired in each function; (3) intrafunction coordination requires that a first-line supervisor be appointed over each pair of operators; (4) interfunction coordination and overall enterprise direction are assigned to an entrepreneur or peak coordinator who heads up the enterprise. The resulting firm thus has three hierarchical levels (peak coordination, first-line supervision, and operations) with a span of control of two between each level. Total employment in such a constant span of control enterprise is given by $\sum_{i=1}^{n} s^{i-1}$, where s is the span of control and n is the number of hierarchical levels. With $s = 2$ and $n = 3$, total employment is 7.

Assume now that the enterprise is gradually expanded until the number of operating employees is doubled while the number of functions is held constant. Assume also that the constant span of control condition of $s = 2$ is preserved. (Gradual expansion will necessarily place the enterprise in a condition of temporary disequilibrium as the

ratio of supervisors to operators is disturbed, but as a transistory
condition this may not be serious.) The question is, What does the
new equilibrium configuration of the firm look like? Note immediately
that, for constant span of control of two, a doubling of the number
of operating employees requires that a new hierarchical level be
introduced. Eight rather than four operators will be at the bottom of
the organizational hierarchy. Each pair will report to a first-line
supervisor; hence there will be four first-line supervisors. The new
hierarchical level appears between these four supervisors and the
office of the peak coordinator. Each pair of first-line supervisors
reports to a middle manager who in turn reports to the peak
coordinator.

The scheme by which the expanded enterprise is organized
naturally defines the content of the middle manager and peak coordination roles. The two alternatives that will be considered here are
(1) the retention of the old organization form, so that each middle
manager heads up one function, and (2) the creation of an organization
parallel to the original one, the two parts to be joined at the top by
an overall peak coordinator. The latter strategy will be referred to as
"multidivisionalization" and is discussed in Chapters 8–10. We focus
here on the former strategy, which will be referred to as amplification.

Amplification would appear to be the "natural" way for the firm
to expand. New employees under this arrangement are simply fitted
into the existing structure. Thus the forces of tradition and inertia
operate in its favor. Such a procedure also appears to be have been
contemplated in the early literature on firm expansion [45, pp. 340–41].
Finally, it corresponds roughly with the historical facts on expansion
of the multifunction enterprise [42, p. 49]. Under this form of organization, the middle managers become heads of functional divisions and
are responsible for intrafunction coordination of the expanded functional activity. Interfunction coordinating responsibility is thus
retained by the office of the peak coordinator, which is also responsible
for overall enterprise direction. One should not be surprised if, as a
result of continued expansion of this sort, the office of the peak coordinator would eventually be overloaded. The goal pursuit consequences
of this condition will be examined in Chapter 3. For our purposes here
it is sufficient to observe that the functional form of organization has
been preserved and that an additional hierarchical level has been
introduced when the firm is expanded as described. Attention will be
focused on the control loss consequences of these changes.

Although the pyramidal structure of organization described above
scarcely offends common experience, it may be well to consider further
the factors that contribute to hierarchy. Hierarchical organization is
a characteristic not merely of business firms but of complex systems

in general—social, biological, and physical [**35**] [**59**] [**142**]. Herbert Simon attributes the near universality of hierarchical structure in complex organizations to their capacity to absorb shock and to the enormous reduction they afford in information transmission requirements [**144**, pp. 99–100]. Hierarchical systems, by decomposing the task into quasi-independent domains, are able to localize the effect of disturbances. Hence, among "systems of a given size and complexity, hierarchical systems, composed of subsystems, are the most likely to appear through evolutionary processes" [**144**, pp. 99–100].

The information-saving characteristics of hierarchical organization can be illustrated, in an extreme way, by considering two alternative organization structures in each of which there are M operators cooperatively engaged in the task. If there is no coordinator, and if the degree of interdependence requires that every member of the group be in contact with every other, $(\frac{1}{2})(M^2 - M)$ two-way communication channels must be provided. If, instead, all communications are channeled through a single coordinator (which introduces an element of hierarchy), only M two-way channels will be required. Thus an enormous reduction in channel requirements is achieved (for any M greater than 3) by the simple introduction of a single coordinator.

This, however, understates the advantages of hierarchy. For if the change in the behavior of any individual in the fully interconnected nonhierarchical system requires that each of the others adapt appropriately, and if the adaptation by each imposes a further need for subsequent adaptations throughout the system, instability against shock may result. That is, to disturb an initial equilibrium position (however obtained) by a change of parameters that exceeds threshold sensitivity may, in a system where every operator is adapting to every other, prevent it ever from restabilizing. This might be partly or wholly overcome if causal orderings among the parts could be identified and subsystems were brought into adjustment sequentially, but this introduces an element of hierarchy of a different sort. How attractive, by contrast, to have a single coordinator note the change and optimally respecify the entire system.

The latter, however, is not feasible except in the simplest of systems. For complex systems where M is large, this is not a genuine alternative. Bounded rationality—by which is meant bounds on the rate at which information can be absorbed per unit of time, limits to the information storage capacity (in an effective retrieval sense), and bounds on the processing ability of the decision-maker—precludes this [**104**, Chap. 6] [**59**, pp. 13, 17, 144]. The principle of reporting to a coordinator, rather than having the M operators attempt unassisted adaptation among themselves, is nevertheless perfectly sound. Bounded rationality merely requires that a multistage hierarchy be introduced to overcome the inherent limitations of the human mind. Presumably this hierarchy would be designed with both causal ordering and coordinating purposes in mind.

Bounded rationality thus should be added to the list of factors that are responsible for a great deal of what we regard as interesting economic behavior. It would seem to be fully as important as uncertainty, and more fundamental, really, than both incomplete information and transaction costs. In the absence of bounded rationality, administrative coordination would, presumably, always obtain over the market. Fully integrated operations would be the rule, and complete information, up to a knowledge of probability distributions or otherwise uncertain events (in the sense of ignorance concerning the state of nature), would prevail.[2]

Given bounded rationality, however, only finite spans of control are feasible. Large systems therefore require that multiple levels of organization be introduced. Coordination will be facilitated by grouping richly interacting activities together, which permits high-frequency, high-intensity interactions to be mediated locally, while overall coordination between weakly interacting parts is provided at a higher level [59] [142]. Such an arrangement corresponds to the functional organization described above. Thus at the bottom we find operators grouped according to functional specialization. The rich interactions within these groups are mediated by first-line supervisors. Interfunction coordination (as well as overall enterprise direction) is supplied by the office of the peak coordinator. The middle-level management performs a linking function. In part it involves resolving differences between and coordinating the activities of first-line supervision on matters that have strictly intrafunctional consequences; partly it is an information processing activity (sorting and summarizing information that has interfunctional implications for higher level review); and partly it entails giving operational content to the instructions of the peak coordinator by directing first-line supervisors appropriately.[3] This last part of the middle management function will subsequently be referred to as operationalizing.

3
LIMITS TO
FIRM SIZE

The compelling reasons to expect complex systems to be hierarchically organized have been sketched out above and have been given elsewhere by others. The limits that hierarachical systems are subject to have been less thoroughly developed. A simple answer, based on the arithmetic of constant span of control enterprise, is that

a hierarchically organized system that combines s previously independent systems requires one additional hierarchical level and, hence,
one additional employee.[4] *Ceteris paribus,* the s independent systems
will have lower costs on this account. But this is trivial. If hierarchical
organization is subject to important size limits, these must be found
elsewhere. A general answer to this matter has been provided by
Kenneth Boulding [**36**, p. 8]:

> There is a great deal of evidence that almost all organizational struc-
> tures tend to produce false images in the decision-maker, and that
> the larger and more authoritarian the organization, the better the
> chance that its top decision-makers will be operating in purely imagi-
> nary worlds. This perhaps is the most fundamental reason for sup-
> posing that there are ultimately diminishing returns to scale.

The argument here articulates this proposition that problems of trans-
mitting accurate images across successive levels in a hierarchical
organization are fundamentally responsible for diminishing returns to
scale. There is, however, less than unanimity on this issue. Indeed,
it has long been disputed whether or in what ways the management
factor is responsible for a limitation to firm size. Although descriptive
treatments of this question have been numerous, these have generally
been too imprecise to permit testable implications to be derived. The
present analysis attempts a partial remedy for this condition by
embedding in a formal model the control loss features of hierarchical
organization that have recently been advanced in the bureaucratic
theory literature. The background to this discussion of control loss as
a limitation to firm size is reviewed in 3.1. A simple model possessing
basic control loss attributes is developed and its properties are derived
in 3.2. The model is elaborated and extended in 3.3, including a discussion of problems to expect in empirical testing.

As indicated earlier, expansion will be assumed to take the form
of amplification within the functional form of organization rather
than multidivisionalization. Not until Chapter 8 will this assumption
be relaxed. In addition, it will be assumed that employees of the firm
behave in strictly functional ways; there is no subgoal pursuit. Information is transmitted and instructions are operationalized with the
sole intent of advancing higher-level objectives. This latter assumption
will be relaxed in the following chapter.

3.1
Background to the Analysis

That the question of the optimum size firm presented a serious
dilemma for the theory of the firm was noted by Knight in 1933.
Thus, he observed [**87**, p. xxiii]:

The relation between efficiency and size is one of the most serious problems of theory, being in contrast with the relation for a plant, largely a matter of personality and historical accident rather than of intelligible general principles. But this question is peculiarly vital because the possibility of monopoly gain offers a powerful incentive to *continuous and unlimited* expansion of the firm, which force must be offset by some equally powerful one making for decreased efficiency (in the production of money income) with growth in size, if even boundary competition is to exist.

Within a year, E. A. G. Robinson [130] proposed what we believe to be a substantially correct answer, namely, that problems of coordination imposed a static limitation to firm size; and Coase generally supports this position [45, pp. 340–41]. Nicholas Kaldor [79], however, argued that problems of coordination vanished under truly static conditions, and hence only declining product-demand curves or rising factor-supply curves could be responsible for a static limitation to firm size. Only in the context of firm dynamics did coordination problems, in his view, constitute a genuine limitation to firm size. But as Robinson was quick to point out, Kaldor's argument rested on his peculiar specification of the static condition as one in which the control problem is defined to be absent. This approach to the economics of the firm he found quite uninstructive for, as he pungently noted, "In Mr. Kaldor's long period we shall not only be dead but in Nirvana, and the economics of Nirvana . . . is surely the most fruitless of sciences" [129, p. 250].

The argument remained there[5] until N. S. Ross [131, p. 148], in a sweeping attack on the economic treatments of this question, took the position that this whole literature bordered on the irrelevant for its failure to incorporate "certain aspects of the theory of organization and management." Recasting the problem in what he regarded as suitable organizational terms, he concluded that "by appropriate measures of decentralization and control the firm may expand without incurring increasing costs of coordination over a range sufficiently wide to cover all possible cases within the limits imposed by scarcity of resources" [131, p. 154]. W. H. Starbuck, in apparent sympathy with Ross, likewise regards the treatment by economists of these issues as entirely too narrow and probably self-serving [147, p. 343].

Mrs. Penrose also finds this literature unsatisfactory, observing that "whether managerial diseconomies will cause longrun increasing costs [requires that] management . . . be treated as a 'fixed factor' and the nature of the 'fixity' must be identified with respect to the nature of the managerial task of 'coordination.' *This identification has never been satisfactorily accomplished*" [122, p. 12]. (Italics added.) She continues to regard the issue as a vital one, however, but argues with Kaldor that it is the dynamics, not the statics of coordination, that give rise to a limitation to firm size. In their view, expansion is contingent on knowledgeable planning and skillful coordination where these are a function of internal experience. Since experience is available in restricted supply, the rate of growth is thereby necessarily restricted. Variations on this argument have since been developed, and some have come to regard the growth rate as the only limitation to firm size.[6]

It is unfortunate (although understandable) that the static limitation argument should continue to be misunderstood in this way. The difficulty is probably traceable to the distinction between truly static and quasi-static conditions. Those who reject the static-limitation argument tend to adopt the former position, while those who advocate it take the latter. This is implicit in the Kaldor-Robinson dispute cited above. Differences of this sort are especially difficult to resolve, but an effort to explicate the quasi-static position may nevertheless be useful.

The problem can be stated in terms of deterministic versus stochastic equilibrium. A steady state is reached in each. But whereas in the former the data are unchanging, in the latter the firm is required to adapt to circumstances which are predictable in the sense that although they occur with stochastic regularity, precise advance knowledge of them is unavailable. Although the deterministic condition provides circumstances in which the usual management functions can be progressively eliminated through the refinement of operations, this is the world of Kaldor's Nirvana and has limited relevance for an understanding of business behavior. Instead, customers come and go, manufacturing operations break down, distribution systems malfunction, labor and materials procurement are subject to the usual vagaries, all with stochastic regularity, not to mention minor shifts in demand and similar disturbing influences of a transitory nature. Throughout all of this, the management of the firm is required to adapt to the new circumstances: request the relevant data, process the information supplied, and provide the appropriate instructions. Coordination in these circumstances is thus essential. If, simultaneously, a general expansion of operations accompanies these quasi-static adjustments, additional direction would be required. But in no sense is growth a necessary condition for the coordinating function to exist.

The question still needs to be faced, however, as to why scaling up the firm should lead to size limitations. Stochastic changes require adaptation whatever the size of firm; one might even argue that the large firm will be able to pool risks and thereby ease the adaptation problem. What are the special problems that large size encounters? Two can be offered. First, expansion (especially if it involves diversification) often exposes the firm to a wider range of environmental and experiential variability and hence makes the problem of peak coordination more severe (recall that all interfunctional coordination is supplied at the top). Second, the information transfer and operationalizing processes that are introduced at middle levels are subject to cumulative error.

Crowding the capacity of the peak coordinator can be partly alleviated by distributing his responsibilities among others. This will be referred to as a capacity-augmenting strategy and it, as well as its consequences, will be considered in Chapter 4. An alternative strategy is to reduce the systems information transmission needs by appropriate redesign. This will be referred to as a process of "decoupling" [59, pp. 24–28] [104, pp. 158–60].

Some of the ways of reducing interdependencies through decoupling are to increase threshold sensitivities between functions, standardize interfaces, introduce buffers (such as inventories), and rely on more flexible (less specialized) resources. Each of these permits the functional divisions to operate in more autonomous ways and thereby reduces the need for frequent cross-functional adjustment, but none is without cost. Moreover, although decoupling devices permit the peak coordinator to conserve his finite energies and better direct them to high-return activities, each experiences diminishing returns. Yet there is no costless choice. Without conscious efforts to decouple, severance will occur in unplanned ways as proliferating variety overwhelms the system's capacity for calculated response. The coordination problem will be solved partly by default; unable to obtain direction from the top, the functional divisions will be forced to coordinate informally among themselves.

For our purposes here, the expense of malcoordination due to decoupling and that involved in information transfer activites will be impounded in what will be referred to as the "control loss" phenomenon. F. C. Bartlett's studies of serial reproduction illustrate how information transfer has cumulative loss effects. His experiments involved the oral transmission of descriptive and argumentative passages through a chain of serially linked individuals. Bartlett concluded from a number of such studies that [22, p. 175]:

> It is now perfectly clear that serial reproduction normally brings about startling and radical alterations in the material dealt with. Epithets are changed into their opposites; incidents and events are transposed; names and numbers rarely survive intact for more than a few reproductions; opinions and conclusions are reversed—nearly every possible variation seems as if it can take place, even in a relatively short series. At the same time the subjects may be very well satisfied with

their efforts, believing themselves to have passed on all important features with little or no change, and merely, perhaps, to have omitted unessential matters.

Bartlett [22, pp. 180–81] illustrates this graphically with a line drawing of an owl which—when redrawn successively by eighteen individuals, each sketch based on its immediate predecessor—ended up as a recognizable cat; and the further from the initial drawing one moved, the greater the distortion experienced. The reliance of hierarchical organizations on serial reproduction for their functioning thus exposes them to what may become serious distortions in transmission.

Although this phenomenon is widely experienced, it was not generally regarded as having special theoretical significance until Gordon Tullock [154, pp. 142–93] argued that not only was authority leakage possible in a large government bureau, but it was predictable and could be expressed as an increasing function of size. Anthony Downs has since elaborated the argument and summarized it in his "Law of Diminishing Control: *The larger any organization becomes, the weaker is the control over its actions exercised by those at the top*" [55, p. 143]. The cumulative loss of control as instructions and information are transmitted across successive hierarchical levels is responsible for this result.

Actually, although the serial reproduction argument has great heuristic value for understanding control loss experience, hierarchical organization rarely relies on pure serial reproduction operations. Also, it should be noted that both Tullock and Downs place their principal emphasis on the opportunities for deliberate distortion afforded by hierarchical organization rather than on the simple control loss condition. So as better to focus on the elementary limits to hierarchical control, the calculated distortion aspect will be deferred to Chapter 3. The respects in which information exchange at middle levels of the enterprise differ from serial reproduction are, however, relevant to an understanding of simple control loss behavior.

As indicated earlier, middle-level officials are more than mere information exchange nodes. They exercise critical judgments in the sorting and summarizing of information to be transmitted forward, in mediating intrafunctional differences, and in providing operational content to instructions received at the top in discharging their supervisory responsibilities. James Emery cites John Gardner regarding the upward flow process as follows: Raw data are "sampled, screened, condensed, compiled, coded, expressed in statistical form, spun into generalizations and crystallized into recommendations" as they are transmitted forward [59, p. 114]. The downward flow can be expressed in opportunity set terms. General instructions are issued at the top which are consistent with a wide range of eventual behavior, not all of which outcomes have the same utility value [**59**, p. 129]. Transmission across levels is designed successively to narrow the region of feasible choice, in a way intended to promote high-level objectives. This successive shrinkage of opportunity sets is what is meant by operationalizing.[7]

In consideration of the limitations that decoupling experiences (which is to say that the coordination problems of the large firm cannot be overcome by mere design changes), hierarchical data flows are a necessary consequence of large size. The transmission losses due to data compression and operationalizing and the malcoordination losses of decoupling will be characterized as simple control loss. To illustrate the control loss phenomenon and keep the analysis tractable, it will be assumed that while expansion places more resources at the disposal of the peak coordinator, introducing an additional hierarchical level reduces the effectiveness of his control by a multiplicative constant α $(0 < \alpha < 1)$.

3.2
The Basic Model

Consider a hierarchically organized business firm with the following characteristics: (1) only employees at the lowest hierarchical level do manual labor; the work done by employees at higher levels is entirely administrative (planning, forecasting, supervising, accounting, and so on); (2) output is a constant proportion of productive input; (3) the wage paid to employees at the lowest level is w_0; (4) each superior is paid $\beta(\beta > 1)$ times as much as each of his immediate subordinates; (5) the span of control (the number of employees a supervisor can handle effectively) is a constant $s(s > 1)$ across every hierarchical level; (6) product and factor prices are parameters; (7) all nonwage variable costs are a constant proportion of output; (8) only the fraction $\alpha(0 < \alpha < 1)$ of the intentions of a superior are effectively satisfied by a subordinate; (9) control loss is strictly cumulative (there is no systematic compensation) across successive hierarchical levels.

The first assumption can be restated as: there are no working foremen.[8] This seems quite reasonable and permits us to simplify the analysis of the relation of output to input. Taken together with assumption (2) which assures that there are no economies of specialization in production (in the relevant range), output can be expressed as a constant proportion of productive input. The distinction between direct labor input and productive labor input should be emphasized. The former refers to the total labor input at the lowest hierarchical level. The latter is that part of the direct labor input which yields productive results. The latter is smaller than the former not by reason of labor inefficiencies but because of the cumulative control loss in the transmission of data and instructions across successive hierarchical levels.

Assumption (3) is innocuous; assumption (4) is plausible and appears to correspond with the facts. This is Simon's conclusion in his study [141] of the theory and practices of executive compensation. The constant β condition is also reported by a recent U.S. Department of Labor study [170, p. 8] of salary structures in the large firm, which found that "the relationship maintained between salary rates for successive grades was more commonly *a uniform percentage spread* between grades than a widening percentage spread" (italics added). An independent check of this hypothesis is also possible from the data on executive compensation included in the Annual Reports of the General Motors Corporation from 1934 to 1942. This is developed in Appendix A.

Assumption (5), that the span of control is constant across levels, is also employed in the wage model tested in Appendix A, although the cumulative distribution relation tested does not uniquely imply this relation.[9] Taken in conjunction with the Department of Labor findings on β, however, the fits reported in Appendix A also lend support to the constant span of control assumption. We nevertheless show in Section 3.3 where this assumption can be relaxed somewhat and the basic results preserved.

Assumption (6) permits us to treat prices in the product and factor markets as parameters. As we will show, this can also be relaxed without affecting the qualitative character of our results. Assumption (7) is not critical, but permits us a modest simplification. Assumptions (8) and (9) are merely restatements of the earlier argument. They are responsible for the control loss attributes of the model. Since much of the exposition in subsequent parts of the chapter will be explicitly concerned with them, we will say no more about them here.

For purposes of developing a model around these assumptions, let:

s = span of control

α = fraction of work done by a subordinate that contributes to objectives of his superior $(0 < \alpha < 1)$; it is thus an internal efficiency parameter.

N_i = number of employees at the ith hierarchical level = s^{i-1}

n = number of hierarchical levels (the decision variable)

P = price of output

w_0 = wage of production workers

w_i = wage of employees at ith hierarchical level
     = $w_0 \beta^{n-i}$ $(\beta > 1)$

r = nonwage variable cost per unit output
Q = output
$\quad = \theta(\alpha s)^{n-1}$
R = total revenue
$\quad = PQ$
C = total variable cost
$\quad = \sum\limits_{i=1}^{n} w_i N_i + rQ$

Without loss of generality, assume that $\theta = 1$. The objective is to find the value of n (the number of hierarchical levels, and hence the size of the firm) so as to maximize net revenue. This is given by:

$$R - C = PQ - \sum_{i=1}^{n} w_i N_i - rQ \tag{1}$$

$$= P(\alpha s)^{n-1} - \sum_{i=1}^{n} w_0 \beta^{n-i} s^{i-1} - r(\alpha s)^{n-1}$$

now

$$\sum_{i=1}^{n} w_0 \beta^{n-i} s^{i-1} = w_0 \left(\frac{\beta^n}{s}\right) \sum_{i=1}^{n} \left(\frac{s}{\beta}\right)^i$$

where

$$\sum_{i=1}^{n} \left(\frac{s}{\beta}\right)^i = \frac{\left(\frac{s}{\beta}\right)^{n+1} - \left(\frac{s}{\beta}\right)}{\frac{s}{\beta} - 1} \simeq \frac{s^{n+1}}{(s-\beta)\beta^n}.$$

Thus, we have

$$R - C = P(\alpha s)^{n-1} - w_0 \frac{s^n}{s - \beta} - r(\alpha s)^{n-1}. \tag{1'}$$

Differentiating this expression with respect to n and setting equal to zero (and letting ln denote natural logarithm), we obtain as the optimal value for n:

$$n^* = 1 + \frac{1}{ln\,\alpha}\left[ln\,\frac{w_0}{P-r} + ln\,\frac{s}{s-\beta} + ln\left(\frac{ln\,s}{ln\,(\alpha s)}\right)\right]. \tag{2}$$

The values of α and $w_0/(P - r)$ in this expression are both between zero and unity, while $\beta < s$ and $\alpha s > 1$. The condition $\beta < s$ must hold for the approximating relation to apply and is supported by the data.[10] The condition $\alpha s > 1$ must hold if there is to be any incentive to hire employees. Not merely diminishing but negative returns would exist were $\alpha s < 1$. Since $ln\,\alpha < 0$, the expression in brackets must be negative, a condition which is virtually assured by the stipulation that the firm earn positive profits.[11] Assuming that the appropriate bounds and inequality conditions are satisfied, the following *ceteris paribus* conditions are obtained from the model:

a) Optimal n increases as the degree of compliance with supervisor objectives (α) increases.

b) Optimal n is infinite if there is no loss of intention ($\alpha = 1$) between successive hierarchical levels. Only a declining product-demand curve or rising labor-supply curve could impose a (static) limit on firm size in such circumstances.

c) Optimal n decreases as the ratio of the basic wage to the net price over nonwage variable costs ($w_0/P - r$) increases. Thus, the optimum size for an organization will be relatively small and the optimum shape relatively flat in labor intensive industries.

d) Optimal n increases as the span of control (s) increases. Intuition would have led us to expect that flatter organizations (fewer hierarchical levels) would be associated with wider spans of control, but obviously this is not the case.[12]

e) Optimal n decreases as the wage multiple between levels (β) increases.

Plausible values for α can be obtained by substituting estimated values for each of the parameters into equation (2). This is done below. In addition, propositions (c), (d), and (e) can be tested empirically by observing that total employment is given by

$$N^* = \sum_{i=1}^{n^*} N_i = \sum_{i=1}^{n^*} s^{i-1}. \tag{3}$$

The sum of this series is given by

$$N^* = \frac{s^{n^*} - 1}{s - 1} \simeq \frac{s^{n^*}}{s - 1}. \tag{4}$$

Taking the natural logarithm and substituting the value of optimal n^* given by equation (2), we have:

$$\begin{aligned} ln\, N^* &\simeq ln\left(\frac{1}{s-1}\right) \\ &+ ln\, s\left\{1 + \frac{1}{ln\, \alpha}\left[ln\, \frac{w_0}{P-r} + ln\, \frac{s}{s-\beta} + ln\left(\frac{ln\, s}{ln\,(\alpha s)}\right)\right]\right\}. \end{aligned} \tag{5}$$

Expressing the optimal size firm in this way avoids the necessity of collecting data by hierarchical levels.

Employment among the five hundred largest industrials in the United States runs generally between one thousand and one hundred thousand employees. For values of s between 5 and 10, which is the normal range [**89**, p. 88], this implies an optimal n of between 4 and 7. If all of our assumptions were satisfied, if there were no additional factors (risk, growth, and so on) acting as limitations to firm size, and for values of β in the range 1.3 to 1.6 and $w_0/(P - r)$ in the range $\frac{1}{3}$ to $\frac{2}{3}$, the implied value of α is in the neighborhood of 0.90. Since other factors are likely to act as limitations to some extent, the true value of α may generally be higher than this. It is our contention, however, for the reasons given above, the values of α less than unity are typical and that the cumulative effects of control loss are fundamentally responsible for limitations to firm size.

3.3
Extensions

Although the basic model developed in the preceding section makes evident the critical importance of control loss as a static limitation to firm size in a way which is more precise than was heretofore available and thus both clarifies the issues and expresses them in a potentially testable form, it is obviously a highly special model and may be properly regarded with scepticism for that reason. We attempt in this section to generalize the analysis in such a way as to make clear its wider applicability. First, the possibility of introducing economies of scale, either through the specialization of labor or in the nonlabor inputs, to offset diseconomies due to control loss is examined. Second, we develop the properties of a model in which the utility function of the firm includes both profits and hierarchical expense. Next, imperfections in the product market are permitted. Fourth, we allow for the possibility of variations in the span of control at the production level. Finally, the compliance parameter (α) is expressed as a function of the span of control.[13]

3.3.1. Economies of scale.   We assume above that economies of scale due to specialization of labor or in the nonlabor inputs have been exhausted so that diseconomies of scale due to control loss give rise to increasing average cost conditions in the range of output under consideration. These assumptions can be made more precise here. For this purpose, we express the parameter θ which converts input to output as a function of n. Over the range where economies of specialization exist $\partial\theta/\partial n > 0$, whereas when these have been exhausted $\partial\theta/\partial n = 0$. Thus, average cost can be expressed as:

$$AC = w_0 \frac{s}{s - \beta} \cdot \frac{1}{\theta\alpha^{n-1}} - r \qquad (6)$$

and AC will decrease so long as $\partial\theta/\partial n > \theta \, ln \, \alpha$. When these two are in balance, constant returns to the labor input will prevail, but as

$\partial\theta/\partial n$ declines (and eventually goes to zero), diminishing returns due to control loss will set in.

In a similar way, the nonwage variable cost per unit output parameter, r, can be expressed as a function of output, where $\partial r/\partial Q > 0$ initially, but eventually $\partial r/\partial Q = 0$. Thus, average costs will at first decline for this reason as well, but the cumulative effects of control loss will ultimately dominate and the average cost curve will rise. Implicitly, the model in Section 3.2 assumes that both $\partial\theta/\partial n$ and $\partial r/\partial Q$ are zero, so that economies with respect to both labor and nonlabor inputs are assumed to be exhausted in the relevant range. Actually, this is somewhat stronger than is necessary for control loss to impose a limitation to firm size; this result would obtain under the assumptions that $\partial^2\theta/\partial n^2 < 0$ and $\partial^2 r/\partial Q^2 > 0$. This latter, however, would lead only to changes in degree and not in kind from those derived above.

3.3.2. Imperfection in the product market. If product price is not treated as a parameter but instead $P = P(Q)$, $\partial P/\partial Q < 0$, we obtain the following expression for optimal n:

$$n^* = 1 + \frac{1}{ln\,\alpha}\left\{ ln\,\frac{w_0}{P\left(1 - \dfrac{1}{\eta}\right) - r} + ln\,\frac{s}{s - \beta} + ln\,\frac{ln\,s}{ln\,(\alpha s)}\right\}, \quad (7)$$

where η is the elasticity of demand.

Obviously, in a perfect product market, where $\eta = \infty$, (7) is identical with (2). As is to be expected, the value of optimal n decreases as demand becomes more inelastic.

3.3.3. Variation in the span of control over operators. It is assumed in the model developed in section 3.2 that the span of control is uniform throughout the organization. Although variations in the span of control among the administrative levels of the organization are generally small, this is frequently untrue between the foremen and operatives. Typically, the span of control is larger here and the reasons are quite obvious: Tasks tend to be more highly routinized, and thus the need for supervision and coordination are correspondingly attenuated. Letting σ be the span of control between foremen and operatives, total employment of operatives is now given by the product of σ and the number of foremen, where this latter is s^{n-2}. Productive output is thus the product of control loss, $(\alpha)^{n-1}$, times σs^{n-2}, or $\alpha\sigma(\alpha s)^{n-2}$. The value of optimal n derived from this version of the model is:

$$n^* = 1 + \frac{1}{ln\,\alpha}\left\{ ln\,\frac{w_0}{P - r} + ln\left(\frac{\sigma + \beta s/(s - \beta)}{\sigma}\right) + ln\left[\frac{ln\,s}{ln\,(\alpha s)}\right]\right\}. \quad (8)$$

Again, it is obvious by comparing this expression with equation (2) that when $\sigma = s$ they are identical and that qualitatively the properties are the same. The additional implication that obtains from this model is that as σ increases, optimal n increases. That is, for α unchanged, increasing the span of control between the foremen and operatives leads to a general increase in the number of levels and, consequently, number of employees in the hierarchical organization, a result which is completely in accord with our intuition.

3.3.4. Compliance and span of control interaction. The difficulties associated with the selection of an optimum span of control have been noted by Simon as follows [**139**, p. 28]:

> The dilemma is this: in a large organization with interrelations between members, a restricted span of control produces excessive red tape. . . . The alternative is to increase the number of persons who are under the command of an officer. . . . But this, too, leads to difficulty, for if an officer is required to supervise too many employees, his control over them is weakened.
>
> Granted, then, that both the increase and the decrease in span of control have some undersirable consequences, what is the optimum point?

More precisely, the dilemma can be stated in terms of compliance (α) and span of control (s) interaction. Whereas the preceding analysis treats the level of compliance (α) and the span of control (s) independently, in fact they are intimately related. Increasing the span of control means that while each supervisor has more productive capability responsive to him he has less time to devote to the supervision of each, and hence a loss of control results. For purposes of examining this behavior, we let

$$\alpha = f(s), \qquad \partial f / \partial s < 0. \qquad (9)$$

Given that α is a declining function of s as indicated, the question next arises: What is the optimum value of s and how is this related to size of firm? Now output is given by $Q = (\alpha s)^{n-1}$, so that for any particular level of output, say $\bar{Q}$, choice of n implies a value for s (and, hence, through [9], α) and conversely.[14] To determine the relation between optimum s and $\bar{Q}$, we observe that since gross revenue is fixed given the level of output, the optimization problem can be expressed as one of minimizing labor costs subject to constraint. Thus, the objective is:
minimize

$$C_L = w_0 \frac{s^n}{s - \beta}$$

subject to

$$(i) \ (\alpha s)^{n-1} = \bar{Q} \tag{10}$$

$$(ii) \ \alpha = f(s).$$

The standard technique for studying the behavior of this system is to formulate it as a Lagrangian and perturb the first-order conditions with respect to $\bar{Q}$. Unfortunately, the resulting expressions cannot be signed on the basis of the general functional relation $\alpha = f(s)$. Assuming, however, that the function is bell-shaped on the right (which intuitively is the correct general configuration), we can replace (9) and, hence, the second constraint, by

$$\alpha = e^{-ks^2}. \tag{9'}$$

The value of the exponent k in this expression can be interpreted as a composite organization form–internal efficiency parameter. As internal efficiency increases, the value of k decreases and α increases at every value of s.

The comparative statics responses of n and s (and hence α) to changes in firm size (as measured by output) and internal inefficiency (k) are shown in Table 2-1. The direction of adjustment of any particular decision variable to a displacement from equilibrium by an increase in either of those parameters is found by referring to the row and column entry corresponding to the decision variable-parameter pair.[15]

That the number of hierarchical levels should increase as output increases is not surprising. That the span of control should decrease, however, is less obvious. Moreover, it contradicts what little data there are on this question. Thus, Starbuck [**147**, p. 375] concludes his systematic survey of the relevant literature bearing on this issue with the observation that the "administrative span of control . . . probably increases with organizational size." Unless our model can be somehow extended to explain this condition, it calls seriously into question the

TABLE 2-1

Comparative Statics Responses

Decision Variable	Shift Parameter	
	Output $(d\bar{Q})$	Internal Inconsistency (dk)
Hierarchical level (dn)......	$+$	$+$
Span of control (ds)........	$-$	$-$
Control effectiveness $(d\alpha)$	$+$	?

validity of the control loss approach to organizational behavior. Thus, one of the merits of formalizing this argument as we have is that we can go beyond mere plausibility arguments to discover the less obvious properties of the model and address the relevant evidence to them. Appendix B concerns itself with this dilemma.

That an increase in k leads to a decrease in the span of control and hence increase in n for a fixed size organization is entirely in accord with our intuition. Indeed, given that control loss is cumulative across hierarchical levels, we would expect that efficiency is relatively high (k is low) and thus the span of control large in large organizations. That organizations such as the Catholic Church successfully operate with relatively flat hierarchical structures is surely partly attributable to the high degree of goal consistency that the organization possesses. Selection and training procedures obviously contribute to this result.

4
CONCLUSIONS

The proposition that the management factor is responsible for a limitation to firm size has appeared recurrently in the literature. But the arguments have tended to be imprecise, lacked predictive content, and consequently failed to be convincing. The present chapter attempts to overcome some of these shortcomings by developing a formal model in which the control loss phenomenon is made central to the analysis.

The fundamental importance of bounded rationality to the argument cannot be too greatly emphasized. Also important is the assumption that expansion follows the amplification process. As will be seen in Chapter 9, a change in the expansion strategy (which substitutes multidivisionalization for functional amplification) has far-reaching size and performance consequences. Ultimately, however, bounded rationality will operate to impose a size limit on the multi-divisionalization process as well.

APPENDIX A
TEST OF THE WAGE MODEL

Our basic wage hypothesis is that $w_i = w_0 \beta^{n-1}$, where w_0 is the base level salary, n is the number of hierarchical levels, i is the particular level in question, and β is the wage multiple. Unfortunately, the General Motors data are reported by wage ranges of unequal size rather than by hierarchical levels. It can nevertheless be used to test our hypothesis by developing the cumulative distribution counterpart of our model.

Taking logarithms of this wage relation, we have $\log w_i = \log w_0 + (n - i) \log \beta$. By assumption (5), the total number of employees at level i is $N_i = s^{i-1}$, where s is the span of control. Taking this logarithm, we obtain $\log N_i = (i - 1) \log s$. Solving for i in this second logarithmic expression and substituting into the first we obtain:[16]

$$\log N_i = \log b_0 - \left(\frac{\log s}{\log \beta}\right) \log w_i, \qquad (A1)$$

or

$$N_i = b_0 w_i^{-b_1}$$

where

$$\log b_0 = (\log s/\log \beta) \cdot [\log w_0 + (n - 1) \log \beta]$$

and

$$b_1 = (\log s/\log \beta).$$

We denote by $N(\bar{w})$ the total number of individuals having a wage greater than $\bar{w}$. This is given by

$$N(\bar{w}) = \int_{\bar{w}}^{\infty} b_0 w^{-b_1}\, dw = \left(\frac{b_0}{b_1}\right) \bar{w}^{(-b_1+1)} \qquad (A2)$$

or

$$N(\bar{w}) = a_0 \bar{w}^{-a_1}$$

where

$$a_0 = b_0/b_1$$

and

$$a_1 = -b_1 + 1.$$

This cumulative form does not require either information about the hierarchical levels or uniform size classes and, hence, can be applied to the General Motors (or any similar class of) wage data. Being derived from our wage-employment hypotheses, it should produce a good fit to the data if these hypotheses are substantially close approximations. The results are reported in Table 2-A1.

As is quickly apparent from inspecting the Table 2-A1 results, the wage model given by (A2) provides an excellent fit to the data. The coefficients of determination adjusted for degrees of freedom all

TABLE 2-A1

Wage Model Fit to General Motors Salary Data, 1934–42*

	1934	1936	1938	1940	1942
No. Obs.	10	11	6	6	6
R^2	.940	.970	.956	.907	.944
Log $\hat{a}_0$	10.022	10.828	10.688	11.859	10.822
	(0.733)	(0.523)	(0.882)	(1.400)	(1.077)
$\hat{a}_1$	-1.904	-2.067	-2.037	-2.297	-2.045
	(0.160)	(0.116)	(0.193)	(0.306)	(0.236)

* Standard errors are shown in parentheses.

exceed .90, and the estimates of the coefficients are both stable over the entire interval and significantly different from zero in every year. Assuming that General Motors salary schedules are not atypical (and since General Motors is frequently regarded as a model of better management practices we might expect imitation from other firms in this respect), we have some confidence that the assumptions underlying our wage model are correct at least for the class of large corporations that we are principally concerned with.

APPENDIX B
A DIGRESSION ON DYNAMICS

The analysis in the text has at least two disturbing implications. First, not only does control loss impose a limit to firm size, but once this limit is reached the firm will stabilize at this level. Since continuing expansion of large firms is common, the model appears to be at variance with reality in this aspect. Second, the model predicts that the span of control decreases with firm size, while the evidence points to the contrary. Either the control loss argument must be fundamentally incorrect, or the model must be amended in one or more respects.

We propose an extension, one that mainly involves allowance for dynamic conditions ignored in our static analysis. At least three factors are operative. First, increases in experience lead to refinements, short-cuts, and routinization, all of which permit increasing the span of control for a fixed level of control loss. And experience is obviously positively related to firm size. Second, although most of the economies of scale resulting from specialization and indivisibilities are ordinarily exhausted at a relatively modest firm size [20, chap. iii], the economies that result from a large data processing capability may well extend considerably beyond this size. Since for a given level of control loss increases in information processing capability permit the span of control to be expanded, the association of an increasing span of control and large firm size may be due in part to this information processing and firm size relation. Third, the rate of change of firm size may have an important influence. Penrose [122, pp. 44–48] has argued persuasively that the dynamics of growth require additional hierarchical personnel than are needed when the expansion is completed. Presumably this is because problems of coordination and control are more serious during periods of expansion. Expressing this argument in span of control terms, an inverse relation is to be expected between span of control and the growth rate. The remaining question then is what, if any, association between growth rate and size is to be expected. The data here are scant, but the results from the stochastic, serial correlation, growth models of Ijiri and Simon [77, pp. 86–87] are at least suggestive, namely, that "firms which grow large experience most of their growth [early in their history] . . . , then reach a plateau." Assuming that this is generally valid, growth rates will tend to be inversely related to firm size. Thus here again we have a dynamic, size-related condition that helps to explain the apparent contradiction between the data relating span of control to firm size and our static analysis.

Taking these dynamic or age-related characteristics into account suggests that, given the value of α, the optimum span of control be expressed as:

$$s = \varphi\,(Q, k, t, d, r, \ldots) \tag{B1}$$

where

$Q = $ output: $\varphi_Q < 0$
$k = $ inefficiency parameter; $\varphi_k < 0$
$t = $ chronological age (a proxy for experience); $\varphi_t > 0$
$d = $ data processing capability; $\varphi_d > 0$
$r = \dfrac{dQ/dt}{Q} = $ rate of change of output; $\varphi_r < 0$

Among the advantages of this formulation is that it permits us to accommodate parts of Mrs. Penrose's theory as a part of our own. Thus, if increases in r reduce the span of control, additional hierarchical levels will be required to sustain the level of output. But for fixed α, cumulative control loss which is given by $(1 - \alpha^n)$ now increases. Hence, costs increase as r increases, and the optimum growth rate is therefore restricted. Although Mrs. Penrose's emphasis is on internal experience and no attention is given to notions such as the span of control, the existence of control loss is implicit in her discussion and our model helps make this clear. Similarly, she observes that "as plans are completed and put into operation, managerial services absorbed in the planning processes will be gradually released" [**122**, p. 49]. Plan realization here implies that r decreases, hence the span of control increases and the release of managerial services follows necessarily.

The above formulation also points up the very real dangers of performing simple correlations between s and Q. For the reasons given above, Q is positively related to t and d and negatively related to r. Inasmuch as φ_t and φ_d are positive while φ_r is negative, the combined effect of these three factors could easily swamp the true effect of Q on s (as predicted by our static model) if simple bivariate analysis were attempted.

Finally it should be emphasized that expansion is assumed to occur by amplification, so that the unitary form structure is preserved. Expansion through multidivisionalization is treated in later chapters.

FOOTNOTES

[1] Technical conditions are sometimes cited to explain the multifunction enterprise; the transfer of hot steel ingot to a rolling mill or a continuous processing chemical plant are examples. But hot steel ingot transfers could be market mediated, and most "continuous" processes are separable into a number of stages across which the market could (and often does) operate. Technical separation that involves large technical costs is evidence of indivisibility. Organizational separation that experiences large transfer costs is evidence of market, not technical, limitations.

[2] Recall that unbounded rationality implies unrestricted information receiving, storage, and processing capability. One might argue in these circumstances that the system will be deterministic except for events that impinge from outside the universe—genuine acts of God. Thus even uncertainty in the probabilistic sense vanishes.

[3] As Arrow puts it, "a manager is an information channel of decidedly limited capacity . . . some decisions, if only trivial ones, must be made at lower levels to avoid overloading the top" [**13**, p. 400].

[4] Thus the number of employees in the combined system is given by $\sum_{i=1}^{n} s^{i-1}$, while total employment of the independent systems is $s \sum_{i=1}^{n-1} s^{i-1}$. The difference, $\sum_{i=1}^{n} s^{i-1} - s \sum_{i=1}^{n-1} s^{i-1}$, is one.

[5] E. H. Chamberlin [**41**, pp. 249–50] objected to some aspects of the argument in his treatment of the divisibility question, but nevertheless acknowledged that problems of coordination arising from increasing complexity eventually were responsible for increasing unit costs.

[6] Thus, John Williamson takes the position that: "One of the more discredited concepts in the theory of the firm is that of an 'optimum size' firm . . . [S]ince firms are not restricted to the sale of a single product or even a particular range of products, there is no more reason to expect profitability to decline with size than there is evidence to suggest that it does. This raises the question as to what does limit the size of a firm. The answer . . . is that there are important costs entailed in *expanding* the size of a firm, and that these expansion costs tend to increase with the firm's growth rate" [**159**, p. 1].

[7] On this, see Emery [**59**, p. 129] and Boulding [**35**, p. 148].

[8] This assumption has been expressed in this way by Mayer [**113**].

[9] Strictly speaking, the empirical results reported in Table 2-A1 support the proposition that the ratio $\log s/\log \beta$ is constant across successive hierarchical levels, not that s and β are identical across levels. Letting $\log s/\log \beta = \gamma$, where γ is a constant, implies that $\beta = s^{1/\gamma}$ at every level. Thus, changes in the span of control would be accompanied by changes in the wage multiple according to the relation $\beta_i = s_i^{1/\gamma}$. That β and s are related in this way seems at least as special as to assume that they are constant across levels. Moreover, in view of the Department of Labor report that β is indeed constant across levels, the constant s condition is implied by our results.

[10] If $\beta > s$, then $(\log s/\log \beta) < 1$ and $a_1 = -(\log s/\log \beta) + 1 > 0$. But as the results in Table 2-A1 show, a_1 is clearly negative, which requires that $s > \beta$, as assumed.

[11] The condition that the firm earn positive profits implies that

$$(P - r)(\alpha s)^{n-1} - \frac{s^n}{s - \beta} w_0 > 0,$$

or

$$\frac{w_0}{P - r} \cdot \frac{s}{s - \beta} \cdot \frac{1}{\alpha^{(n-1)}} < 1.$$

This requires that

$$\left[ln \frac{w_0}{P - r} + ln \frac{s}{s - \beta} + ln \frac{1}{\alpha^{(n-1)}} \right] < 0.$$

Since $ln [1/\alpha^{(n-1)}]$ is approximately of the same magnitude as $ln [ln s/ln (\alpha s)]$, or if anything is likely to exceed it, the condition that the firm earn positive profits is tantamount to requiring the bracketed term in equation (2) to be negative.

[12] This result should be interpreted with some care. It assumes that α is unaffected by increasing the span of control. Within any given firm, this is possible only if the increase in the span of control results from a management or technical innovation. Otherwise, increasing the span of control would lead to an increase in control loss. With this caveat in mind, the result indicated in the text is less counterintuitive. See 3.3.4.

[13] The properties of a model in which the utility function of the firm includes both profits and hierarchical expense components are developed in the appendix to Chapter 4, section 1.

[14] Actually, two values of s and α are consistent with each feasible choice of n: a high α, low s pair and a low α, high s pair. Of these two, the high α, low s position is always preferred since, with output fixed, gross revenues are unaffected by choice of s (and the associated value of α), while increasing s for a given n leads to higher employment and hence costs increase. More precisely, costs vary roughly in proportion to s^{n-1}, and the lower the value of s the lower the associated labor costs.

[15] The responses to changes in k are unambiguous. Those for changes in $\bar{Q}$ hold over all relevant values of α ($\geq .7$) and s (≥ 2).

[16] The derivation of equation (A1) is similar to Simon [**141**]. Simon does not, however, go on to derive the cumulative relationship given by equation (A2), which is ordinarily the only testable version of the model. A similar derivation to ours can, however, be found in Davis [**50**, chap. ix].

3

subgoal pursuit and the managerial discretion phenomenon

It will be assumed here and, except for some qualifying remarks in Chapter 10, throughout this book that the office of the peak coordinator regards its principal responsibility to be that of maintaining enterprise viability and that profit maximization is an effective proxy for this organizational objective. The question then is why, if these assumptions are satisfied even roughly, the view should now be widely embraced [30] [67] [112] that the separation of ownership from control poses a threat to stockholder interests.[1]

Of the various explanations, the one that we would propose for serious consideration turns on the distinction between the peak coordinator (who is an individual) and the process of peak coordination (which is a function). It is the function that is powerful, and while the peak coordinator participates in the peak coordination process in an important way, he may not, for reasons related to bounded rationality, dominate it. As a result, his preferences may somehow be compromised.

The argument will be facilitated by focusing on the strategic decision-making process. Section 1 discusses hierarchical organization and strategic decision-making. The argument is interpreted with the assistance of an elementary feedback control model. The way in which the processes of "natural" enterprise expansion described in the previous chapter (amplification rather than multidivisionalization) transform the character of strategic decision-making with pervasive goal consequences is treated in section 2. Subgoal pursuit and the managerial discretion phenomenon are considered in section 3.

1
HIERARCHICAL ORGANIZATION AND STRATEGIC DECISION MAKING

One repeatedly hears remarks—usually facetious, but sometimes expressed in dead earnest—that the behavior of an organization is dominated by its clerks and secretaries (or some other lower-level group). Although there is usually an element of truth to this, the power referred to is also ephemeral: It is apt to be extinguished if it is exercised. The position taken here—and, with qualifications, throughout this book—is that "in view of the hierarchical structure that is typical in most formal organizations, it is a reasonable use of language to employ organizational goal to refer particularly to the constraint sets and criteria of search that define roles at the upper level" [143, p. 21]. Almost certainly the office of the peak coordinator will be included in the upper-level classification. But what other groups qualify for inclusion, when, and with what consequences?

Consider in this connection a general control model of the firm and its relation to hierarchical structure. The main organizing device that will be used for examining differences in hierarchical control processes is W. Ross Ashby's model of what he terms an "ultrastable" system [17]. This model is a "first principles" treatment of the control problem, and hence is not by itself able to deal with all the ramifications of alternative control techniques. It does, nevertheless, provide a useful frame of reference, both for considering the ways by which control can be exercised and in characterizing major differences between alternative organization forms.

1.1
The Basic Model

Ashby's initial development of the model of an ultrastable system had the simple objective of identifying the minimum specifications for a system to adapt successfully (in the sense of maintaining viability) against disturbances of both a local and a general nature. The model was not conceived, therefore, in a normative or optimizing tradition, but merely as a means of identifying the essential control components necessary to sustain the system and the relationships these bear to each other. Moreover, the model was mainly intended to deal with biological and mechanical control systems rather than, as used here, for an examination of organizational control.

Stafford Beer, however, has since extended the Ashby model to consider corporate control, but his principal interest is in normative design rather than in positive analysis [29]. Beer's elaboration of the system is much more extensive than we shall require, and his emphasis on normative issues directs attention away from the rudimentary questions of positive economics that are of primary interest to us here. We shall, therefore, rely more on a simple interpretation of the Ashby model than on Beer's version in this chapter, although the latter will prove useful in several respects.

As noted above, Ashby is concerned with the problem of providing the minimum specifications for a system to adapt appropriately (in the sense of maintaining survival, if nothing else) to environmental change of two types. First, the system experiences frequent, small changes the adaptation to which requires only a change in degree. Second, the system experiences infrequent, large changes, the adaptation to which requires a change in kind. Assuming that the organism is already in a state of equilibrium, changes of the first type require only that the system preserve the state while changes of the second type require that it be able to shift to a new stable form [17, pp. 131–32]. Ashby then shows that the appropriate system will be one with double feedback. A direct feedback loop will exist between the environment and the "main variables" of the reacting part, and this will permit adjustment against the small, frequent disturbances. The second feedback loop will pass through the "essential variables" to a step-function generator, and this permits adjustments to large, infrequent disturbances that threaten to push the essential variables out of control limits under the existing specifications. As Beer puts it [29, pp. 290–91]:

> . . . an ultrastable system is capable of resuming a steady state after it has been disturbed *in a way not envisaged by its designer*. This is the really powerful feature of a homeostatic control mechanism. It is all very well for a system to be, as it were, programmed to respond to disturbances in a sensible way. The difficulties into which viable systems, whether natural or artificial, characteristically run are due to environmental disturbances of an unexpected kind.

Although Ashby never uses the term "performance program," it is a broadly accurate way of characterizing much of the behavior that he is concerned with and is a term that has found widespread use in the organization theory literature [**104**, pp. 141–48]. His adaptive response processes will, therefore, be described in performance program terms. First, however, consider the variables in his system and the schematic connections between them.

The "environment" (*E*) is exogenous to the system.[2] Sources of disturbance of both kinds originate there. The environment can thus be viewed as a variety generator; system survival requires that appropriate adaptive responses be selected against each configuration of parameters that is presented. The system consists of a reacting part (*R*) in which the main variables (or decision variables) are located, a set of essential variables (*V*), and the step-mechanisms (*S*). The connections between the environment and each of these system components are shown in Figure 3-1.

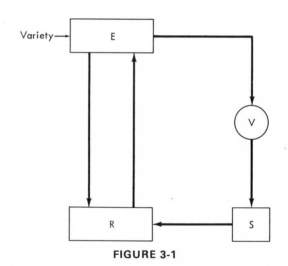

FIGURE 3-1

Assume that the system is initially in a state of equilibrium. This means that the performance programs supplied to the reacting part (*R*) by the step-mechanisms (*S*) are such that the reacting part is able to select values on its main variables (decision variables) that yield performance results which satisfy the control limits on its essential variables (*V*) under the conditions presented by the environment (*E*). Small changes in the condition of the environment are adapted to by the reacting part within the constraints imposed by existing performance programs. Thus small changes in *E* induce self-organizing responses in *R* that satisfy the essential variables at *V* without any change in the step-mechanisms *S*. So long as the adaptations at *R* continue to yield performance results which satisfy the essential variables without change in S, the adaptive response will be termed one of degree but not of kind. If, however, a large change in E occurs, the existing performance programs imposed by S on R may be poorly suited to generate the appropriate response. In this case the values of the main variables would yield performance results which are unsatisfactory (fall outside the control limits at V) and this induces a change in the step-mechanisms. This will cause a new set of performance programs to be supplied to the reacting part, and the main variables in the reacting part will now be selected under this new set of constraints. The appropriateness of this new set of performance programs will then be determined by ascertaining whether the essential variables are returned to values that are within the control limits. If they are, the step-mechanisms will fix on this new set of performance programs. If they are not, the step-mechanisms will introduce a second set of performance programs (and will continue to shift) until the resulting behavior at R restores the essential variables to their control limits. Changes of this type will be termed changes in kind. Ashby proves that double feedback is a *necessary condition* for a system to possess the type of adaptive behavior described: "*Any* system that has essential variables with given limits, and that adapts by the process of testing behaviors by how each affects ultimately the essential variables, must have a second feedback formally identical (isomorphic) with that described here. This deduction holds equally for brains living and mechanical" [17, p. 85]—and, as Beer observes, organizational as well [29, p. 378].

Data transmission between the parts must be brought into appropriate correspondence if such a system is to perform satisfactorily. More precisely,

> when an organism is adapting by discrete trials, the essential variables must change the step-mechanisms at a rate slower than the rate at which the main variables change. Too rapid a change at the step-mechanisms means that the appropriateness (or not) of a set of values does not have time to be communicated round. . . . If it takes ten years to observe adequately the effect of a profound re-organization of a Civil Service, then such re-organization ought not to occur more frequently than at eleven-year intervals [17, pp. 218–19].

It is important to note that Ashby does not say that the adjustment to a new set of performance programs should be allowed to go to completion. Rather, the effect of any change should be observed "adequately" before it is decided that the particular adaptation is inappropriate. Obviously inference techniques for projecting accurate estimates of eventual effects based on early observations will be very valuable in such a system.

1.2
The Model Interpreted

It is interesting to note that this system can be interpreted as a three-level hierarchy, and closely corresponds in this respect to the description of corporate organizations given by Simon [**144**, p. 98]:

> An organization can be pictured as a three-layered cake. In the bottom layer, we have the basic work processes—in the case of a manufacturing organization, the processes that procure raw materials, manufacture the physical product, warehouse it, and ship it. In the middle layer, we have the programmed decision-making processes, the processes that govern the day-to-day operation of the manufacturing and distribution system. In the top layer, we have the nonprogrammed decision-making processes, the processes that are required to design and redesign the entire system, to provide it with its basic goals and objectives, and to monitor its performance.

The reacting part clearly corresponds to Simon's lower level of basic work processes; the step-mechanisms presumably discharge the programming functions assigned to the middle layer; the essential variables correspond to the top layer of nonprogrammed goal formation and control processes.

In terms of the description of hierarchical functions given earlier, the bottom layer (reacting part) includes the operators and first-line supervisors, the middle layer (step-mechanisms) corresponds to the middle managers, and the top layer (essential variables) is the peak coordinating function. What might be characterized as the strategic decisions, which involve long-run planning and resource allocation[3] as well as adaptation to really large environmental disturbances, are (intendedly) discharged at the top. One would expect that the preferences of the executives on whom this responsibility devolves will be ones which decisively "count" in characterizing the firm's objective function. The peak coordinator himself is naturally one of these executives; his preferences, by assumption, favor profit maximization. If, however, the office of the peak coordinator is overcome by proliferating variety and the capacity-augmenting strategy mentioned in the previous chapter is adopted (which involves sharing these duties), his preferences may not be prevailing. It is to this matter that we turn now.

2
ENTERPRISE EXPANSION AND
STRATEGIC DECISION MAKING

For the reasons described in Chapter 2, enterprise expansion that takes the form of amplification eventually crowds the capacity of the peak coordinator's office. Two strategies were proposed to help overcome this condition. One involved an attempt to alleviate this condition by cutting down on coordinating requirements through the use of decoupling devices. The other is a capacity-augmenting strategy and is the approach of interest to us here.

Among the several augmenting alternatives that are available, the dominant solution has involved sharing the peak coordinating function with the heads of the functional divisions. As Chandler and Redlich point out, large unitary form corporations adopted this device around the turn of the century to help overcome the bounded capacity problem. As they put it [**43**, p. 9]:

> The head of each functional division was a specialist and supreme in his own sphere. Usually a vice-president, he had his managing director for dealing with the routine activities of his department. The vice-presidents, as individuals, planned the broader developments within their functionally determined divisions. Collectively, together with the president and chairman of the board, they guided the destinies of their vast business empires.

Although initially these functional division chiefs may have been engaged mainly in the coordination of operating matters, their knowledge and expertise also made them natural candidates to assist the peak coordinator with broader aspects of his duties, including the strategic decision-making function. Indeed, this transformation is quite explicit in the citation above. Overall enterprise direction thus came to be determined jointly by the office of the peak coordinator together with these functional division chiefs.

As a result of this change in the nature of the role of these functional executives, the mapping described earlier that relates ultrastable system component to hierarchical level is no longer one-to-one. The above described functional vice-presidents are now engaged in both strategic decision-making (essential variable) and operationalizing (step-function) activities. This is an unusually powerful combination. The goal formation consequences of this evolutionary development of the large unitary form organization remain to be discovered.

3
SUBGOAL PURSUIT AND
THE MANAGERIAL DISCRETION PHENOMENON

3.1
Subgoal Pursuit

Given this transformation in the character of the strategic decision-making process, it is no longer obvious that the goals of the enterprise can be usefully represented as those of the peak coordinator. For this to obtain would require that opportunities for discretion be absent or that functional division chiefs should identify exclusively with enterprise-wide objectives in discharging their responsibilities. Since, by assumption, the firms in question are ones for which discretionary opportunities exist, only the latter is of interest to us here.

That the heads of the functional divisions should adopt the same profit maximization posture as the peak coordinator seems unlikely. For one thing, it would require that they undergo role transformations of an extreme sort. Functional identifications must prevail when operating duties are being discharged, while enterprise-wide considerations must obtain during their participation in the strategic decision-making process. That an individual with operating responsibilities should disregard these (except as they have strictly functional significance to the peak coordination function) when he wears his strategic decision-making hat is to require adaptability of an uncommon sort. (This is not to suggest that individuals cannot or do not regularly undergo significant attitudinal transformations as they move from one level in the hierarchy to another, say as a result of promotions.[4] But here we are dealing with the coexistence of two roles. That neither should affect the other seems unlikely.)

It could be argued, of course, that the roles are somehow offsetting: while the heads of the functional divisions bring parochial attitudes into strategic decision-making, they compensate by bringing global attitudes into functional activities. As a result, any disinclination to favor profits in the one role is offset by a sensitivity to higher-order considerations in the other. This argument experiences two difficulties. First, the introduction of enterprise-wide considerations into operating matters may be counterproductive. Each part of the enterprise is expected to perform its specialist function according to the prescribed rules. Groups that are forever contemplating the wider consequences of their activities and adapting accordingly may be generating more problems than they solve. Second, even if there are beneficial offsetting effects, the real question is one of degree. What net effects are to be expected? Since the functional division chief has near-exclusive responsibility for the welfare and performance of his functional division but only partial (and ill-defined) responsibility for the enterprise-wide side of his assignment, a net functional-favoring orientation seems likely.[5]

Internal natural selection processes are also apt to favor this outcome. Candidates for promotion are those who distinguish themselves in their respective functional activity. Moreover, even if a division chief were successfully to make the enterprise-wide transformation in dealing with strategic affairs, unless his peers undergo a similar transformation the system generates forces that encourage him to adopt an advocacy posture. Without his aggressive support, the interests that he is expected to represent go unattended, and the need for his replacement is apt both to be perceived among his associates and to be demanded by his subordinates. A nonpartisan chief may thus be nonviable in these circumstances. That mixing strategic and operating responsibilities should have this effect on the strategic decision-making process is supported by the historical survey of Chandler and Redlich [43, pp. 10–11]:

> ... planning for the maintenance and expansion of the enterprise as a whole ... meant that the senior officers had to make basic decisions with respect to several very different functional activities. The executive committee had to allocate funds among departments and thus decided whether to expand or contract in sales, manufacturing, the control of raw materials, engineering, etc. In so doing, it had to face a new specific difficulty. Since this top committee was made up of department heads, i.e., of functional specialists, the final policy tended to be the result of negotiations and compromise between the different departments. In addition, the top level team, so composed, had neither enough time, nor enough impartial information to handle over-all problems satisfactorily. Its members spent most of their working day on departmental matters, and the information on which the executive committee acted was biased just because it was framed by these executives in their capacities as functional operating officers. Factual and analytical reports were usually presented so as to favor one of the alternatives under discussion, although this was not always done consciously.

3.2
Managerial Discretion

Managerial discretion can be viewed in two distinct stages. First, what is the opportunity set to which the strategic decision-makers have access? Second, what forms does the exercise of managerial discretion take? Each will be considered in order.

3.2.1. Opportunity sets. It will be assumed that the firm is constrained to take up a position of nonnegative profits. Any collection of decision variables that satisfies this condition will fall within the firm's opportunity set [28]. This may also be termed the region of enterprise viability. The management's opportunity set is the firm's opportunity set reduced by the amount of minimum profits demanded (π_0) to forestall a management displacement effort. Symmetrically, this will be termed the region of management viability.

Opportunity sets of several types will be distinguished (for each type, the enterprise and management opportunity sets differ by an additive constant π_0):[6]

1. *Maximal potential opportunity set.* This set will obtain if the firm selects the best organization form for its scale and type of activity. Location on the boundary of this set presumes full compliance

by lower-level participants in the organization with expressed managerial preferences.

2. *Actual potential opportunity set.* This set will be the same as the maximal set only if organization form has been chosen optimally. Otherwise it will be smaller than the maximal set to reflect inferior choice of organization form.

3. *Effective opportunity set.* This is the set to which the strategic decision-makers in the firm have access when allowance is made for noncompliance by lower-level participants. The effective opportunity set will be identical to the actual opportunity set only if lower-level participants behave in strictly functional ways.

"Strictly functional" will be interpreted to mean a day's work for a day's pay with no calculated attempt to influence outcomes by distorting information. Nonfunctional activity involves either on-the-job leisure or information distortion. Both will be assumed to be a function of higher-level example and thus will result from imitative rather than original behavior. In the absence of evidence of subgoal pursuit in the strategic decision-making process, lower-level behavior will be assumed to be chiefly functional. Nonfunctional behavior of either sort will therefore be reflected in an imitative efficiency parameter. This is a strong version of Geoffrey Vickers contention that "Imitation and emulation are at least as important psychic forces as the fear of kicks or the desire for carrots" [**158**, p. 47].

3.2.2. Managerial discretion. Efficient choice will naturally place the firm on the boundary rather than inside of its effective opportunity set. This may, of course, be inside of its actual potential set on account of noncompliance, which in turn may be inside the maximal potential set on account of inferior choice of organization form. Whatever these effects, it will be assumed that the management locates on the boundary of its effective opportunity set. Where on the boundary the firm will operate depends on what factors the heads of the functional divisions are prone to give consideration. How is the firm's utility function, as revealed through the strategic decision-making process, influenced by the participation of these functional division chiefs?

Almost certainly, profits will remain as one component of the effective objective function. Conceivably this could be represented simply by stipulating a "consensus" profits constraint (equal to or greater than minimum profits demanded), but this seems somewhat arbitrary and solves the problem of a tradeoff between profits and other goals in a particularly severe way. Instead, profits will be included explicitly in the objective function as one of several goals to which the strategic decision-making process attaches positive value. That it should be the only goal, however, is doubtful—at least in the type of organization structure described here where profits are the exclusive responsibility of none of the functional divisions.

A second objective, and a consideration that the functional division chiefs can be expected to be especially responsive to, is hierarchical expense, or "staff." As Alfred Marshall observed, the selective expansion of operations may easily be perceived by the management as having benefits that can be distributed quite generally throughout the management hierarchy [**110**, pp. 321–22]. Indeed, since promotional opportunities within a fixed-size firm are limited (while to increase jurisdiction has the same general effect as promotion but simultaneously produces the opportunity for advance to all [**139**, pp. 117–18] [**152**, pp. 101–2]), the incentive to expand staff may be difficult to resist. Being a means to promotion, expansion of staff serves to advance both salary and dominance objectives simultaneously. In addition, staff can contribute to the satisfaction of security and professional achievement objectives as well [**21**, p. 159].

Organization theorists have observed that "the modern organization is a prolific generator of anxiety and insecurity" [**152**, p. 24]. This insecurity is partly due to uncertainty with respect to the survival of the organization as a whole. More important (in the sense of being more immediately relevant to its individual members) is the security of the parts with which the individuals identify. Attempts to reduce perceived sources of insecurity can be expected. Indeed, the direction these efforts will take can be anticipated. If the surest guarantee of the survival of the individual parts appears to be size, efforts to expand the separate staff functions can be predicted.

A "professional" inducement to expand staff arises from the typical view that a progressive staff is one that is continuously providing more and better services. An aggressive staff will therefore be looking for ways to expand. Although in choosing directions for expansion the relative contribution to productivity will be considered, the absolute effect on profit may be neglected. As long as the organization is able to satisfy its requirements for acceptable level of performance, the tendency to value staff apart from reasons associated with its productivity produces a predisposition to extend programs beyond the point where marginal costs equal marginal revenues.

As indicated above, the functional division chief who does not share these preferences is not apt to be viable for long. His subordinates will realistically view their individual prospects and collective success in terms of the size and prominence of their own operations in relation to that of other functional divisions. To act conservatively may be to decline relatively, with the possibility that more aggressively constituted divisions will begin to crowd or pre-empt activities to which the division in question might otherwise logically lay claim. To engage instead in partisan representations is to fulfill expectations and realize local gains simultaneously. Thus, except possibly in circumstances where firm viability itself is in jeopardy (in which case a different set of executives with different preferences might emerge), advocacy would appear to be in an internal natural selection sense the favored posture. Assigning a positive value to staff or hierarchical expense is therefore to be expected.

A third objective that seems not implausible, at least in a munificent environment, is slack or on-the-job-leisure. The reluctance explicitly to include such a concept in the theory of the firm is perhaps attributable to a recognition that on-the-job leisure is a general condition characteristic, to a greater or lesser extent, of every line of human endeavor. The interesting question, however, is whether this behavior is invariant or adjusts to relative prices. The latter assumption, which is the more general, will be employed here, and some modest evidence will be adduced on its behalf. Although the argument is tentative, it seems potentially too important to dismiss. Except for efficiency losses attributable to an inferior choice of organization form (which has not previously been examined in an efficiency context), leisure losses would appear to be the most likely candidate to generate nontrivial static allocative efficiency losses. Otherwise one is left mainly with selling expense and Marshallian triangles to manipulate.[7] The former is notoriously difficult to evaluate rigorously, while the latter does not take on quantitative significance for any reasonable set of assumptions [71] [91] [163]. Since even a relatively small leisure loss[8] can, by comparison, effect a large welfare loss, it seems injudicious to rule out such effects from the outset.

FOOTNOTES

[1] The first detailed statement of this view was that of Berle and Means [31]. For a similar statement of concern that was left undeveloped, see Keynes [84].

[2] Beer develops the proposition that "the environment of a system not only affects it [but] the system *belongs* to the environment." He thus introduces the notion of a "coenetic variable," which is defined as "the common causal determinant of the state of both the environmental disturbance and the [system] at the same time" [29, p. 285]. This is a useful way to formulate the problem, but for simplicity the exogenous relation will be employed here.

[3] R. N. Anthony characterizes strategic planning as a process [10, pp. 24–25]:

> . . . having to do with the formulation of long-range, strategic plans and policies that determine or change the character or direction of the organization. In an industrial company this process includes planning that affects the objectives of the company; the acquisition and disposition of major facilities, divisions, or subsidiaries; policies of

all types, including policies as to management control and other processes, the markets to serve and distribution channels for serving them, the organization structure . . . , research and development of new product lines . . . , sources of new permanent capital and dividend policy, and so on.

Also see [**59**, p. 119] [**125**, pp. 245–46].

[4] As Simon notes, Thomas Becket is an example of a highly institutionalized personality [**139**, p. 214, n. 20].

[5] In conjunction with the preceding footnote, it is relevant to point out that the goal tensions experienced by Becket in his dual role as Chancellor of England and Archbishop of Canterbury were resolved (much to the dismay of Henry II) mainly in favor of the archbishopric—which would appear to be roughly consistent with the suggestion advanced in the text.

[6] This assumes that π_0 is independent of the opportunity set, which oversimplifies. See Chapter 6.

[7] This assumes that all efficiency-adjusted output is counted equally in expressing national income. Some might weight different components (e.g., defense expenditures) differently. See [**132**, Chap. 17].

[8] This presents a problem, however. Is leisure loss to be counted as the full value of output sacrificed, or is it a source of satisfaction properly to be regarded as partially offsetting?

4

managerial discretion in the unitary form corporation: static aspects*

The purpose of this chapter and the following one will be to investigate the equilibrium and the comparative static and dynamic properties of firms that have expanded by means of amplification—which is to say that the functional or unitary structure has been preserved as the firm becomes large. This process results in the introduction of additional hierarchical levels with control loss consequences (see Chapter 2) and transforms the nature of strategic decision-making with the goal pursuit effects described in the previous chapter.

As indicated earlier, it will be assumed that the executives in the firm whose preferences decisively count are those who participate

*Portions of this chapter have been reprinted from O. E. Williamson, *The Economics of Discretionary Behavior: Managerial Objectives in a Theory of the Firm* (Chicago: Markham Publishing Company, 1967), Chap. 4.

directly in the strategic decision-making process. It will also be assumed that a consensus among them is reached (see [**160**, Chap. 8]) in specifying what, in effect, can be regarded as the goals of the firm. A variable proportions model in which staff and profit constitute the principal components of the utility function is examined in section 1. A roughly parallel treatment of a fixed proportions model that includes a control loss effect is given in section 2. Revenues are substituted for staff as a proxy for the size aspirations of the management in the model treated in section 3. An appendix is included in which slack as well as staff and profits enters the utility function.

1
A VARIABLE
PROPORTIONS MODEL

The variable proportions model developed in this section has two components in the utility function: staff and profit. Both the geometry and the calculus are laid out in some detail for this model since later models (see the appendix) can be regarded as a variant of it.

The following terms enter into the analysis:

$$R = \text{revenue} = PX; \quad \partial^2 R/\partial X\partial S \geq 0$$
$$P = \text{price} = P(X, S; E); \quad \partial P/\partial X < 0; \quad \partial P/\partial S \geq 0;$$
$$\partial P/\partial E > 0$$
$$X = \text{output}$$
$$S = \text{productive staff expense}$$
$$mS = \text{slack staff expense}$$
$$(1 + m)S = \text{total staff expense}$$
$$m/(1 + m) = \text{fraction of total staff expense taken as slack}$$
$$E = \text{the condition of the environment (a demand shift parameter)}$$
$$\theta C = \text{production cost} = \theta C(X); \quad \partial \acute{C}/\partial x > 0$$
$$\theta = \text{imitation parameter} = \theta(m); \quad \theta' > 0, \; \theta'' > 0$$
$$\Pi = \text{reported profit} = R - \theta C - (1 + m)S$$
$$\pi_0 = \text{minimum (after tax) profit demanded}$$
$$T = \text{taxes, where } t = \text{tax rate and } \bar{T} = \text{lump-sum tax}$$
$$\pi - \pi_0 - T = \text{discretionary profit}$$
$$U = \text{the utility function}$$

We begin with a statement of the basic managerial discretion model, including an examination of its equilibrium and comparative static properties. An application of the model to examine the effects of regulatory restraint is given in 1.2.

1.1
The Basic Model

With staff and profit entering into the utility function, the firm's objective is taken to be

$$\text{maximize:} \quad U = U(S, \pi - \pi_0 - T)$$
$$\text{subject to:} \quad \pi \geq \pi_0 + T$$

The constraint can be rewritten as $\pi - \pi_0 - T \geq 0$. Assuming diminishing marginal utility and disallowing corner solutions, it follows that the firm will always choose values of its decision variables which will yield positive utility with respect to each component of its utility function. The second component is $\pi - \pi_0 - T$. If it is always to be positive, then constraint will always be satisfied as an inequality. Thus the constraint is redundant and the problem can be treated as one of straightforward maximization.[1] Substituting the functional relationships for profit into the expression yields:

$$\text{maximize:} \quad U = U[S, (1 - t)(R - C - S - \bar{T}) - \pi_0]$$

The following first-order results are obtained by setting the partial derivatives of U with respect to X and S equal to zero.[2]

$$\frac{\partial R}{\partial X} = \frac{\partial C}{\partial X} \tag{1}$$

$$\frac{\partial R}{\partial S} = \frac{-U_1 + (1 - t)U_2}{(1 - t)U_2} \tag{2}$$

From Equation 1 we observe that the firm makes its production decision in the conventional fashion by equating marginal gross revenue to the marginal costs of production. However, Equation 2 reveals that the firm will employ staff in the region where the marginal value product of staff is less than its marginal cost. That is, the firm will operate where $\partial R/\partial S < 1$, whereas the usual short-period profit maximization model would employ staff only to the point where the equality between marginal costs and benefits obtains. Equation 2 can be rewritten as

$$\frac{\partial R}{\partial S} = 1 - \frac{1}{1 - t}\frac{U_1}{U_2}$$

where U_1/U_2 is the marginal rate of substitution between profit and staff. *Ceteris paribus*, an increase in the ratio reflects a shift in tastes in favor of staff. In a profit maximizing organization this ratio is zero.

These relationships are displayed graphically in Figure 4-1. With staff plotted along the ordinate and output along the abscissa, isoprofit contours are imbedded in the XS plane. These contours are elliptical with major axes running from southwest to northeast.[3] Connecting points of tangency between the isoprofit contours and a series of horizontal lines at successively greater levels of staff traces out the locus $R_x = C_x$—i.e., the locus of optimal output given the level of staff expense. Similarly the points of tangency between the isoprofit contours and a series of vertical lines drawn at successively greater levels of output yields the locus $R_s = 1$. Their intersection, K, corresponds to the short-run profit maximization position.

Since the equilibrium relations are $R_x = C_x$ and $R_s < 1$, the utility-maximizing firm will take up a position somewhere along the locus $R_x = C_x$ but above the locus $R_s = 1$. Point A in Figure 4-1 represents such a position. Thus, the utility-maximizing firm will choose a larger value of staff, and this will in turn give rise to a larger value of output than would be chosen by the firm that maximizes short-run profit.

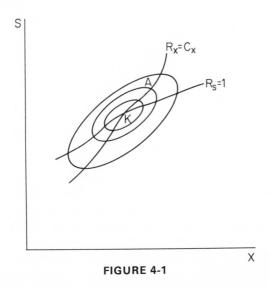

FIGURE 4-1

The locus $R_x = C_x$ specifies the pairs of (X, S) combinations along which the firm that has its utility function augmented to include a staff component will locate. For every value of staff there exists an optimal value of output, say $\hat{X}$, where $\hat{X} = f(S)$. Given the condition of the environment, profit depends on the choice of X and S, that is, $\pi = g(X, S; E)$. If, however, X is chosen optimally, then

$$\pi = g(\hat{X}, S; E) = g[f(S), S; E] = g'(S; E)$$

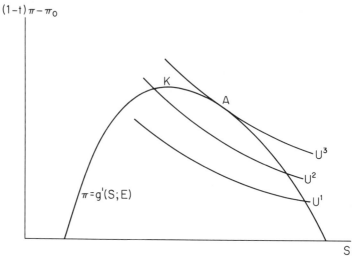

FIGURE 4-2

Thus, profit can be plotted as a function of staff. This is done in Figure 4-2 with profit along the ordinate and staff along the abscissa. By introducing indifference curves between profit and staff, the equilibrium results can be interpreted somewhat differently. Again, the point K represents the profit-maximizing position and A, the point where the tangency between the indifference curves and the profit curve obtains, is the position at which the utility-maximizing firm will locate.

Several generalizations suggest themselves immediately. First, for the firm to select the point K requires that the slope of the indifference curves in the region around K be zero; that is, the marginal rate of substitution between profits and staff must be zero. Since $MRS = -(d\pi/dS) = [(\partial U/\partial S)/(\partial U/\partial \pi)]$, this implies that the marginal utility of staff in the vicinity of K must be zero. Either staff must be "objectively" valued only for its contribution to profit or the benefits associated with expanding staff must be exhausted before K is reached. If the argument regarding the positive preference for staff is accepted, the first of these can be dismissed and the second represents a limiting condition. Considering the variety of ways in which staff contributes to managerial satisfactions, the zero marginal utility condition seems unlikely to be realized.

A second observation is that if the profit curve is very sharply peaked, the resulting tangency will be one where the value of staff (and output) selected will not be far removed from the profit maximization position. As the profit curve becomes flatter, however, and as the indifference curves become more steeply sloped (i.e., as staff becomes relatively more highly valued), the tangency shifts progressively to the right.

Having established the equilibrium conditions, the comparative statics properties of the model remain to be developed. That is, we want to displace the equilibrium. In particular, we want to find how the system adjusts to a change in the condition of the environment (the demand-shift parameter E), a change in the profits tax rate (t), and a lump-sum tax ($\bar{T}$).

It will facilitate the argument to compact the notation and designate each decision variable by Z_i and each parameter by α_j. Then the function $U(X, S; E, t, \bar{T})$ can be represented as $U(Z_1, Z_2; \alpha_1, \alpha_2, \alpha_3)$. The general form[4] for determining the response of the pth decision variable to a change in the kth parameter is:

$$\left(\frac{\partial Z_p}{\partial \alpha_k}\right)^0 = \frac{-\sum_{i=1}^{2} \dfrac{\partial^2 U}{\partial Z_i \partial \alpha_k} D_{ip}}{|D|}, \qquad \begin{array}{l} p = 1, 2 \\ k = 1, \ldots, 3 \end{array}$$

where D_{ip} is the cofactor of the ith row and the pth column of D and $|D|$ is the determinant of the second partials $\partial^2 U / \partial Z_i \partial Z_j$. The sign matrix D is

$$D = \left\| \begin{array}{cc} - & + \\ + & - \end{array} \right\|$$

Second-order conditions for a maximum require that D be positive.[5]

The signs of the values $\partial^2 U / \partial Z_i \partial \alpha_k$ for $Z_i = X, S$ and $\alpha_k = E, t, \bar{T}$ are as follows:[6]

$$\left\| \frac{\partial^2 U}{\partial Z_i \partial \alpha_k} \right\| = \begin{array}{c|ccc} & E & t & \bar{T} \\ \hline X & + & 0 & 0 \\ S & + & +? & - \end{array}$$

TABLE 4-1

Comparative Statics Responses for the Staff Model

		Parameter		
		E	t	$\bar{T}$
Variable	X^0	+	+?	−
	S^0	+	+?	−

The comparative statics responses, shown in Table 4-1, are obtained directly and without difficulty from the sign relationships alone. The direction of adjustment of any particular decision variable to a displacement from equilibrium by an increase in a parameter is found by referring to the row and column entry corresponding to this pair.

That the response to an increase in the profits tax rate is not unambiguous is due to a combination of substitution and income effects. As shown in [**160**, pp. 61–65], the net substitution effect of staff to an increase in the profits tax rate is always positive, whereas the "income" effect is always negative. The gross substitution effect is the combination of these two separate effects so that its sign depends on their relative magnitudes. As shown in [**160**, pp. 61–65], the gross substitution effect will usually be positive although, when the firm encounters adversity and has difficulty in satisfying its minimum profit the response may be negative. The direction of response of output to a change in the profits tax rate is identical to that of staff. Indeed, it is a derived rather than a direct effect: in the absence of the staff component in the utility function, output would be unchanged.

These income and substitution effects can also be interpreted graphically by an extension of the apparatus used in Figure 4-2. In the construction of that figure it was shown that $\pi = g'(S)$. It is likewise true, therefore, that $(1 - t)\pi - \pi_0$ can be expressed as a function of staff, where $(1 - t)\pi - \pi_0$ is discretionary profit (Figure 4-3).

The profit as a function of staff curves are drawn for a tax rate of $t = 0$ and $t = t_1$, where $t_1 > 0$. At tax rate $t = 0$, the optimum position for the firm occurs at A, where tangency between the profit

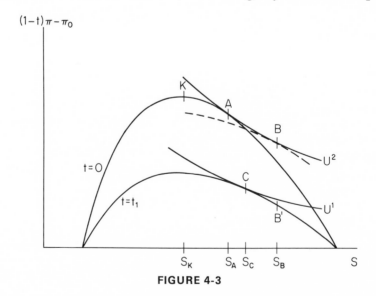

FIGURE 4-3

curve $t = 0$ and the indifference curve U^2 occurs. When the tax rate is increased to t_1, tangency of the resulting profit curve and the indifference curves occurs at C. As drawn, the optimal choice of staff increases ($S_C > S_A$).

The adjustment can be broken up into an income and a substitution effect by introducing a *compensated* tax change. Thus the dashed curve through A is a vertical displacement of the curve $t = t_1$. If the firm were awarded a lump-sum bounty simultaneously with the increase in the profits tax just large enough for it to continue to realize the utility represented by U^2, its profit curve would be the dashed curve shown. Since the slope of the curve t_1 is everywhere less than the corresponding slope of the curve $t = 0$, tangency between the dashed curve and the indifference curves will occur to the right of A. The point designated B represents such a position, and the shift from A to B is the *net substitution effect*. Since profit and staff are substitutes, the net substitution effect is unambiguously positive; that is, when the "price" of taking satisfaction in the form of profit increases, the compensated tax adjustment always leads to a substitution of staff for profit and $S_B > S_A$.

If the indifference curves were vertical displacements of one another, the curve U^1 would be tangent to the profits curve $t = t_1$ at B'. The vertical displacement condition, however, is not quite realistic. It represents a condition where, given the level of staff, the marginal rate of substitution across successive indifference curves is constant. Instead, the marginal rate of substitution will normally fall as profit declines. That is, at lower levels of profit, the increase in staff required to offset a specified reduction in profit and still maintain the same level of utility becomes larger. Thus the indifference curve U^1 is drawn so that the marginal rate of substitution at each level of staff is everywhere smaller than it is along the indifference curve U_2. Hence tangency occurs not at B' but at C. The shift from B to C represents the *income effect*. Were the vertical displacement condition to hold between indifference curves, the income effect would be zero. In the usual circumstance where the marginal rate of substitution falls as profit declines, the income effect will be negative and $S_C < S_B$.

By postulating that the marginal rate of substitution behaves in this prescribed way instead of permitting it to vary without limitation, I impose a restriction on the utility function that may seem objectionable. I submit, however, that the restriction is perfectly reasonable. It merely guarantees that the staff component in the utility function is not an inferior good. Whereas special assumptions of this sort are unwarranted in the analysis of consumer behavior where the arguments that enter the utility function are deliberately left in an unspecified general form (and hence the possibility of inferior good must be admitted), the components of the utility function under study here are fully specified and, hence, the analysis can be bounded appropriately. Indeed, where generality is attained only at the expense of relevance, a specialization of the analysis that removes uninteresting or implausible contingencies is altogether warranted.

Invoking this principle in the present case dictates the following choice: since each of the expenses for which a positive preference has been indicated is surely a normal good and since leaving the inferior good possibility open merely produces confusion, the inferior good contingency is disallowed. Indeed, Scitovsky's analysis of entrepreneurial behavior is essentially an application of this principle and rests on a stronger specialization of the utility function than the one I employ. In his analysis the marginal rate of substitution, given the level of activity, is constant across successive levels of profit (see [**160**, p. 18, n. 6]). In the present analysis, this constant marginal rate of substitution relationship represents a limiting condition.

The gross substitution effect is the combination of the net substitution and income effects and thus depends on the relative magnitudes of these two effects. As shown in [**160**, pp. 61–65], the gross substitution effect will normally be positive ($S_C > S_A$), although as adversity is encountered and the firm is hard pressed to satisfy its minimum profit constraint, it may become negligible and could become negative. As long as the firm is enjoying comparative prosperity, however, the gross substitution effect will generally be positive and staff will be increased in response to an increase in the profits tax rate.

The effects of a progressive tax rate can be investigated by letting $T = h(\pi)$ be the profits tax. Then discretionary profit will be $\pi - h(\pi) - \pi_0$, and, since $\pi = g'(S)$, this can be expressed as a function of staff. This is shown in Figure 4-4, where the responses to a constant and progressive tax rate are examined. Three profit curves are drawn. The top curve represents a zero tax condition. The solid curve below it shows profit under a progressive profits tax. The dashed curve shows profits under a constant profits tax. The progressive tax rate produces a profit curve flatter at the top than does the constant tax rate. Thus tangency between the indifference curves and the profit curve is shifted significantly to the right (at C). Actual profit is given by C' and the distance between C and C' is the amount of tax collected.[7] To summarize, under the progressive profits tax, actual profit is reduced from π_A to $\pi_{C'}$, due to expanding staff from S_A to S_C, and a tax of CC' is collected.

The constant profits rate t_1 is chosen so that tangency between the resulting profit curve and the indifference curves occurs at a point

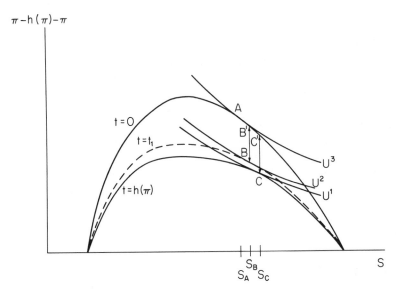

$\pi - h(\pi) - \pi$

FIGURE 4-4

that yields precisely the same amount of tax as was collected under the progressive tax program. Thus the length BB′ is the same as CC′. Since the marginal tax rate under the constant profits tax is less than it would be under the progressive profits tax plan, there is less incentive for the firm to absorb profits and take its satisfactions through staff. Thus $S_B < S_C$, $\pi_B > \pi_C$, and $\pi_{B'} > \pi_{C'}$. These results hold over the entire range of possible progressive versus constant profits tax rates as long as tax collections under both arrangements are required to be equal.

The effects of a lump-sum tax can also be examined with this type of diagram. To increase the lump-sum tax shifts the profit curve vertically downward. If the indifference curves were vertical displacements of one another, tangency would occur at precisely the same level of staff expense. Since, however, the marginal rate of substitution decreases as profit decreases (given the level of staff), the indifference curves become somewhat flatter and tangency obtains at a lower value for staff.

As is well-known, the short-run profit-maximizing firm is entirely unresponsive to both a change in the profits tax rate and to the levy of a lump-sum tax. The implications of the utility maximization analysis as contrasted with those of the usual profit maximization analysis are thus significantly different and appear to be testable.

1.2
Application to Public Utilities

Since the types of departures from profit-maximizing behavior that are said to exist in public utilities (and other regulated industries) appear to be derivable by a direct application of the proposed model, it may be worthwhile to demonstrate the relevance of the model to this class of firms separately. Alchian and Kessel have discussed this kind of behavior previously [4], but they have not attempted to develop their argument in the context of a model. The behavior they describe follows as a logical consequence of the managerial discretion models developed above.

The rates that a public utility is permitted to charge are set at levels which are intended to allow the utility to cover its costs and earn a fair rate of return [18, p. 1052]. Ordinarily, rates are not adjusted continuously as conditions change but are revised only periodically. In the short run, therefore, a utility may earn above or below normal profit, but this is not a situation that will be long continued; profit will eventually be restored to a fair level by rate adjustments.

Since above-normal profit cannot be long continued and since supernormal profit may invite the early attention of the regulatory commissions, the management of a public utility that has other than profit-maximizing objectives has an incentive to hold profit at or below some "safe" level. In the absence of other restrictions, one would expect that profit would be absorbed in ways which are especially productive of managerial satisfaction; in the context of the present model, this would be as staff.

That the argument is not wholly speculative is at least suggested by R. J. Gordon's study of comparative airline efficiency. He found that differential efficiency between airlines was mainly accounted for by excess personnel [68, p. 83]. Moreover, the magnitude of estimated cost excesses was not trivial: "If the industry had been able to save a *third* of the estimated potential cost savings . . . its rate of return would have been doubled" [68, p. 90]. Also, the extent of cost excesses were found to vary directly with the degree to which an airline had access to favorable route advantages, which is to say monopoly power [68, pp. 90–91]. Although, as Gordon concedes, the data and analysis are crude, the results are too strong to be easily dismissed.

Conceivably, if these tendencies are general, regulatory agencies will inspect for an "expense balance": staff expenditures may not be permitted to exceed some maximum proportion of total output.[8] It may for these reasons be necessary to augment the above model by introducing two additional restraints if the effects of regulation on firm behavior are to be adequately assessed. The objective of the firm is therefore expressed as:

$$\text{maximize:} \quad U = U[S, \pi - (\pi_0 + T)]$$

subject to: (i) $\pi \geq \pi_0 + T$

           (ii) $\pi \leq \bar{\pi}$

         (iii) $S \leq kX$

For the reasons given previously, the minimum profit constraint $(\pi_0 + T)$ is redundant, but the maximum profit constraint $(\bar{\pi})$ and the expenditure balance restraint (kX) may be encountered. The problem restated, using the method of the Lagrangian multiplier, becomes:

$$\text{maximize } L(X, S, \lambda_1, \lambda_2) = U[S, (R - C - S)(1 - t) - \pi_0]$$
$$- \lambda_1[R - C - S)(1 - t) - \bar{\pi}]$$
$$- \lambda_2(S - kX),$$

where $(-\lambda_i)$ are Langrange multipliers.

Setting the partial derivative of L with respect to X, S, λ_1, and λ_2 equal to zero yields:

$$\frac{\partial R}{\partial X} = \frac{\partial C}{\partial X} - \frac{\lambda_2 k}{(U_2 - \lambda_1)(1 - t)} \tag{3}$$

$$\frac{\partial R}{\partial S} = 1 - \frac{U_1 - \lambda_2}{(U_2 - \lambda_1)(1 - t)} \tag{4}$$

$$(R - C - S)(1 - t) \leq \bar{\pi} \tag{5}$$

$$S \leq kX \tag{6}$$

When equations (5) and (6) are satisfied as inequalities, both $\lambda_i = 0$ and equations (3) and (4) become identical to (1) and (2). When either constraint is encountered, however, the corresponding λ_i is positive. Consider the effects that obtain when the constraint represented by equation (5) becomes binding while (6) is satisfied as an inequality. Then $\lambda_1 > 0$ and $\lambda_2 = 0$, so that marginal gross revenue continues to be set equal to the marginal costs of production but now staff expense must be increased so as to satisfy the equality in equation (4).[9] If instead the constraint represented by equation (6) becomes binding while (5) is satisfied as an inequality, output must be expanded so that the firm operates in a region where the marginal gross revenue

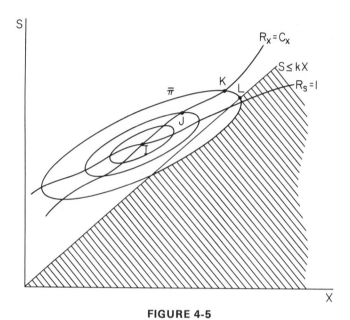

FIGURE 4-5

is less than the marginal costs of production (whether price is greater or less than the marginal costs of production in these circumstances cannot be determined a priori). Staff expense will be reduced so as to satisfy the constraint given by (6) and the marginal relation (4). The effects of having both constraints binding can be shown by examining Figure 4-5.

Maximum profit attainable is given by the intersection of the loci $R_x = C_x$ and $R_s = 1$. This is point I. Assume that the unregulated utility-maximizing position is given by point J (on the locus $R_x = C_x$). If only the maximum profit constraint is binding, the firm moves to the isoprofit contour $\bar{\pi}$ at point K (still on the locus $R_x = C_x$). If, in addition, the expense balance constraint is binding, the firm takes up a position at point L, where now $R_x < C_x$, on the ray $S = kX$. (The shaded region here is the region of admissible choice.) An overall evaluation of the effects of regulatory behavior should thus address itself to both of the constraining relations, if indeed both are believed to be operative.

2
A FIXED
PROPORTIONS MODEL

We consider here a managerial model of the above type for which a fixed proportions technology between staff and production is assumed to prevail. More precisely, the productivity relations described in our treatment of the control loss phenomenon in Chapter 2 are presumed to hold. The principal decision variable, therefore, is firm size.

Only modest changes are necessary to develop a utility-maximizing model of the staff type for the fixed proportions technology. Designating staff expense as H and treating this as all wage expense above the operating level, we have

$$H = \sum_{i=1}^{n-1} w_0 \beta^{n-i} s^{i-1} \simeq w_0 \frac{\beta s^{n-1}}{s - \beta}. \qquad (7)$$

We represent the utility function by U and, given the assumption that staff and profit are the principal components, the objective becomes: maximize

$$U = U(H, R - C) \qquad (8)$$
$$= U\left[w_0 \frac{\beta s^{n-1}}{s - \beta}, \; P(\alpha s)^{n-1} - w_0 \frac{s^n}{s - \beta} - r(\alpha s)^{n-1} \right].$$

Treating n as the only decision variable and all other variables in this expression as parameters, optimal n is now given by:

$$n^* = 1 + \frac{1}{\ln \alpha} \left[\ln \frac{w_0}{P - r} + \ln \frac{s - (U_1/U_2)\beta}{s - \beta} + \ln \left(\frac{\ln s}{\ln \alpha s} \right) \right]. \qquad (9)$$

Comparing this expression with that obtained in equation (2) of Chapter 2, we observe that the only difference is the presence of a $(U_1/U_2)\beta$ term in the brackets of equation (9), where U_1 is the first partial of the utility function with respect to staff, and U_2 is the first partial with respect to profit. Obviously, if staff is valued objectively only for the contribution that it makes to profit, U_1 is zero and (9) becomes identical with (2). If, however, the management displays a positive preference for hierarchical expense so that the ratio U_1/U_2 is not zero, the optimal value of n^* in the utility-maximizing organization will be larger than in the corresponding profit-maximizing organization with identical parameters.

The response of n^* to an increase in each of the parameters is identical with that given on page 30 with the exception of β. Whether n^* will increase or decrease in response to an increase in β depends on whether U_1/U_2 is greater than or less than unity respectively.

The response of n^* to an increase in the demand-shift parameter (E), the tax rate parameter (t), and a lump-sum tax, or equivalent, $(\bar{T})$ is positive, positive $(?)$, and negative respectively, subject to the stipulation that both components of the utility function be normal goods, and recognizing that the profits tax response is subject to offsetting income and substitution effects.[10]

3
REVENUE—PROFITS MODELS

It might be argued that revenue is a better proxy for the "size aspirations" of the management than is hierarchical expense. Inasmuch as revenue bears a less direct relation to what might reasonably be regarded as expense preference, the rationale for such a substitution is not altogether clear. The substitution would, however, bring the analysis into closer relation with the revenue maximization hypothesis advanced by William Baumol [**23**]. It also fits the argument of Chapter 8 (see section 2.2.3). For purposes of completeness, a utility function $U = U(R, \pi)$ is postulated, and both variable and fixed proportions versions of the model are examined.

3.1
Variable Proportions

Consider the utility function $U = U[R, (R - C - S - \bar{T})(1 - t) - \pi_0]$, which is identical to that postulated in 1.1 but for the substitution of R for S as the first component of the utility function. Setting partial derivatives of the utility function with respect to output (X) and staff (S) equal to zero and solving we obtain:

$$\frac{\partial R}{\partial X} = \frac{U_2(1 - t)}{U_1 + U_2(1 - t)} \frac{\partial C}{\partial X} \tag{10}$$

$$\frac{\partial R}{\partial S} = \frac{U_2(1 - t)}{U_1 + U_2(1 - t)} \tag{11}$$

By contrast with equations (1) and (2), where it was observed that production and staff decisions displayed asymmetry, here we observe that the marginal value products of both output and staff are less than their corresponding marginal costs by identical proportions. The comparative statics properties of this model are, under reasonable assumptions, the same as were obtained for its staff counterpart in section 1 above.

3.2
Fixed Proportions

Consider the utility function $U = U[P(\alpha s)^{n-1}, (P - r)(\alpha s)^{n-1} - w_0(s^n/s - \beta)]$, which is identical to that postulated in 2.1 but for the substitution of R for H as the first component of the expression. Taking the derivative with respect to n, treating all other variables as parameters, optimal n is now given by:

$$n^* = 1 + \frac{1}{\ln \alpha}\left[\ln \frac{w_0}{P\left(1 + \frac{U_1}{U_2}\right) - r} + \ln \frac{s}{s - \beta} + \ln \left(\frac{\ln s}{\ln (\alpha s)}\right)\right] \quad (12)$$

A strong similarity to equation (9) is noted. Whereas there a U_1/U_2 term appeared in the second of the bracketed expressions, here it appears in the first. The effect, here as there, of a positive U_1/U_2 ratio is to cause the optimal value of n to increase over the value it would take on in a profit-maximizing organization with identical parameters.

Designating the value of n^* in equation (9) as n_1^* and that in (12) an n_2^*, and expressing U_1/U_2 as $(U_1/U_2)_1$ in (9) and $(U_1/U_2)_2$ in (12), we have, taking the difference of n_1^* and n_2^*:

$$n_1^* - n_2^* = \frac{1}{\ln \alpha}\left\{\ln \left[1 + \left(\frac{U_1}{U_2}\right)_2 \frac{P}{P - r}\right] + \ln \left[1 - \left(\frac{U_1}{U_2}\right)_1 \frac{\beta}{s}\right]\right\} \quad (13)$$

Inasmuch as $\ln (\alpha)$ is negative, this expression will be negative or positive depending on whether the sum of the two logarithms in brackets is positive or negative respectively. If $(U_1/U_2)_2$ and $(U_1/U_2)_1$ are roughly the same, the difference is apt to be negative.[11] Thus, substituting revenue for staff in the firm's utility function will, under these circumstances, ordinarily lead to an increase in firm size.

APPENDIX
THE STAFF-SLACK MODEL

1
THE STAFF-SLACK MODEL WITH VARIABLE PROPORTIONS

We generalize the argument here to provide for the possibility of slack that, in an originating sense, takes the form of unproductive hierarchical expense. The possibility that imitation spreads the effects of slack to production costs is also included. In addition to (or in place of) those terms defined earlier, the following terms now enter the analysis:

m = excess fraction of staff expense which takes the form of slack

$(1 + m)S$ = total staff expense (in money terms)

θC = production expense

θ = imitation premultiplier = $\theta(m)$; $\theta' > 0$, $\theta'' > 0$, $\theta(0) = 1$

π = profits = $R - \theta C - (1 + m)S$

The firm's objective is now taken to be

$$\text{maximize:} \quad U = U(S, mS, \pi - \pi_0 - T)$$

$$\text{subject to:} \quad \pi \geq \pi_0 + T,$$

where again the mimimum profit constraint is assumed to be redundant. Substituting the functional relationships for profit into the utility expression yields

$$\text{maximize:} \quad U = U\{S, mS, [R - \theta C - (1 + m)S - \bar{T}](1 - t) - \pi_0\}.$$

The following first-order conditions are obtained by setting the partial derivatives of U with respect to X, S, and m equal to zero.

$$\frac{\partial R}{\partial X} = \frac{\partial C}{\partial X} \tag{1'}$$

$$\frac{\partial R}{\partial S} = \left(1 - \frac{1}{1-t}\frac{U_1}{U_3}\right) + m\left(1 - \frac{1}{1-t}\frac{U_2}{U_3}\right) \tag{2'}$$

$$U_2 = \frac{1-t}{S}(\theta'C + S)U_3 \tag{3'}$$

If $m = 0$ then, since $\theta(0) = 1$, equations (1') and (2') reduce to (1) and (2) respectively. If, however, positive slack exists, output will be set at a level such that marginal gross revenues exceed the real (or unadjusted) marginal costs of production. Also, if $m > 0$, the marginal revenue product of staff need not, although it probably will, be less than its marginal cost. (It will be less if $U_1 + mU_2 - m(1 - t)U_3 > 0$.) As equation (3') reveals, the "optimum" degree of slack involves a balance between marginal utility gains (U_2) and weighted marginal utility losses (U_3), where the weights include profits tax and imitation consequences.

The comparative statics responses shown in Table 4-A1 are somewhat conjectural. For reasonable specifications of the utility function (mainly that all components are normal goods),[12] the responses shown ordinarily will, but may not, obtain.

The special ambiguity associated with the responses to the profits tax rate parameter is again attributable to mixed income and substitution effects.

TABLE 4-A1

Comparative Stastics Responses Staff-Slack Model

		Parameter		
		E	t	$\bar{T}$
	X°	$+$	$+?$	$-$
Variable	S°	$+$	$+?$	$-$
	m°	$+$	$+?$	$-$

2
THE STAFF-SLACK MODEL WITH FIXED PROPORTIONS

The utility function here includes staff, slack, and profits components. It takes the form $U = U(H, mH, \pi)$, where m is the slack variable. Also we include an imitation relation θ at the production level (where $\theta = \theta(m)$, $\theta' > 0$, $\theta'' > 0$, $\theta(0) = 1$). Thus the objective is to maximize

$$U = U\left[w_0 \frac{\beta s^{n-1}}{s - \beta}, mw_0 \frac{\beta s^{n-1}}{s - \beta}, (P - r)(\alpha s)^{n-1}\right.$$

$$\left. - (1 + m)w_0 \frac{\beta s^{n-1}}{s - \beta} - \theta w_0 s^{n-1}\right].$$

The decision variables are n and m. Setting the partial derivatives of U with respect to each decision variable equal to zero and solving we have

$$n^* = 1 + \frac{1}{\ln \alpha}\left\{\ln \frac{w_0}{P - r} + \ln\left[(1 + m)\frac{\beta}{s - \beta} + \theta\right.\right.$$

$$\left. - \left(\frac{U_1}{U_3} + \frac{U_2}{U_3}m\right)\frac{\beta}{s - \beta}\right] + \ln\left[\frac{\ln s}{\ln (\alpha s)}\right]\right\} \qquad (4')$$

$$\frac{U_2}{U_3} = 1 + \theta'\left(\frac{s - \beta}{\beta}\right) \qquad (5')$$

If $m = 0$, in which case $\theta = 1$, $(4')$ becomes identical to (9).[13] The marginal rate of substitution between profit and slack for positive m is given by $(5')$; this will be unity in the case $\theta' = 0$. Optimal n and m here need to be determined simultaneously.

The comparative statics properties of this model are obtained only with difficulty. Assuming the utility function to be additive in each component, optimal n will generally adjust to changes in the parameters as described in Chapter 2, page 30 and in 2.1 above. This cannot, however, be established on purely qualitative grounds.

FOOTNOTES

[1] Although this is a convenience, it is by no means a necessity. Thus, an inequality constrained maximization problem can be handled by making use of the Kuhn-Tucker theorem.

[2] In these expressions, U_1 is the first partial of the utility function with respect to S and U_2 is the first partial with respect to $(1 - t)(R - C - S - \bar{T}) - \pi_0$.

[3] That this is the correct relationship follows from the assumption that $\partial^2 R/\partial X \partial S > 0$. Under this assumption, the effect of increasing staff is to shift the marginal revenue curve of the standard price-quantity demand curve to the right so that necessarily, whatever the shape of the marginal cost of production curve, the optimum output increases as staff increases. To preserve this property in the construction of an isoprofit map on the output-staff plane requires that the isoprofit curves have major axes running from southwest to northeast. See n. 5, below for further discussion of the sign of $\partial^2 R/\partial X \partial S$.

[4] See P. A. Samuelson, *Foundations of Economic Analysis* (Cambridge: Harvard University Press, 1958), pp. 12–14.

[5] If D is an $n \times n$ matrix, second-order stability conditions for a maximum require that the principal minors alternate in sign beginning with a negative. It might be noted that I assign $\partial^2 U/\partial X \partial S$ a positive sign in the D matrix. This follows from my assumption that $\partial^2 R/\partial X \partial S$ is positive. From a strictly theoretical standpoint it is not essential that this be positive in order to preserve stability. All that is necessary is that the 2×2 matrix be negative definite. From a practical standpoint, however, it is difficult to imagine how $\partial^2 R/\partial X \partial S$ could be anything other than positive (or, as a limiting condition, when the effects of staff on price are exhausted, zero). That is, as output increases, staff unchanged, we would generally expect that the change in gross revenue that would obtain from increasing staff incrementally would be larger than the corresponding change that would occur at lower values of output. This same assumption is made in the profit maximization models examined in the following chapter. If the demand function is multiplicative, $\partial^2 U/\partial X \partial S$ will be positive unambiguously.

[6] Although the sign of $\partial^2 U/\partial X \partial E$ is certain to be positive as indicated, I need to appeal to a "reasonableness" argument to assign a positive sign to $\partial^2 U/\partial S \partial E$. The argument, very simply, is that as the environment moves from a buyers' market to a sellers' market (i.e., as E increases), an incremental increase in staff activity yields a larger increase in gross revenue than the same increment would have produced under less favorable environmental conditions. The results are unaffected if $\partial^2 U/\partial S \partial E$ is zero but ambiguities develop if $\partial^2 U/\partial S \partial E$ is permitted to become negative. In this case, the model has to be specialized and particular demand and cost expressions introduced. The effects of shifts in E on the level of activity of the firm are examined in more detail in Chapter 5.

[7] Actual profit is given by C′ only when $\pi_0 = 0$. Otherwise actual profit is given by profits at C′ plus π_0. However, the value of π_0 in no way affects the general properties of the results.

[8] My treatment of this possibility was suggested by my reading of a draft paper by Milton Kafoglis on "Output of the Firm Under Earnings Restraint." A revised version has since appeared in the *American Economic Review*, September 1969, **59**, 583–89.

[9] Output will also be increased as a result; but the marginal condition $R_x = C_x$ will hold.

[10] These parameters are omitted from the specification of the utility function in (11), but are introduced in the way shown in section 1 above.

[11] Assuming that $(U_1/U_2)_1 \cong (U_1/U_2)_2$, the bracketed expression will be positive if $1 > \beta/s\,[(P - r)/P + (U_1/U_2)_1]$. For the range of parameter values for β and s given in Chapter 2, for $(P - r)/P$ as large as 0.9 and $(U_1/U_2)_1$ as great as 1.0, the inequality will hold.

[12] This will always obtain if $U_{ij} = 0$, $i \neq j$. This is the most convenient specification of the utility function to work with.

[13] U_1/U_3 in (4') corresponds to U_1/U_2 in equation (9) in this case.

5

managerial discretion
in the unitary form
corporation:
dynamic aspects*

Among the shift parameters considered in the previous chapter is the so-called demand-shift parameter. Not surprisingly, output, staff, and slack can all be expected to move directly with the condition of the environment. Our purpose here is to characterize this adjustment behavior more completely. Can one, for example, explain the quite massive adjustments to changes in the condition of the environment which have been observed elsewhere [**160**, Chap. 6] in a more satisfactory way than the models in Chapter 4 permit?[1] Can the Rayner-Little evidence on "higgledy-piggledy" growth be explained? What implications for pricing behavior can be extracted?

*Portions of this chapter have been reprinted from O. E. Williamson, "A Dynamic Stochastic Theory of Managerial Behavior," in *Prices: Issues in Theory, Practice, and Public Policy*, eds. A. Phillips and O. E. Williamson (Philadelphia: University of Pennsylvania Press, 1967), pp. 11–31.

We examine in this connection a phenomenon which will be referred to as "syndrome behavior." Although this phenomenon has been noted in a variety of contexts previously, it has always been invoked in an *ad hoc* way. It is my contention, however, that behavior of this sort is characteristic of complex organizations generally, and that the unitary form organization, because of the high incidence of subgoal pursuit, is especially subject to it. A more systematic treatment of this condition as it influences the conduct and performance of the unitary form corporation is therefore indicated.

The managerial models developed in the preceding chapter are deterministic, treat the environment as exogenous, and assume that adaptations to changing conditions are always ones of degree and not changes in kind. In fact, however, firms operate in a somewhat uncertain world, future conditions of the environment are not wholly unrelated to the current behavior of the firm, and shifts in the prevailing "managerial philosophy" as a function of the condition of the environment appear to occur sometimes. This last, it would appear, is what Kaysen is alluding to when he inquires: "Need the function a particular firm seeks to maximize be invariant over time? If the [answer to this question is]...negative, as I think [it] clearly [is], the definiteness of our behavioral rule begins to fade" [**83**, p. 43]. If I interpret him correctly, the utility function of the firm undergoes occasional transformation, and this gives rise to shifts in the *modus operandi*. If this is true, however, we are left with the need for a meta-theory to tell us when such transformations can be expected to occur. Lacking this, explanations of observed shifts will be quite *ad hoc*.

A dynamic-stochastic model having probabilistic properties, and for which the size of the opportunity set is a function of firm behavior, is developed in section 1. The model provides a possible explanation for the changing managerial philosophy condition referred to by Kaysen. An interpretation of the Rayner-Little evidence on "higgledy-piggledy growth" is provided in section 2. An extension of the model to consider its implications for pricing behavior is given in section 3.

1
A DYNAMIC STOCHASTIC MODEL
OF DISCRETIONARY BEHAVIOR

The utility function of the firm is assumed to be given by

$$U = U(D, \pi) \tag{1}$$

where D is a portmanteau variable indicating the level of discretionary spending and π is reported profits. Discretionary activity is manifested here, as in Chapter 4, by the expansion of staff over profit-maximizing levels, as slack, and by the imitation of lower-level operatives which takes the form of on-the-job leisure. Inasmuch as we are concerned here with discrete rather than continuous adjustments, and since, for illustrative purposes, numerical values will be employed, the profit and utility functions must both be specialized.

Reported profit is jointly determined by the amounts of discretionary spending and the condition of the environment (E). Thus we have:

$$\pi = \pi(D; E); -1 < \frac{\partial \pi}{\partial D} < 0, \frac{\partial \pi}{\partial E} > 0 \qquad (2)$$

That π_D is less than 0 is due of course to the other-than-profit objectives of discretionary behavior. That it exceeds -1 implies that a positive productivity is associated with composite expenditures of this sort so that D does not represent a pure profit drain.[2] More precisely it is assumed that

$$\pi = \pi^* - \gamma D^\theta; 0 < \gamma < 1, \theta \geqslant 1, \qquad (2')$$

where π^* is the maximum profit attainable, and

$$U = \alpha_1 D^{\beta_1} + \alpha_2(\pi^* - \gamma D)^{\beta_2}; \alpha_1, \alpha_2 > 0; 0 < \beta_1, \beta_2 < 1 \qquad (1')$$

Thus, given the condition of the environment, which defines π^*, maximum U is obtained where:

$$\frac{\partial U}{\partial D} = \alpha_1 \beta_1 D^{\beta_1 - 1} + \alpha_2 \beta_2 (\pi^* - \gamma D)^{\beta_2 - 1}(-\gamma) = 0. \qquad (3)$$

Syndrome properties are introduced in 1.1. A representative solution to the resulting model is given in 1.2.

1.1
Syndrome Analysis

Dynamic stochastic properties are introduced into the model by assuming that the firm can adopt either of two postures, a utility-maximizing or a profit-maximizing stance, and that transitions from one environmental condition to another follow a simple Markov process in which the transition probability is a function of the current state of the system. Consider two conditions of the environment, prosperity and adversity, and designate these H and L respectively. Representing managerial posture by M (U max) and the stockholder posture by S (π max), the following conditions characterize the transition probabilities:

$$\begin{cases} P(L; H, M) > P(L; H, S) \\ P(H; L, M) < P(H; L, S) \end{cases} \qquad (4)$$

Thus the probability that the system will shift to a low-level condition of the environment, given that it starts in a high-level position, will be greater if the firm adopts a managerial stance than if it is operated as a profit-maximizing concern. Similarly, the probability that the system will shift to a high-level position, given that it originates in a low-level position, will be lower if the firm adopts a managerial posture.

That the inequality conditions shown in (4) should hold derives from our assumption that the opportunity set is larger when the organization is run more aggressively. Thus, adopting a managerial posture yields high current satisfaction but only at the expense of "shrinking" future choice sets. A decline in the condition of the environment is therefore more probable and an improvement less probable when the organization is operated along managerial lines than when a profit-maximizing posture is adopted. Opportunities that the profit-maximizing organization will recognize or develop will simply go unrecognized or undeveloped if the managerial syndrome prevails.

The assumption that only two postures are possible requires some justification. It is, at the very least, an oversimplification to represent behavior in this way. At the same time, however, it possesses a certain intuitive plausibility. Organizational behavior frequently displays "syndrome" properties. Either the organization is run as a "tight ship" or is permitted to run slack. Intermediate positions are difficult to sustain. Thus, although top management might desire to restrict the exercise of discretion to activities which it controls directly, while the remainder of the organization is run along strictly profit-maximizing lines, in fact this option may be unavailable. Lower-level compliance is conditional on higher-level example [**160**, p. 97]. Where this is lacking, control problems multiply, and the costs of securing intended behavior from lower-level operatives may become prohibitive. Thus the stance adopted by top management tends to characterize the entire operation. Since fine discriminations are difficult to express beyond the dichotomy between slack and no slack, limiting attention to "managerial" and "profit-maximizing" postures seems warranted.

Although behavior along these lines has been previously noted by other investigators (including allusions to it in *The Economics of*

Discretionary Behavior [**160**, pp. 60–61, 122, 169–170]), it has never previously been developed in a systematic way. It is nevertheless of interest to note some of the contexts in which it has been raised. Morris Adelman observes of the behavior of the domestic coal operators and railroads that "it was the . . . fear of nuclear power that jolted them out of a self-pitying routine . . . and led to the present delivered coal prices, which are expected to go even lower. Both coal and railroads were suffering a profit squeeze; they 'deserved' and needed higher prices and profits in order to generate the funds needed to modernize and reduce costs to serve national welfare and security . . . and so on. But the threat of losing markets coerced them into cutting costs to improve profits; and where there was money to be made, money was found" [**2**, p. 113]. Thus, with the future condition of the environment hanging in balance, the coal operators and railroads chose a shift in their managerial postures. Slack was taken in, costs were reduced, and markets preserved.

Similarly, Albert Rees observes (without endorsing) that, in response to an increase in wage rates, employers may "discover . . . neglected opportunities. In this case total costs and prices could be lower after the wage increases than before, and the larger sales of the product could offset the adverse effect on employment of the change in methods of production. This is one variety of the so-called 'shock effect' [i.e., threshold adjustment] argument. The argument can turn on improved personnel practices, changes in hiring standards, or reduction of wastes of various sorts rather than on the introduction of new equipment" [**127**, p. 89]. That Rees is reluctant to make more of this argument is probably due to the fact that a simple increase in wage rates, unless accompanied by adversity of other types, is not usually sufficiently severe to induce the shift in managerial postures described above. Yet occasionally such wage changes may contribute to these adjustments, and this probably explains the existence of "shock effects" in the folklore of labor economics.

As a third example of behavior that has syndrome attributes, consider Harvey Leibenstein's treatment of what he calls "X-efficiency." His survey of the literature on productivity change leads him to conclude that variations in the condition of the environment induce differential management responses. In situations where competition in the product market is ineffectual, the management is inclined to choose the "easy life," while where competitive pressures are intensive, a sharp reduction in slack-type expenditures occurs [**91**, pp. 392–415].[3]

Such uncomplicated posturing can be found in virtually any large organization in which the behavior of subordinates is conditional on higher-level example. Recognition of this sometimes leads to attempts at creating artificial austerity (turning off lights in the White House?) in the hope of inducing economy measures at operating levels, but these are rarely successful. To achieve the desired effect, the efforts to achieve restraint must be both genuine and pervasive. Intermediate positions, being difficult to articulate, are easily misread and therefore hard to sustain. This leads to dichotomous shifts in behavior which are sometimes regarded as evidence of lack of sophistication, but in fact they represent organizational efforts to achieve coherence and orderliness in the face of complexity.

1.2
A Representative Solution

We therefore take syndrome behavior to be a standard attribute of life in the large corporation. Our objective here is to provide a more basic rationale for such behavior than has been given previously. For this purpose we assume that the firm is operated so as to maximize expected discounted utility and show how with this goal the posture of the firm is conditional on the state of the environment. Sequential, stochastic decision problems of this kind can be solved by dynamic programming. The algorithm developed by R. A. Howard is particularly well suited to dealing with problems of this sort [74]. Since optimal behavior cannot be specified independently of the rewards and transition probabilities characterizing each state, consider the following "representative" problem.

The values of the parameters in the utility function are assumed to be:

$$\alpha_1 = 1; \; \alpha_2 = 2$$
$$\beta_1 = \beta_2 = \tfrac{1}{2}$$
$$\gamma = \tfrac{1}{3}; \; \theta = 1$$

Under these circumstances it can be shown that the optimum value of D in equation (3) is $\hat{D} = \tfrac{9}{7}\pi^*$. The values of maximum profit as a function of the condition of the environment together with the associated values of discretion, reported profit, and utility as a function of the posture of the firm are shown in Table 5-1. The value of maximum profit is a function of the current period and immediate future period of the environment only. If the system originates in a high-level position and remains there for the next period, maximum profit is 28. If it originates in a high-level position, but a shift to a low-level position occurs, the transitional maximum profit is 14, etc. If utility is maximized in the current period, a managerial posture is adopted and

TABLE 5-1

Pay-off Relations

Condition of the Environment (Current, Immediate Future)	Posture	π^*	$\hat{D}$	π	U
(H, H)	M	28	36	16	14
	S	28	0	28	10.6
(H, L)	M	14	18	8	9.9
	S	14	0	14	7.5
(L, L)	M	7	9	4	7
	S	7	0	7	5.3
(L, H)	M	10	12.9	5.7	8.4
	S	10	0	10	6.3

the corresponding value of $\hat{D}$, π, and U are given by the "M" row, while if a profit-maximizing posture is adopted the associated values of $\hat{D}$, π, and U are given by the "S" row. It is interesting to note that with $D = \frac{9}{7}\pi^*$, the level of discretionary expenditures exceeds the level of maximum profit attainable, yet reported profit remains positive. This is possible, of course, because discretionary spending is not a pure profit drain—a possibility which, in some respects at least, appears to be at variance with Shorey Peterson's conclusion that "there is little room for . . . waywardness" in the management of the firm [**123**, p. 14].[4]

It remains only to specify the transition probabilities. These are given in Table 5-2. As is apparent by inspection, the probabilities assigned satisfy the conditions given by the inequalities in (4). It will also be noted that for the transition probabilities specified, the system

TABLE 5-2

Transition Probabilities

Initial Condition of the Environment	Posture	Transition Probability to Succeeding Condition of the Environment	
		H	L
H	M	0.8	0.2
	S	0.9	0.1
L	M	0.1	0.9
	S	0.3	0.7

will have a tendency to remain in whichever environmental state it originates. Thus, although shifts between levels will occur, the system will display persistence properties within a level—a condition which is probably in accord with reality.

Assume that the discount rate is 11 percent, so that $1/(1 + r)$ is 0.9. This completes the basic data, and we are now in a position to derive the optimality conditions for our problem. For this purpose it is useful to summarize the expected immediate utility of each state-action pair in Table 5-3. Thus if the system originates in state H and the management adopts posture M, the system will remain in H with probability 0.8 and realize a utility of 14 and go to L with a probability of 0.2 while realizing a utility of 9.9, so that the expected utility of being in state H and adopting posture M is 13.2. The other results in Table 5-3 are derived similarly.

TABLE 5-3

Expected Immediate Utility

| Originating State | Posture | Transition State | | | | Expected Immediate Utility |
| | | H | | L | | |
		Probability	Utility	Probability	Utility	
H	M	0.8	14	0.2	9.9	13.2
	S	0.9	10.6	0.1	7.5	10.3
L	M	0.1	8.4	0.9	7.0	7.1
	S	0.3	6.3	0.7	5.3	5.6

There are four possible decision rules, which may be designated as

$$a_1 = \binom{M}{M}, \quad a_2 = \binom{M}{S}, \quad a_3 = \binom{S}{S}, \quad a_4 = \binom{S}{M},$$

where the first component in each column vector represents the posture to be taken in state H and the second is the posture to be taken in state L. Fortunately it is not necessary to evaluate all possible variations in order to obtain an optimum policy.

Since rule a_1 is the rule having the highest expected immediate utility in each state, consider it as the initial test policy. The corresponding transition probabilities and expected immediate utilities are:

$$P_1 = \begin{bmatrix} 0.8 & 0.2 \\ 0.1 & 0.9 \end{bmatrix}, \quad U_1 = \binom{13.2}{7.1}$$

Let $V_i = \begin{pmatrix} v_{iH} \\ v_{iL} \end{pmatrix}$ be the vector of discounted utility associated with decision rule a_i. As Howard shows [74, p. 81],

$$V_i = \left[I - \frac{1}{1+r} P_i \right]^{-1} U_i$$

so that for decision rule 1 we have

$$\begin{pmatrix} v_{1H} \\ v_{1L} \end{pmatrix} = \left[\begin{pmatrix} 1 & 0 \\ 0 & 1 \end{pmatrix} - 0.9 \begin{pmatrix} 0.8 & 0.2 \\ 0.1 & 0.9 \end{pmatrix} \right]^{-1} \begin{pmatrix} 13.2 \\ 7.1 \end{pmatrix}$$

Solving, we obtain $v_{1H} = 102.4$ and $v_{1L} = 86.2$. Thus the expected discounted utility of decision rule 1 is 102.4 if the firm originates in H and 86.2 if it originates in L.

To test whether rule a_1 is optimal, suppose that a_1 is used in all periods but the first but that in the first period S replaces M. Denoting the expected immediate utility of using posture S in the state H by U_{SH} the expected discounted value of this strategy, if the system originates in H, is:

$$\hat{V}^1_{SH} = U_{SH} + 0.9[P(H; S, H)v_{1H} + P(L; S, H)v_{1L}]$$
$$= 10.3 + 0.9[(0.9)(102.4) + (0.1)(86.2)]$$
$$= 101.2$$

Since this is less than 102.4, the strategy of using M in H is preferred. If the system originates in L, the expected discounted value of the strategy of replacing M by S in the first period is

$$\hat{V}^1_{SL} = U_{SL} + 0.9[P(H; S, L)v_{1H} + P(L; S, L)v_{1L}]$$
$$= 5.6 + 0.9[(0.3)(102.4) + (0.7)(86.2)]$$
$$= 87.7$$

and since this exceeds 86.2, a shift to posture S when the system is in state L is indicated. Our revised policy thus becomes rule $a_2 = \begin{pmatrix} M \\ S \end{pmatrix}$. Repeating the above procedure for V_2 we have:

$$\begin{pmatrix} v_{2H} \\ v_{2L} \end{pmatrix} = \left[\begin{pmatrix} 1 & 0 \\ 0 & 1 \end{pmatrix} - 0.9 \begin{pmatrix} 0.8 & 0.2 \\ 0.3 & 0.7 \end{pmatrix} \right]^{-1} \begin{pmatrix} 13.2 \\ 5.6 \end{pmatrix}$$

The resulting values are $v_{2H} = 106.3$ and $v_{2L} = 92.4$. The test routine thus leads to the adoption of a better policy than a_1. Here the firm takes a managerial posture when it experiences prosperity but acts as a profit-maximizer under adversity.

Can this policy also be improved upon? To test this we assume that rule 2 is in force in all periods but the first, while in period 1 posture S is adopted when H prevails and posture M if L prevails. The resulting test quantities $\hat{V}^2_{SH}$ and $\hat{V}^2_{ML}$ are 105.8 and 92.3 respectively, each of which is lower than corresponding criterion quantities 106.3 and 92.4. Thus rule a_2, under which a managerial posture is adopted when the environment is in the high-level range and a profit-maximizing stance when adversity sets in, is optimal.

By way of summary we note that the utility function of the firm is independent of the condition of the environment and, contrary to Kaysen's conjecture, remains invariant over time. The model nevertheless generates shifts in management posture as the condition of the environment shifts. As noted above, this is a property that appears to be roughly consistent with the observed behavior of oligopolistic firms required to adapt to adversity. It thus gives us confidence in the analysis in this respect. Moreover, the model can easily be extended to include intermediate conditions of the environment if this should be desirable. As long, however, as syndrome behavior of the type described above characterizes managerial options, we would not expect that this would produce behavior significantly different from that already obtained.

2
RAYNER AND LITTLE
ON FIRM GROWTH

A. C. Rayner and I. M. D. Little have examined the earnings growth of English companies in an effort to establish "whether past growth leads to further growth; in other words, whether a successful management continues to do well" [126, p. 1]. A variety of tests are performed to this end. The general conclusion which they reach is that, discouragingly, "earnings growth occurs in an almost purely random manner" [126, p. 62].

Among the possible explanations that they advance for this disturbing result is that, conceivably, "the quality of the management changes rather rapidly from good to bad and back again" [126, p. 63]. They are able, however, only to motivate this in an *ad hoc* way and are manifestly uncomfortable with such an explanation. The theory advanced here helps to overcome this difficulty: the alternation phenomenon which Rayner and Little conjecture is not merely possible but is to be expected in firms with syndrome properties and utility functions of the type described. For the reasons given above, syndrome properties would appear to be characteristic of complex organizations generally. For reasons given earlier and developed in subsequent chapters, the utility function described is apt to be most characteristic in unitary form organizations. If the "exceptions" noted by Little and Rayner tend to be multidivision rather than unitary form enterprises, the evidence would further support the approach to firm behavior described here and in the chapters which follow.

None of this is to suggest that we have supplied the whole of the explanation for the empirical results which Rayner and Little report. It is sufficient merely to observe that (1) their conjecture can in this way be provided with deeper level rationality properties, and (2) their evidence provides some tentative support for the theory advanced here.

3
PRICING IMPLICATIONS

The principal remaining issue for our purposes here is to develop the pricing implications, if any, of shifts between managerial and profit-maximizing postures as the environment alternates between munificent and penurious conditions. This is an issue on which the model in no specific sense leads to an identifiable set of consequences, but in some general sense the syndrome behavior imputed to the management may have relevance for understanding oligopolistic pricing practices. The highly conjectural character of this discussion should nevertheless be recognized.

Since price itself possesses no intrinsic utility-producing properties, efficient utility maximization requires that it be chosen in a strictly instrumental way. The factors that determine this choice are therefore those which enter the utility function, namely discretion and profit. Given the level of expenditures on hierarchical expense, price should be set at profit-maximizing levels unless as yet unidentified discretionary considerations dictate otherwise. Consider in this connection whether, in addition to all those long-run profit-related pricing considerations described by J. K. Galbraith in his treatment of stabilization policy [63]—namely, stability of interfirm relations, customer loyalty, the effect of price on the condition of entry, strategic wage bargaining, etc.—there also exist long-run discretion-related objectives which influence pricing practices.

There are at least two such candidates. The first is simple sluggishness; the second is strategic smoothing. The first of these is a purely leisure-related phenomenon. The second contributes to discretionary objectives generally. Of these two only the second seems likely to have quantitative significance. It may be more "convenient" for the sales and billing departments to maintain prices, but this produces such a local, limited variety of satisfaction that profit considerations would normally be overriding. With respect to strategic smoothing, however, the calculated suppression of price increases so as to produce backlogs may be very much in the management's interest. It provides, in Galbraith's words, a cushion of "unliquidated monopoly gain" [**63**, p. 127] which can be drawn upon when the environment becomes less bountiful. Obviously a policy of backlogging could not provide permanent protection against a persistent decline in the condition of the environment. But temporary insularity and an opportunity for gradualist adjustment might be achieved by a calculated policy of strategic smoothing. To the extent, therefore, that we have confidence in the discretion model derived above, and if a strategic smoothing policy can be shown to contribute to utility-maximizing objectives within the context of this dynamic stochastic model, we will have more confidence in this policy of incomplete market clearing (through deferring price increases during prosperity) that Galbraith describes.

Extending the model to allow for smoothing is relatively easy. Essentially it amounts to buying a transition option (i.e., a backlog) by sacrificing current profits. Thus suppose that backlogging implies a 2-unit reduction in the value of maximum profits attainable when prosperity prevails, so that $\pi_H{}^*$ under backlogging becomes 26, but that this permits an increase in the value of transition profits from 14 to 20. The expected immediate utility of choosing to backlog is, of course, lower than would be realized without backlogging. When the effects of current behavior on future conditions are taken into account, however, it can be shown that the optimal policy is to "buy" the transition option at the cost of a reduction in current period profits and adopt, as before, a managerial posture when the environment originates in condition H and a profit-maximizing posture when it originates in L. It can also be shown that if, for some reason, the profit-maximizing posture were to be employed under H, the backlogging option would not be chosen. Expected discounted future profits (as contrasted with utility) would be reduced.[5] Thus for those firms which are operated as utility- rather than profit-maximizers, the spreading of profits through strategic smoothing may play a decisive role in decisions to restrict the use of price as a rationing device during periods of economic prosperity.[6] In this respect, the model may be regarded as one having "administered" pricing properties. This lagged-response analysis, as it applies both to price increases and decreases, should nevertheless be distinguished from the usual treatments of administered pricing conditions. These latter are concerned with such phenomena as ratchet effects, mark-ups, and nonresponsiveness—none of which is implied by the present model.

4
CONCLUSIONS

The main purpose of this chapter has been to advance a possible explanation for the massive shifts in managerial attitudes that have been observed to occur in response to changes in the condition of the environment. Previous studies of this phenomenon have attributed the shift from a managerial to a profit-maximizing posture after the onset of adversity as being due to management's fear of stockholder dissatisfaction and threats of take-over raids. I do not mean to dismiss this possibility here. What I wish to emphasize is that if syndrome behavior is characteristic in large, complex organizations, the management may adopt such a posture when adversity sets in whether there is stockholder discontent or not. The critical linkage here is that future choice sets are a function of current behavior, and if prospects for recovery from a current condition of adversity are significantly improved by shifting to a profit-maximizing stance, discounted utility can be increased by foregoing current satisfaction. This dependency of opportunity sets on behavior appears to be an important consideration which present theories of the firm generally omit. Although there are obviously other ways of establishing such a connection, the one used here seems both simple and useful and is easily extended.

One possible extension has already been indicated; namely, the possibility of "buying" a transition option by choosing to backlog orders when the environment is munificent. This means, of course, that price in these circumstances is not used as a rationing device by which to clear the market completely. Excess demand is permitted to develop and persist, which implies that current profits are, to some extent, sacrificed. Among the advantages of backlogging, of course, is that a certain smoothing of rewards is possible, so that the transition to adversity can be made more gradual. Only the crudest version of such a transition option was presented above, but it illustrates the point, and more elegant variations of this model can easily be designed and investigated.

The incentive to use backlogging for reasons of strategic smoothing lends support to the argument advanced by Galbraith that oligopolistic firms will have access to a certain amount of "unliquidated monopoly gain" during periods of prosperity. As he points out, this may partially frustrate efforts by the monetary authority to contain inflation. Large firms, in his view, are able to delay the effects of monetary restraint and cause it to operate unevenly. Small firms feel the effects more quickly than the large firms which resort to liquidation of their reserves. Although a thoroughgoing study of this condition, if it exists, would require a better-specified model than that employed here, the approach to the dynamics of discretionary behavior proposed above should prove useful if such an analysis were attempted.

FOOTNOTES

[1] An additional example of massive adjustments, induced partly by unfavorable product market experience and reinforced by the threat of takeover, is afforded by Allis-Chalmers. In an open letter to the stockholders asking their support (printed, among other places, in a full-page ad in the May 6, 1969 *Wall Street Journal*), Mr. David C. Scott, the new president and chairman of the board, claimed the following accomplishments:

> Your Company's quarterly report for the period ending March 31, 1969 shows record sales and substantial improvement in earnings.... Here is the record:
> Sales increased to $211.2 million, *the highest first quarter in Allis-Chalmers history.*
> Earnings for the three months increased to $5.1 million, *the second highest amount in more than a decade....*
> *We achieved this increase in sales and earnings while substantially reducing the number of employees and overhead.* Since September over 3,400 nonproduction employees have been removed....
> There are other parts of your management's program that are important. *These include reduction of the corporate staff from 1,510 to 125 people; creation of more manageable profit centers; and raising new equity capital.* (Emphasis in original.)

Although accounting "cosmetics" may partly explain the earnings experience of Allis-Chalmers (see *Fortune*, May 15, 1969, pp. 234, 240), the employment changes would appear to be real.

[2] This is not to say that some components of D are not pure profit drains. As a composite, however, positive productivity exists both at the margin and in total.

[3] For similar much earlier views on the relation between competition and efficiency, see A. T. Hadley [**69**, p. 383].

[4] In his critique, Kaysen summarizes Peterson's position as follows [**83**, p. 41]:

> In the representative firm, even the representative large managerial firm, margins between revenues and costs are too narrow, and both minuend and subtrahend too fluctuating ... to permit management any significant departure from the goal of profit maximization. If departures exist they are transitory or trivial, not appropriate material for theory building.

[5] The dependence of the argument on the choice of particular parameter values should be appreciated. We nevertheless suspect that the behavior described will emerge under a wide range of "reasonable" assumptions. At the very least, it is more likely to emerge if firms are utility-maximizers than if they are neoclassical profit-maximizers.

[6] The sales maximization and growth-maximization hypotheses [**23**] [**106**] could be brought within this dynamic stochastic framework, but only in a limited sense.

With respect to the sales-maximization hypothesis, this is accomplished by making the prospect of future revenues conditional on the managerial posture adopted during adversity. If a profit-maximizing stance is adopted, the prospect of future revenues is improved. The reason why such an improvement in future prospects should occur, however, is not obvious in a firm (such as a sales-maximizer) which is not generating slack. Thus, although in purely formal terms the accommodation can be made, a different rationale for this behavior than that provided above is required.

Marris' model is less easy to accommodate in this regard, although his generalization of the growth-maximization model to include both the growth rate and the valuation ratio in the utility function [106, pp. 260–265] facilitates such an attempt. Yet again it is necessary to supply a different motivation for the alternation phenomenon than that employed above.

6

competition in the
capital market
in relation to unitary
form behavior*

It has been assumed throughout that competition in the product
market is, for any of the reasons given in Chapter 1, somehow attenuated. It has also been assumed that the firm is organized along the
lines of the unitary form, which involves bringing operating executives
into the strategic decision-making process. The predictable consequences for firm behavior of these two structural conditions have been
investigated in Chapters 4 and 5. Implicit throughout is the assumption that competition in the capital market does not somehow restore
selection on profit-maximizing values of the firm's decision variables.
This hitherto neglected assumption will be considered here.

* Portions of this chapter have been reprinted from O. E. Williamson, "Corporate
Control and the Theory of the Firm," in *Economic Policy and the Regulation of Corporate Securities*, ed. H. G. Manne (Washington, D. C.: American Enterprise Institute,
1969), pp. 281–336.

It will be convenient to separate the argument about competition in the capital market into new and old parts. The new part is concerned with the relation of organization form to both strategic decision-making and *internal* control processes and will be deferred to Chapter 9. This aspect of the argument has never previously been made in connection with competition in the capital market—although, inasmuch as the modern proponents of the competition in the capital market argument have never explicitly addressed the organization form issue, possibly this is what they have had in mind all along.[1] The analysis here assumes that the traditional or unitary form organization prevails, and focuses on what will be referred to as the old part of the argument; namely, on external control processes. At a minimum, it can be regarded as having historical (pre-1945) relevance.

Broadly, the questions to be considered are these: Can the capital market, operating through external controls, either constrain or otherwise induce the management to operate the firm in what is effectively a profit-maximizing manner? What machinery does the capital market have access to for this purpose, and what limitations does this machinery experience?

The possibility that direct capital market controls will be efficacious is briefly considered in section 1. The role of incentive controls is examined in section 2. The managerial displacement mechanism is treated in section 3. Note that the issue is not whether controls of these types, individually or collectively, have any effects but rather whether they are efficacious in achieving the results imputed to them.

1
DIRECT CAPITAL
MARKET CONTROL

The possibility that the capital market *directly* influences the efficiency of operations in the firm "by meting out rewards and punishments in the form of cheaper or more expensive capital funds" [27, p. 79] will be dealt with only briefly here. The argument, roughly, is that the stock market in conjunction with the investment banking community meters funds in a way which effectively restricts managerial discretion. Baumol's recent examination of this position finds it wanting in both logical and empirical respects. He concludes with the observation that there exists [27, p. 76]

> . . . an impressive set of grounds which, together with . . . theoretical analysis, indicates that the infrequent use of the Exchange by the American corporation is neither a historical accident nor a manifestation of irrational behavior.

The upshot is that the stock market is only infrequently given the opportunity to discipline directly the vast majority of the nation's leading corporations and that there seems to be little reason to expect imminent and dramatic changes in this circumstance. If we look to the stock market as a direct regulator of the efficiency of America's corporate enterprise we must find other means for it to accomplish this assignment.

Rayner and Little likewise concluded from their investigation of the capital market's metering capability that, judging at least from the gross performance measures upon which one might reasonably expect the capital market to rely, a dependable relation between the past and subsequent performance of a firm was not evident [126]. Conceivably, however, capital market controls can effectively be brought to bear by indirection.

2
CONTROL BY
INCENTIVE

Control by incentive relies mainly on pecuniary appeals to the top management to provide "profit-maximizing leadership." Assuming that these appeals are successful, the top management is then expected to secure behavior that conforms to its profit-maximizing preferences from the membership of the lower hierarchical levels of the enterprise. The basic question here is the following: Is the a priori quality of the control by incentive position compelling, or does it suffer from serious limitations?

One type of incentive control would be to rely on bonuses that are awarded on the basis of an ex post evaluation. The efficacy of controls of this sort will be considered briefly in Chapter 10. Suffice it to observe here that those who believe that incentives can be effective in inducing profit-maximizing behavior do not appear to assign special importance to the bonus mechanism. They emphasize instead incentive systems that rely for their power on the movement of the share price of the firm's securities.

The incentive techniques of this indirect sort that have received greatest attention are the use of stock options and insider trading. Note that in neither case does the issue turn on whether incentives of either type have *any* effects, but rather on whether they are efficacious in producing the intended effects. Also note the premise on which all incentive arguments rest: if special pecuniary inducements are lacking, the management cannot be expected to select on profit-maximizing values of the firm's decision variables.

2.1
Stock Options

Baumol conjectures that "by far the most important reason for management's concern for the behavior of the price of company stock is the stock option whose value to the recipient executive depends directly on the performance of the Company's securities" [**27**, p. 81]. As he points out in an appendix, the coincidence of interest between the management holding stock options and the stockholders is likely to be incomplete with respect to such matters as dividend policy, but he nevertheless regards the stock option to be the most effective of the indirect, capital market controls.[2]

Without disputing this judgment, there are at least two additional reasons for believing that the stock option may fall short of the mark as a device by which to eliminate the conscious exercise of managerial discretion in the pursuit of other-than-profit goals. These can be characterized as the "moving equilibrium" and "free-ride" problems. The first of these requires that the firm's performance be viewed dynamically. Thus, although the management that is promoting own-goals through the internal absorption of resources can undertake (in principle at least) a once-for-all, *ceteris paribus*, shift in the level of performance simply by releasing these resources and diverting them to profit purposes, the resulting gains are (1) one-time only, and (2) the management now has the burden of sustaining the shift (unless environmental change permits otherwise) lest these gains be dissipated. Except in connection with the strategic smoothing of performance in the face of environmental variability (which would involve not once-for-all but alternation behavior between utility- and profit-maximizing postures),[3] such a result may appear relatively unattractive by comparison with the alternative of enjoying both stock option benefits and the benefits of operating the firm in a utility-maximizing way.[4]

An additional problem with the argument that the award of stock options results in effective, indirect managerial control involves the "free-ride" problem. As everyone recognizes, the overall performance of the enterprise is the resultant of a multitude of inputs. The incentive for any one option holder to give greater emphasis to profitability considerations so as to realize a once-for-all capital gain is attenuated if this preference cannot easily be communicated to other option holders and agreement among them obtained, and if the policing of any agreement reached is difficult. The policing problem results from the difficulty of assigning causality in complex, dynamic systems such as the modern corporation. This same difficulty is experienced in Henry Manne's insider trading model, and I therefore defer further examination of the causality problems to the discussion of insider trading (as Manne conceives it), which follows immediately.

2.2
Insider Trading

The insider trading argument is mainly attributable to Henry Manne [100]; indeed, his is the only systematic development of the issue. Although, as will be evident, we find reason to disagree with much of it, his analysis represents an important and perceptive contribution to the study of capital market operations. The argument being somewhat novel, and his being the most complete development, we will follow him throughout in the critique.

Insider trading influences corporate behavior in two respects. First, it acts directly on incentives. In addition, by serving indirectly as an information disclosure device, it provides an essential support to the displacement mechanism. The incentive aspects will be examined here; the displacement argument is considered in section 3.

As Manne views corporate behavior, insider trading is *the* means by which the incentives for entrepreneurial activity in the large corporation are effectively preserved: the individuals in the corporation who are responsible for its successes must be able to appropriate the gains. Insider trading facilitates this result by serving as a compensation scheme by which insiders with advance knowledge of corporate developments are able to capitalize on this knowledge through buying (or selling) the firm's stock prior to market disclosure. Assuming that the individuals who are knowledgeable are likewise the ones responsible for the corporate change in question, this supposedly affords them an opportunity to receive compensation commensurate with their contributions.[5]

If insider trading really works, it overcomes both the moving equilibrium and free-ride problems that the stock option incentive scheme is subject to. For every increase in stock price there exists an opportunity for insider gains. Those who are responsible for the movement are presumably able to appropriate the gain; free riders are somehow excluded from participation. Since everyone occupying an entrepreneurial position experiences this same performance incentive, aggressive individual pursuit of profits results. Collectively the system achieves profit-maximizing performance.

To state the argument in these bold terms is virtually to answer it. Essential for it to operate as described are the following conditions: (1) since every movement in stock prices represents an opportunity for gain, actions that have negative profit consequences or which give rise to rippling effects must be annihilated; (2) the executive ascension system must be one which assures that entrepreneurial types reach entrepreneurial positions; (3) opportunities for gain must not be seriously impaired by large size; (4) the information disclosure system must assure appropriability without impairing the performance of the firm in other respects; and (5) aggressive individual profit pursuit must not result in suboptimization. This is a formidable set of conditions to have satisfied. Let us consider the properties of insider trading with respect to each.

Since money can be made on downside as well as upward movements in stock prices, a certain uneasiness over the properties of this reward procedure is natural. Manne's answer to it is that downside movements are checked by the displacement mechanism and the professional ethic of executives [**100**, p. 150]. The efficacy of the displacement mechanism is examined in section 3; suffice it to observe here that displacement experiences nontrivial threshold expenses. Although professional ethic is, perhaps, too often dismissed out of hand, somehow an incentive system that permits the officers of the firm to benefit at the expense of their shareholders,[6] yet simultaneously precludes the manipulation of information, is unsettling. One should like an explicit statement of its properties.

Manne is fully aware that his theory must address the question of executive ascension. He observes that the promotion process in the large corporation may not be calculated to attract entrepreneurial types: it is necessary in "large American corporations . . . [to] perform a kind of salaried apprenticeship before entrepreneurial rewards become available" [**100**, p. 123]. He suggests, however, that this can be overcome if entrepreneurial talent can be recruited outside the corporation and injected in at the top [**101**, p. 268]—a supply hypothesis which (although the criteria are somewhat imprecise) is not clearly supported by the data. Inspection of Table 6-1 reveals that the internal promotion process has been the predominant route to high executive position in the large corporation: the number of years of prior employment with the corporation before reaching executive position among corporations ranked in the 500 largest industrials varies from 16 years for a vice-presidency to 17 and 21 years for the presidency and chairmanship of the board respectively. Firms in the size class 401–500 have somewhat lower prior employment statistics, but within the range 1–400 there does not appear to be any significant size-related trend. On the surface, these statistics do not augur well for the external talent supply hypothesis.

Next consider the attenuation problems that are characteristic of large size. Simultaneity is one of them: The effects of any particular initiative in the large firm may be swamped by developments else-

TABLE 6-1

Number of Years of Prior Service of Executives
in 500 Largest Industrial Corporations, 1967

Range from which Sample was Drawn from Population of Firms Ranked by Sales, Largest 500 Industrials*	Number of Years with Present Employer Prior to Appointment to Present Position				
	Chairman		President		Vice-President
	mean	std. dev.	mean	std. dev.	mean
1–100	24.9	11.2	19.6	13.3	18.7
101–200	23.4	11.9	22.4	6.3	17.8
201–300	18.9	11.5	17.0	9.8	14.4
301–400	21.7	18.7	21.4	9.5	13.7
401–500	16.6	21.5	5.2	5.7	10.3
1–500	21.3		16.9		15.7

* Ten firms were selected from each of the five size classes.

Source: Derived from Dun's Reference Book on Corporate Management's, First Edition, New York, 1968.

where. Second, even holding other things constant, as the corporation grows in absolute—and particularly large, conglomerate—size, the effect of a given entrepreneurial development on share price becomes attenuated. The opportunities for insider trading gains (from a fixed sum of capital) are thereby reduced [100, p. 143]. In the absence of countervailing considerations, it would appear that the efficacy of insider trading is impaired by large size. The insider trading theory performs worst where it is needed most.

The requisites of the information disclosure system that would assure appropriability by the responsible entrepreneurial types are not described by Manne. Yet an examination of this is absolutely essential if the insider trading argument is to go through. It is not obvious that the information hoarding which insider trading would seem to require would also have ideal properties from the standpoint of the firm. The conflict is between the necessity to provide "impacted" information (so as to prevent the disclosure of significant developments to free riders) and the demands for effective information exchange within a complex, hierarchical organization. Can an information system be designed for the unitary form organization that avoids the free-ride problem without impairing coordination and inducing subgoal pursuit of a debilitating sort? This seems doubtful. Significantly, Manne never traces out for a change of major proportions how causality is to be established. Simon's observations with respect to major issues are relevant in this connection: "No man is likely to be aware of all of the decisions entering into the process or of who made them, or of the interaction through a period of time that modified decisions at one point or another" [**139**, p. 222]. Establishing causality for a connected series of incremental changes (possibly with lagged responses of various sorts) is all the more difficult. Moreover, it is clearly no answer, as Roger Sherman points out, to call insiders with information "entrepreneurs" simply as a matter of definition [**138**, p. 104].

Aggressive individual profit pursuit likewise (and for similar reasons) poses difficult problems in a complex, interconnected system. Either decomposability of a sort not feasible in the unitary form organization or collective action that would impair the disclosure attributes of this reward mechanism would seem to be required. Otherwise, individual behavior calculated to have local profitability consequences will often result in suboptimization instead.

This is not to say that large organizations are inherently incapable of rewarding executives for high-quality performance, but only that insider trading is not an obvious candidate to assume this burden. An alternative approach to the problems of providing the requisite incentives to the management of the large corporation will be considered in Chapter 10.

3
CONTROL BY DISPLACEMENT

If, for reasons such as those given above, incentives are not sufficient to secure profit-maximizing selection, the stick is substituted for the carrot. Managements that respond insufficiently to pecuniary incentives are displaced. A new group of executives is moved in at the top; the elimination of deviant (non-profit-maximizing) behavior is expected to follow. The argument has been stated by Alchian and Kessel in the following terms [**5**, p. 160]:

> Both the competitive and monopoly model imply that the assets of an enterprise, be it a monopolist or competitive firm, will be utilized by those for whom these assets have the greatest economic value. One might object to this implication of similarity between competition and monopoly by arguing that, when a monopolistic enterprise is not making the most of its pecuniary economic opportunities, it runs less risk of being driven out of business than a similarly mismanaged competitive enterprise. The answer to this is that despite the absence of competition in product markets, those who can most profitably utilize monopoly powers will acquire control over them:

competition in the capital markets will allocate monopoly rights to those who can use them most profitably. Therefore, so long as free capital markets are available, the absence of competition in product markets does not imply a different quality of management in monopolistic as compared with competitive enterprises. Only in the case of nontransferable assets (human monopoly rights and powers like those commanded by Bing Crosby) does classical theory, given free capital market arrangements, admit a difference between competition and monopoly with respect to the effectiveness with which these enterprises pursue profits.

If by free capital market is meant a market that operates costlessly, the argument would appear to be unexceptionable. To the extent, however, that this market experiences nontrivial frictions (costs), incomplete policing of monopoly power may obtain. Whether competitive and monopolistic markets possess the indicated similarities can then no longer be established a priori. An examination of the displacement mechanism is thus indicated.

By contrast with the control by incentive argument, control by displacement relies more on the environment for its support. For one thing, as Manne has pointed out, displacement which takes the form of merger often involves a rival, a customer, or a supplier of the firm [99]. Product market experience is thus brought directly to bear, and this may be important since underachievement may be more evident among these firms than to other surveillance agencies. Moreover, if for any of the reasons given below, merger is not the device by which displacement is achieved, the comparative performance indicators which the environment provides can still serve as useful standards for the evaluation of the firm by alternative displacement agencies. Thus, in both of these respects, the product market provides a variety of support to the displacement argument that is not readily apparent when control operates through incentives. Note, however, that in contrast to the economic natural selection process, the product market here does not act on enterprise viability (the opportunity set of the firm); rather it limits the region of management viability. This latter is a less well specified condition. Also note that, as with control by incentive, the existence of a displacement mechanism is not in dispute but only its efficacy.

Superficially, at least, displacement through the capital market does not appear to be delicately conceived. Consider in this connection Shorey Peterson's argument that the capital market constitutes an effective control mechanism. He takes the position that, "Far from being an ordinary election, a proxy battle is a *catastrophic* event whose mere possibility is a threat, and one not remote when affairs are in *conspicuous* disarray." Indeed, even "stockholder suits . . . may be provoked by evidence of *serious self-dealing*" [**123**, p. 21]. (Italics added.) But as recent history has made abundantly clear, atomic weapons with their catastrophic consequences are ill-suited to support military campaigns involving even half a million men. The principle is perfectly general: controls that have significant discreteness properties are appropriate only when an offense reaches egregious proportions. Otherwise, the remedy is too strong even to be invoked. Peterson concedes as much in his references to "conspicuous" disarray and "serious" self-dealing, and the evidence tends to bear him out [**72**] [**164**]. Therefore, assuming only that management avoids actions which cross the threshold of what Knauth has referred to as obvious and ignominious failure [**86**, p. 45], the proxy contest or the derivative suit appears to be an inappropriate candidate for the task at hand.

Stockholder initiative, however, is not the only way by which displacement can be achieved. Mergers have become increasingly important as a displacement mechanism. Merger opportunities that promise monopoly power or scale economies should be detected relatively quickly. Extant firms (rivals, suppliers, customers) can be expected to display a sensitivity to changes in the extent or character of the market and to technological developments which promise merger gains. In the face of vigorous antitrust enforcement of the merger statutes against horizontal or vertical combinations, monopoly advantages may go unrealized. Certain scale economies may on this account also be sacrificed [**163**]. Potential economies attributable to inferior organization form or subgoal pursuit by the incumbent management, however, are less dependent on horizontal or vertical connections for realization. Any displacement agency (possibly a conglomerate organization) possessing the requisite skills can presumably achieve economies of these types.

This argument will be developed further in Chapters 9 and 10. For our purposes here it is sufficient to note that in order for takeover to be attractive it is necessary, first, to detect the existence of such opportunities for gain and, second, to formulate a strategy that will permit takeover at reasonable cost. Outsiders relying on published accounting and related data together with scraps of internal information, variously obtained, naturally experience an inference problem in determining whether and in what degree opportunities for takeover gain exist. By comparison with an internal control agency, outsiders in this respect stand at a serious disadvantage. If, in general, imperfect knowledge ordinarily leads to estimates of outcomes that are biased downward, which seems likely, a nontrivial inefficiency threshold may need to be crossed before interest in takeover is even generated.

Once the potential for takeover gain has been identified, it is further necessary to achieve displacement at a cost which preserves a positive net gain. Two types of costs need to recognized. First is the expected cost of making a successful displacement offer. Second is the transition cost of bringing the acquired firm under control.

Until recently, the principal techniques for achieving displacement have been the proxy contest and "voluntary" merger. Only in the past several years has the tender offer come to be widely used.

Manne characterizes the proxy contest as "the most dramatic and publicized of the takeover devices . . . , but also the most expensive, and most uncertain, and the least used" [**99**, p. 114]. Costs here are of two types: a premium in the price of shares generally develops when a proxy contest is announced; in addition there are the costs of the solicitation. Considering the difficulty of making a persuasive case for displacement to the shareholders,[7] these efforts are usually made only after the corporation has experienced a succession of bad years and even then are frequently unsuccessful.[8]

The premium in the case of a merger takes the interesting form of a side payment to the existing management. As Manne puts it, "Under almost all state statutes the board of directors of a corporation must approve a merger before it is submitted to shareholders for a vote. . . . Therefore, the existing managers of a corporation [assuming that they control the board of directors] are in a position to claim for themselves the full value of control" [**98**, pp. 1437–38]. Actually, this is probably somewhat too strong. As Manne later points out, the outsider can threaten a proxy fight or resort to a tender bid if the premium extracted by the incumbent management is excessive [**98**, p. 1438]. In addition, the value of the side payment is also constrained by what can be defensibly represented to the stockholders and what promises made to the incumbents are enforceable. "The most obvious kind of side payment to managers is a position within the new structure, either paying a salary or making them privy to valuable market information" [**99**, p. 118].[9] Yet this kind of arrangement is also risky; the existing management would doubtless prefer a lump-sum award, but this is not easily defensible.[10] The difficulty of arranging side payments will tend to reinforce the natural "enterprise sovereignty" objectives of incumbent managements.[11]

The tender offer has the advantage that such negotiations can be bypassed by appealing directly to the stockholders—although it stands a better chance of success if the incumbent management can be induced to support it. The bidder offers existing shareholders a premium over the recent market price on the condition that some minimum percentage response (usually sufficient to bring total holdings over 50 percent, unless the shares are to be used only as a basis for a proxy contest) be obtained. The bidder must obviously value control of the corporation at something higher than the share premiums he is prepared to offer. Assuming that the prospective earnings under the present management are fully reflected in the going price of shares (i.e., the stock is not simply undervalued), this means that a nontrivial inefficiency threshold must be crossed before a tender offer premium (in the range, probably, of 10 to 25 percent) will be made.[12] Thus, so long as *detectable* inefficiency by the incumbent management falls short of this threshold value, or unless either control is desired for nonpecuniary as well as pecuniary reasons or market power effects can also be anticipated, displacement efforts through tender offers are not to be expected.[13] Hayes and Taussig conclude from their 1940–65 study of takeovers that the cash tender offer "represents the only quick reasonably priced approach when resistance is expected. While the record of success here, too, is not outstanding—only 29 successful takeovers during the past ten years out of 83 contested bids—the investment is much smaller than that required for a proxy fight" [**72**, p. 137]. Note, however, that displacement efforts need not be successful for the capital market to have performance consequences. The incumbent management anxious to forestall later attempts may be induced to clean up its own house. Still, if the probability of successful takeover is low, the incentive for a displacement agency to make the initial move will be attenuated.

As with most threatening innovations, the takeover bid has induced an adaptive response. Thus, managements which, only a few years ago, may have passively resigned themselves to the consequences of takeover, once the bid appeared, now call into action a variety of defensive measures that can increase the cost of takeover considerably. The following chronology, from the April 15, 1969, issue of *Forbes*, of the Northwest Industries attempt to take over B. F. Goodrich is illustrative:[14]

THE ATTACK

August-Dec. 20: Loew's Theatres builds up a position totaling at least 358,450 shares in B. F. Goodrich (3%). Loew's Chairman Laurence A. Tisch is a member of the Northwest executive committee. Tisch assures the Goodrich board through John Weinberg of Goldman, Sachs, investment bankers to both Goodrich and Northwest, that he's "only an investor."

Dec. 23: Tisch is informed that Heineman [president of Northwest] would like Northwest to take a position in Goodrich.

Jan. 8: Northwest board grants authority to purchase Goodrich stock.

Jan. 20: Northwest executive committee decides Northwest will make a tender offer for Goodrich. Terms are released to the press.

THE DEFENSE

Jan. 20: Chairman Keener of Goodrich criticizes the method of offer. Jan 21: Goodrich purchases Gulf Oil's 50% interest in Goodrich-Gulf, a synthetic rubber producer, in exchange for 700,000 new Goodrich shares. This move puts 5% of Goodrich's stock in friendly hands. This is a standard defensive move and Northwest sues, claiming Goodrich paid too high a price in order to dilute Northwest's position. Jan. 29: Northwest demands Goodrich's stockholder list. Goodrich refuses.

Jan. 30: Goodrich requests temporary injunction against Northwest alleging violations of Federal Securities Laws, another delaying tactic.

Feb. 3: Goodrich's injunction denied on condition Northwest files registration statements by Feb. 7.

Feb. 6: Northwest files registration statement. Sues to compel Goodrich to produce stockholder list.

Feb. 21: Goodrich sends stockholders proxy materials for Mar. 25 annual meeting. Included is a press release from Congressman Wilbur D. Mills indicating possible changes in the tax laws unfavorable to conglomerates. The political terrain is changing.

Feb. 27: Northwest's request for a preliminary injunction against Goodrich-Gulf deal denied. Lawyers term the decision "a landmark" in defense against takeover attempts. Reason: It recognizes that managements can defend against takeovers they deem unwise.

Mar. 5: Goodrich acquires Motor Freight Corp. for 55,145 Goodrich shares. Motor Freight routes closely duplicate those of the Chicago & North Western Railway.

Mar. 7: Goodrich files supplemental petition with the Interstate Commerce Commission asserting that the Motor Freight acquisition made it necessary for Northwest to get ICC approval on the proposed merger.

Mar. 10: Goodrich sends stockholders a letter mentioning the falling price of Northwest's stock. After firing this barrage, Goodrich loses some ground; it sends Northwest its stockholder list and makes available daily transfer sheets.

Mar. 21: Northwest sues Goodrich contending proxy materials contain misleading statements and requests the postponement of Goodrich annual meeting.

Mar. 24: Northwest suit defeated.

Mar. 25: Goodrich holds annual meeting. Substantial majority of stockholders approve two of four management proposals designed to impede outside takeover attempt. One particular victory involves staggered election of directors; even if Heineman were to win, he couldn't now get a majority on the board until 1971.

Mar. 26: Antitrust Division of the Justice Department asks Northwest to delay proposed tender offer for Goodrich, saying that the proposed acquisition "raises very serious and substantial questions under Section 7 of the Clayton Antitrust Act."

As things now stand, all that Northwest Industries has to show for its efforts are a staggering bill for legal services, high-interest debt and a greatly tarnished reputation. It is also holding 600,000 shares of Goodrich stock that yields only 3.7% and may be difficult to unload. Moreover, with its stock at 80, down more than 40%, Northwest will have to sweeten its offer for Goodrich to the point where the dilution involved will be formidable.

In losing the initiative, Northwest too, has probably lost the support of the arbitragers, the all-important allies of any takeover campaign. These are the financial houses who buy up stock in the attacked company in order to tender it at an assured profit. This, in effect, puts big blocks of stock in hands, which, if not friendly, are certainly cooperative. But arbitragers don't like to lose. As Heineman's chances have faded, so have the arbitragers'.

Thus, in the unlikely event that General Heineman can yet turn defeat into victory, it may well be a victory that costs more than it is worth. Whether Heineman is finally defeated or not, the battle of Akron could well turn out to be the Gettysburg of the Wars of the Takeover.

Subsequently the Antitrust Division of the Department of Justice asked for and, on May 22, was granted a temporary restraining order to prevent Northwest from proceeding with its tender offer for Goodrich. Although its request for a preliminary injunction was denied on July 11, Northwest was nevertheless forbidden to combine with Goodrich or exercise any substantial control, should its tender offer be successful, until a Justice Department suit to block the merger could be decided on the merits—which, considering probable appeals, could take years. The matter, however, is moot. The Northwest offer, which was finally declared effective on July 18, expired unsuccessfully on August 11. Northwest obtained through the tender offer only about a 10 percent response. This brought its total position in Goodrich up to about 20 percent, well short of the amount needed to secure control. Lest a later offer be forthcoming, the Justice Department has indicated that it will seek a permanent injunction. The Justice Department complaint, which broke new antitrust ground, noted that, in terms of assets, Northwest was the 55th largest industrial and Goodrich the 86th and that together they would create the nation's 38th largest industrial.

The above discussion, which is concerned only with transaction costs, incompletely characterizes the costs of achieving displacement.

Transition costs also need to be considered. A displacement agency may not be able merely to correct existing deficiencies. It may also have to contend with serious side effects which its success in turning out the incumbents induces. Middle management may perceive the change at the top as a threat to its security, and dysfunctional behavior, with its attendant effects on performance, may develop. Although these costs may be once-for-all, they need not be trivial—as more than one successful raider has come to appreciate.

4
OVERVIEW

Surveillance from the capital market surely bounds the opportunity set within which the management of an oligopolistic firm feels free to operate. At the same time, however, it is important to note that the *external* control relationship that the capital market bears to the firm severely limits the extent to which capital market controls can be expected to be efficacious.

As conventionally formulated (and even, although to a somewhat lesser extent, when reinterpreted in the context of the multidivision form), there are substantial reasons to expect that capital market controls will incompletely realize the intended effects. With respect to the incentive aspect of this argument, several defects were noted. First, given that the management is responsive to a multidimensional objective function, which is implicit in the incentive argument from the outset, one must assert that relative "prices" are such as to induce a corner solution if profit maximization is to be realized. At the very least, this requires the proponents of such views to explore the characteristics of the utility surface. Second, the efficacy of the incentive argument is seriously weakened by the evidently difficult imputation problems which are encountered. Who deserves what? These give rise to free-ride problems. Third, the incentive system can be beaten. Characterizing the issue in moving equilibrium rather than static terms reveals this. Overall, therefore, incentive controls must clearly be regarded as imperfect.

When the incentive system fails, the threat system is invoked. This is control by displacement. It is also subject to significant limitations. First, the market for corporate control would appear to be imperfect—either by reason of barriers to entry into this market or high inference expense. Second, given existing institutions, this market experiences significant transaction costs in accomplishing displacement. Thus the firm must cross a nontrivial threshold before the threat of displacement will even be activated. Third, even if institutional arrangements were altered so as to reduce the transaction costs, the transition costs which a displacement agency experiences inhibit a change. The discreteness characteristics of the changeover thus also stand as a bar to its employment. Finally, even if a displacement occurs, the new management may eventually become subject to the organizational aspirations of its predecessors, so that the correction achieved does not persist. Altogether, one concludes that, individually and collectively, capital market controls experience weaknesses sufficient to warrant much of the expressed concern over the separation of ownership from control in the large corporation—at least in an environment in which the unitary form structure prevails. Whether and for what reasons the multidivision structure requires a qualification in this judgment remains to be discovered.

FOOTNOTES

[1] At least two considerations weigh against this, however. First, if the argument in Chapter 9 is substantially correct, it is too important not to note explicitly. Second, the proponents of the capital market position have relied extensively on external control processes.

[2] Baumol actually identifies four ways by which efficiency may be induced by reason of indirect capital market controls: (1) the management may be concerned that the price of its securities is "well behaved" (stable); (2) the threat of management displacement by disaffected stockholders; (3) the importance which lenders assign to the performance of the corporation's stock; and (4) the efficiency incentives provided to the management through stock options.

The first and third of these would appear to be of second-order importance and in any case are clearly subject to gaming behavior by the management. Thus it can be shown that utility-maximizing managements (where the utility function reflects, in addition to profits, a positive managerial preference for hierarchical staff, emoluments, and leisure) will respond to changing environmental conditions in such a way as to attenuate intertemporal variations in performance in comparison with a profit-maximizing management. (See Chapter 5.) The likelihood that the variation in stock prices will be reduced by such behavior follows directly. To the extent, therefore, that management assigns additional importance to stock price stability (for either reasons 1 or 3), this is apt merely to enhance its already natural incentives to attenuate earnings variability—which is to say that it will have a greater tendency to absorb profits as corporate personal consumption during periods when the environment is munificent and, correspondingly, reduce slack during adversity.

[3] See Chapter 5.

[4] That the latter is potentially available can be seen by considering a simple model. Let $P_{it} \equiv k_i E_{it}$, where P_{it} is the stock price of firm i at time t, k_i is price earnings ratio of firm (assumed to be invariant over the period in question), and E_{it} is the earnings per share of firm i in period t. Let $E_{it} \equiv \theta_{it} E_{it}^*$, where E_{it}^* is the maximum attainable earnings per share of firm i in period t (which obtains when the firm is operated strictly as a neoclassical profit-maximizer), and θ_{it} is the ratio of actual to maximum earnings per share. Now assume that E_{it}^* is a function of the condition of the environment; namely, $E_{it} = f_i(Z_t)$, where Z_t is exogenous. Then the decimal fraction change in share prices from period t to $t + 1$ is given by the equation:

$$\frac{P_{it+1} - P_{it}}{P_{it}} = \left(\frac{\theta_{it+1}}{\theta_{it}}\right) \frac{\{f_i(Z_{t+1})\}}{f_i(Z_t)} - 1.$$

It follows that $\Delta P_{kt}/P_{kt} = \Delta P_{jt}/P_{jt}$ if the right-hand side of this expression is equal for both k and j. Assuming that the environmental response ratio is approximately the same, this requires only that $\theta_{kt+1}/\theta_{kt} = \theta_{jt+1}/\theta_{jt}$—which obviously holds if $\theta_{it+1} = \theta_{it}$ for all i. Thus, subject to the condition that the value of θ selected is sufficiently high to avoid displacement, *relative* stock prices will fully reflect environmental change, whatever the initial value of θ, while the management that has selected an initial value of θ less than unity will simultaneously have access to opportunities for discretion.

The analysis should, however, be qualified in two respects. First, for the reasons given in Chapter 5, the opportunity set to which the firm has access in future periods may not be independent of current period behavior. The argument is not necessarily vitiated, but this does imply that tradeoffs are involved in selecting values of θ different from unity. Second, a lower bound on the admissible value of θ (greater than that which direct examination of the firm's performance would permit) may obtain if objective performance evaluations regarding the size of the opportunity set (based, for example, on the comparative record of high-performance rivals) are possible. Despite the fact that such achievement indicators are only crude (other things are never equal between firms), the admissible value of θ can, nevertheless, be bounded in this way.

[5] Manne regards salaries as a wholly inappropriate way to compensate entrepreneurial services; bonuses are too conspicuous and experience causality problems; and stock options are neither sufficiently flexible nor high-powered enough to have this result [**100**, pp. 134–38].

[6] Manne insists that stockholders are not damaged [**100**, Chap. 7], but the argument is strained. See Malkiel for a critique of this position [**97**].

[7] For a discussion of defensive strategies, see Hayes and Taussig [**72**, pp. 142–47].

[8] During the period 1956–60, only nine out of twenty-eight proxy fights for control were fully successful [**72**, p. 137].

[9] Documentary support for this is found in A. K. McCord's letter to Westinghouse Air Brake Stockholders, informing them that he had been offered "an option to purchase Crane Stock and Benefits after retirement, possibly by a consulting arrangement" if he would support Crane's merger bid [**56**].

[10] In the event, of course, that the existing management does not have effective control over the board of directors, the management may be bypassed. If side payments extracted by board members are typically lower than by managers, and I would judge this to be the case, the cost of displacement in these circumstances will be correspondingly lower.

[11] Joe S. Bain characterizes enterprise sovereignty as "the virtual deterrent to mergers inhering in the difficulty of potential participants in agreeing on terms, and fundamentally to the reluctance of individual ownership-management units to yield up their sovereign controls over their operations" [**20**, p. 184].

[12] It is doubtful that the premium could go much lower if the offer is to attract sufficient support to be successful. It could, however, go higher. Manne notes simply that "tender bids are invariably made at a price considerably above the current market price of the company's shares" [**98**, p. 1435]. Hayes and Taussig report in their recent survey that "the median premium offered by bidders was 16% over the market two days before the offer." Premiums ranged from zero to 44%, "with the premium tending to be on the higher side when management resistance was encountered" [**72**, p. 140].

[13] The argument oversimplifies by focusing strictly on the efficiency conditions. There are also financial inducements to takeover. These include what are vaguely referred to as stock market dynamics, unutilized debt financing opportunities that permit accounting profit gains, and access to cash flow for reinvestment purposes. Debt financing and captive cash flow inducements are attributable in large part to tax laws which permit interest expense to be deducted before payment of taxes and subject dividend payments to double taxation. For further discussion, see Chapter 10.

[14] The chronology is reprinted by permission of *Forbes* magazine.

THE
MULTIDIVISION
FORM
ORGANIZATION

7

the multidivision
form
innovation

The multidivision form innovation described here and examined in the succeeding chapters can be regarded as an adaptive response of the capitalist system to the evident problems that the large, unitary form organization experienced. For purposes of compactness, the multidivision form and the unitary form structures will be referred to as M-form and U-form structures respectively.

A brief review of the earlier (U-form) argument is given in section 1. The M-form innovation is described in section 2. Imitation of the M-form innovation and recent variations on it are considered in section 3.

1
THE LARGE, UNITARY FORM CORPORATION
IN PERSPECTIVE

Lest the argument be regarded as a negative evaluation of the unitary form structure quite generally, it should be emphasized that the adjective "large" is used here deliberately. The U-form structure is the "natural" way to organize multifunctional tasks. Even in the multidivision form enterprise, the unitary form is preserved at lower levels of the organizational hierarchy. The problems that the U-form encounters are attributable to the difficulties of control that develop if the firm indefinitely continues to expand within this structure and to the discontinuities experienced in moving to the multidivision form.

1.1
Expansion and Its Immediate Consequences

Expansion of the U-form enterprise in a manner that preserves the U-form structure has been referred to in earlier chapters as radial amplification. The functional basis of decomposing the enterprise is preserved all the way to the top under this form of expansion. Finite spans of control naturally require that additional hierarchical levels be introduced in the process.

Adding hierarchical levels can, if only for serial reproduction reasons, lead to an effective loss of control through incomplete or inaccurate transmittal of data moving up and instructions moving down the organizational hierarchy. Although various decoupling devices may be devised to reduce these transmission needs, these are costly and subject to diminishing returns. Decoupling merely alleviates but does not overcome the need for intrafunctional and peak coordination.

Information flows rarely take the form of simple serial reproduction, however. Rather, data are summarized and interpreted as they move forward and instructions are operationalized as they move down. Both processes provide additional opportunities for control losses to develop. These can occur in quite unintentional ways. If, however, the functional units of the firm view the hierarchical structure as affording opportunities to pursue local goals, deliberate distortions may be introduced into the hierarchical exchange process. Control losses of simple and calculated varieties together constitute what is referred to as compound control loss. Cumulative losses of these types stand eventually as an efficiency bar to the further expansion of the firm.

The office of the peak coordinator not merely is involved in the interfunctional coordination of operating matters but also has principal responsibility for strategic planning. As the enterprise successively expands, the capacity of this office to discharge these functions is eventually overcome. The usual means for augmenting this capacity is to bring the heads of the functional divisions into the peak coordination process on both operating and strategic matters. The natural posture for these functional executives to take is one of advocacy in representing the interests of their respective operating units.

1.2
Discretionary Behavior

The partisan interests of these functional executives who participate in the strategic decision-making process may be partly antagonistic and self-canceling. If profits can be made to yield, however, the game is not zero sum. Also one might expect that the interests of this group of executives in reaching a position on rather than within the opportunity set would encourage cooperative behavior. The utility function constructions proposed indeed assume that a consensus is reached among the executives who participate in the strategic decision-making process and that this places the firm on its opportunity set (in an ex ante expectation sense) at a position that maximizes the utility of this core group.

The extent to which these discretionary preferences are significant depends jointly on the size of the opportunity set and the characteristics of the utility function. Foremost among the factors that influence the size of the firm's opportunity set is the condition of competition in the product market. Where the attenuation of product market competition is substantial, a nontrivial enterprise opportunity set can be presumed. Subject to the condition that performance exceed a minimum level sufficient to avoid displacement, and assuming compliance among lower-level participants, the management is free to locate anywhere on or within this opportunity set.

Although profits can be expected to remain an important component in the management's utility function, there is also apt to be a persistent and collective pressure to provide more and better services. An expansionary bias in favor of staff expenditures is a common consequence. A permissive attitude toward slack may also develop, with imitative consequences among lower-level participants. Such imitation effectively increases the relative price of slack in relation to other components of the utility function, and in this respect discourages slack experience at the top.

The comparative static and dynamic-stochastic properties of models of the firm developed on these assumptions seem plausible and are not contradicted by the conspicuous evidence. Also of interest in this regard are the special applications of the argument to public utility behavior and price smoothing. The former is a direct application of the basic argument to a situation where the discretionary behavior in question might be expected to be especially prevalent. That such behavior has been reported by Gordon [68] and others [5] tends to give one modest confidence in the underlying construction. The price smoothing argument is somewhat *ad hoc* but is nevertheless obtained as a reasonable extension of the underlying argument. Again, there appears to be modest evidence to support the behavior in question.

1.3
Control through the Capital Market

The capital market has access to a variety of controls over the corporation, but all of them operate through an external control relationship between the capital market and the firm. This constitutes a more serious limitation than is often appreciated. The possibility of monitoring firm performance through the direct metering of funds is impaired by the internal financing which most firms in the discretionary category have access to. The use of incentive devices of various sorts is impaired by the imprecision with which they apply and by the adaptive responses which they permit. The displacement threat which the capital market poses is subject to serious inference problems and experiences nontrivial displacement costs if the incumbent management is disposed to resist the takeover effort. Recent refinements of the tender offer technique that appear to have reduced these costs have been partially offset as incumbent managements have devised a variety of defensive weapons. Taken together with the antipathy expressed to takeovers of large firms by Congress and the regulatory agencies, this technique stands in real jeopardy. The important role that the tender offer has and should continue to play in revitalizing moribund managements should be appreciated, however—a subject to which we return in Chapter 9. But for the effects on takeover of the M-form innovation discussed there, capital market controls can scarcely be relied on effectively to extinguish residual opportunities for discretion that the product market affords. This is not to suggest that the capital market is wholly inefficacious in supplying incentives or enforcing lower bound performance, but in neither case are the controls it has access to delicately conceived.

2
THE MULTIDIVISION
INNOVATION

The historical development of the multidivision form has been traced by Alfred Chandler, Jr., in his superlative book titled *Strategy and Structure*. He reports that the M-form innovation was initially devised in the early 1920s, apparently quite independently, by Du Pont and General Motors; somewhat later, but still independently, it was adopted by Standard Oil of New Jersey and Sears [42]. It has been widely imitated and "rediscovered" since.

The immediate cause for the innovation to be introduced was the onset of adversity. In Du Pont, the "company's financial statement for the first half of 1921 provided the shock that finally precipitated a major reorganization. In those six months, as the postwar recession became increasingly severe, the company had lost money on every product except explosives" [42, pp. 126–27]. At General Motors, an inventory crisis together with the collapse of the auto market in 1920 produced the change [42, pp. 156–57]. Partial reorganization at Jersey was induced by excessive inventories, falling profits, and a declining market share [42, p. 230], but it was not until earnings fell to the lowest level in 1927 of any year since 1912 (from $117.7 in 1926 to $40.4 million in 1927) that major organization changes were induced [42, p. 256]. Although profit pressures at Sears were less dramatic, they also contributed to the change [42, pp. 321–23].

The basic reason why the innovation became necessary, however, is traceable to more fundamental reasons than transitory market conditions. Chandler summarizes the defects of the unitary form, and consequently the needs for the multidivision structure, in the following way [42, p. 369]:

> The inherent weakness in the centralized, functionally departmentalized operating company . . . became critical only when the administrative load on the senior executives increased to such an extent that they were unable to handle their entrepreneurial responsibilities efficiently. This situation arose when the operations of the enterprise became too complex and the problems of coordination, appraisal, and policy formulation too intricate for a small number of top officers to handle both long-run, entrepreneurial, and short-run, operational administrative activities. To meet these new needs, the innovators built the multi-divisional structure with a general office whose executives would concentrate on entrepreneurial activities and with autonomous, fairly self-contained operating divisions whose managers would handle operational ones.

Illustrative of overloading conditions is the report of the troubles experienced by Du Pont following its diversification moves but prior to its adoption of the multidivision form [42, p. 111]:

> Broad goals and policies had to be determined for and resources allocated to functional activities, not in one industry but in several. Appraisal of departments performing in diverse fields became exceedingly complex. Interdepartmental coordination grew comparably more troublesome. The manufacturing personnel and marketers tended to lose contact with each other and so failed to work out product improvements and modifications to meet changing demands and competitive developments.... Each of the three major departments— Purchasing, Manufacturing, and Sales—made its own [forecasts] and set its own schedules.

Thus, as the complexity of its various yet interconnected activities progressively increased, its ability to supply the requisite coordination became strained and even collapsed. Unable meaningfully to identify with or contribute to the realization of global goals, managers in each of the functional parts attended to what they perceived as operational subgoals instead [42, p. 156]. The experience of Ford in operating the giant River Rouge plant as a U-form organization in the 1920s affords a similar example (although, it should be noted, others have interpreted the problems of Ford mainly in personality rather than structural terms [120, Chaps. 8, 11]).

The difficulties that the large, U-form enterprise became subject to (and which the M-form innovation was presumably designed to relieve) can be expressed in terms of indecomposability, incommensurability, nonoperational goal specification, and the confounding of strategic and operating decisions. Incommensurability made it difficult to specify the goals of the functional divisions in ways which clearly contributed to higher-level enterprise objectives. Indecomposability made it necessary to attempt more comprehensive coordination among the parts; for a given span of control, this naturally resulted in a high degree of control loss between hierarchical levels. Moreover, to the extent that efforts at coordination broke down and the individual parts suboptimized, the intrinsic interconnectedness between them virtually assured that spillover costs would be substantial. The confounding of strategic and operating decisions served further to compromise organizational purpose. These are the fundamental reasons why the U-form enterprise eventually encountered serious operating difficulties. Adversity merely made these structural conditions the more apparent.

Functional organization nevertheless was and is the natural way to decompose simple tasks. Preserving the functional form as the firm is gradually expanded is also to be expected. Eventually, however, the U-form structure defeats itself. This will obtain even if the U-form entrerprise undergoes a simple radial amplification in size without concurrent diversification. If accomplished through diversification, coordination within the functional form can be expected to present even more severe problems.

The organizational innovation that was devised as a response to these conditions involved substituting quasi-autonomous operating divisions (organized mainly along product, brand, or geographic lines) for the functional divisions of the U-form structure as the principal basis for achieving compartmentalization. Inasmuch as each of these operating divisions is subsequently divided along functional lines (see Figure 7-1), one might characterize these operating divisions as scaled down, specialized U-form structures. Although this is a considerable oversimplification (operating divisions may be further subdivided by product, geographic, or brand subdivisions before the final U-form structure appears), the observation has at least heuristic merit.

This simple change in the decomposition rules might not, by itself, appear to have other than superficial consequences. Indeed, for the reorganization to be fully effective really requires more. The peak coordinator's office (shown in Figure 7-1 as the "general office") also has to undergo transformation and an elite staff needs to be supplied to assist the general office in its strategic decision-making (including control) responsibilities. Chandler characterizes the reasons for the success of the multidivision form as follows [**42**, p. 382–83]:

> The basic reason for its success was simply that it clearly removed the executives responsible for the destiny of the entire enterprise from the more routine operational activities and so gave them the time, information, and even psychological commitment for the long-term planning and appraisal. . . . The new structure left the broad strategic decisions as to the allocation of existing resources and the acquisition of new ones in the hands of a top team of generalists. Relieved of operating duties and tactical decisions, a general executive was less likely to reflect the position of just one part of the whole.

The nature of the transformation and the reasons for it were not unperceived by those who engineered the change. Among those who had been instrumental in bringing about the reorganization of General Motors was Donaldson Brown.[1] As the following statement (which was made in 1924, when he was a vice president of General Motors) reveals, the change was undertaken self-consciously; the intended results were apparently clear [**37**, pp. 195–96]:

> Each division is equipped with a self-contained organization having complete jurisdiction over manufacture, sales, and finance, subject to control from the central authority. The ordinary, everyday questions of policy, embodying even such important matters as production schedules, inventory commitments, design of product, and methods

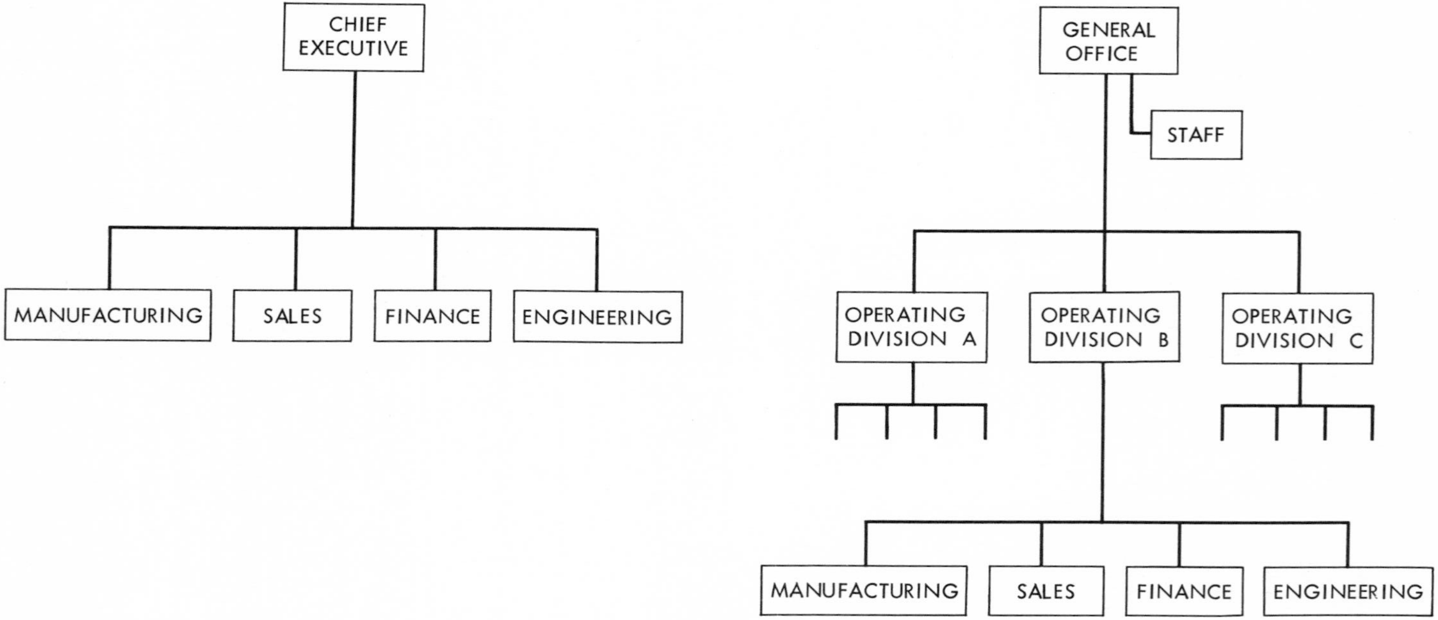

UNITARY FORM

MULTI-DIVISION FORM

FIGURE 7-1

of distribution, are left ordinarily within the consideration and decision of the divisions themselves, under certain general limitations, and in every way the men on the firing line are inspired with a sense of responsibility for results.

The central organization embraces talent in automotive engineering and research, and experts dealing with important problems of improved methods in manufacture and distribution, all of whom serve in a more or less advisory capacity. Apart from these important adjuncts, and certain necessary activities in finance and accounting, law, and related matters, the central organization deals almost exclusively with questions of policy. The president is general manager of the corporation in fact, but controls the operations by the establishment of principles and the interpretation of policies, and refrains from entering into questions of operating detail except in cases where the two are inseparable. The Executive and Finance Committees, as active bodies subject to the board of directors, have final jurisdiction over the entire business through the enunciation of policies and by direct action in matters involving essential points of policy.

3
IMITATION
AND SUBSEQUENT DEVELOPMENTS

Imitation of the M-form innovation was at first rather slow. For one thing, however obvious its superior properties may have been to the innovators, others were naturally skeptical. In some industries (such as those engaged in metal processing) the divisionalized structure was not as easy to create as in others where distinct product or brand lines were readily established. In others, administrative inertia appears to have been substantial. Up through the 1930s, only a handful of firms had accomplished the transformation [**42**, Chap. 7]. A number of firms which by 1940 had reorganizational changes in the works postponed these with the onset of World War II. Since 1945, however, large firms quite generally have undergone a reorganization along M-form lines.[2]

Among the imitators, a change in the chief executive was frequently essential to bring the reorganization off. Chandler observes this to have been the case at Goodyear [**42**, p. 436], General Electric [**42**, pp. 456–57], IBM [**42**, p. 458], International Harvester [**42**, p. 460], and Ford and Chrysler [**42**, pp. 462–63], among others. Occasionally firms were observed to make the change without the pressures of adversity or the retirement of key personnel, and no doubt this has become more common as the merits of the M-form structure have become more widely appreciated. But adversity appears to have been an essential goad for those who were first to innovate; and among those who were the early imitators, "the essential reshaping of administrative structure nearly always had to wait for a change in the top command" [**42**, p. 472].

The early 1950s witnessed a variant on the M-form structure that, in the 1960s, has become widespread: the conglomerate organization.[3] This was a natural extension of the M-form organization to include a deliberately diversified (multimarket) structure. Although many of the first firms to adopt the M-form structure were diversified to some extent, they usually limited this to a general class of activity (e. g., chemicals) or otherwise maintained a relatively high product specialization ratio despite multimarket occupancy (e. g., autos). The conglomerator, by contrast, has regarded the M-form as a vehicle by which to move aggressively into multiple markets without special concern for the conventional product variety constraints.

A recent statement of the advantages and properties of the M-form structure, particularly in conjunction with conglomerate operations, was provided by Harold Geneen, speaking as chairman and president of International Telephone and Telegraph Corporation. ITT under his leadership had undertaken an extensive diversification program and provided it with an M-form structure. Geneen expressed the opinion that the effectively managed M-form organization has superior properties (both with respect to strategic decision-making and program execution) to a similarly well-managed U-form enterprise and attributed this to its surpassing goal formation, staff support, and control characteristics. As he put it: "We select the most purposeful goals at the corporate [general management] level . . . and concentrate local autonomy at the daily operation [division management] level. We monitor both at the corporate level" [**65**, p. 16]. The elite staff of the general office is available to assist the operating divisions, but its principal function is to help assure that the strategic objectives of the general office are realized. This division of effort between the general office and the operating divisions "separates the day-to-day problems of the [operating] division from the long-term corporate responsibilities for growth and future above-average returns" [**65**, p. 16].

Geneen then went on to observe that the multidivision structure performs functions which are closely related to those traditionally associated with competition in the product and capital markets [**65**, p. 17]:

> The philosophy of varied industry and a unified multi-layer management, provided it stays in direct touch with the field, . . . produces the most logical, efficient growth pattern for the corporate vehicle as we know it. . . .
>
> By entering *many* industries, it brings the resources and purposes of more efficient companies into the competition for resources. . . . The

varied-industry company, far from reducing competition, actually *increases* competition.

Although self-diagnosis is often unreliable and sometimes self-serving, one may not want to dismiss these observations altogether. The conglomerate phenomenon is now more than fifteen years old and has long since passed the point at which quantitative substantiality could be claimed. That the rationale for so pervasive a condition should so long remain a matter of mystery or indifference among academics (economists, lawyers, and organization specialists alike) perhaps suggests that the views of operating types be accorded more than ordinary weight. Skeptics may nevertheless be encouraged that one of the few academics who have explicitly addressed themselves to the M-form structure, Richard Heflebower, concludes that its quasi-market properties are not unlike those described by Geneen [**73**, p. 18]:

> The top executive group becomes an "activated board of directors" whether or not they are the legally constituted board. . . . Such an executive group—where men are members of the group because they are top officers—does not "manage" in the usual sense of the word. . . . Instead the role of such a group is more like that of an investment manager with the power to choose the particular users of funds . . . and to judge performance of those whom it authorizes to use the capital.

FOOTNOTES

[1] Actually, General Motors had been organized more along the lines of a holding company than a U-form organization. Chandler observes that its "diversity of activities proved almost impossible to manage effectively through the overdecentralized holding company [that Durant had devised]. . . . Sloan's transformation of Durant's tiny top office into a coordinating, appraising, and policy-making general office made possible the rational and profitable management of such an enterprise" [**42**, p. 372].

[2] Those who adopted the M-form structure later often expressed their reasons for going to this structure and explained its properties in terms strikingly similar to those given by Donaldson Brown in 1924. Consider the following 1956 statement of IBM regarding its then recent organization changes (which it characterized as a "new" pattern for progress) [**76**]:

> . . . the new alignment of the various areas is based on products. Each of the product divisions will, within the framework of policy established by the Board of Directors and general management, operate almost as an individual company with its own manufacturing, sales, and service functions. Each of these divisions is equipped with special skills and product knowledge to concentrate on developing the full potential of a specific market.
>
> Further strength is given the organization with the creation of the Corporate Staff, which, being separate from the operating organization responsible for developing, producing, selling and servicing goods, can closely examine the special areas of the business and assist the operating executives in solving problems in these areas.

[3] Conglomeration has much earlier origins, but not until the 1950s did it assume public policy significance. For an early 1950s discussion, see [**57**].

8

properties
of the
multidivision form

The observations of the businessmen and academics cited in the previous chapter are broadly consistent and lead to the following summary statement regarding the characteristics and advantages of the multidivision form:

1. The responsibility for operating decisions is assigned to (essentially self-contained) operating divisions.
2. The elite staff attached to the general office performs both advisory and auditing functions. Both activities have the effect of securing greater control over operating division behavior.
3. The general office is principally concerned with strategic decisions involving planning, appraisal, and control, including the allocation of resources among the (competing) operating divisions.
4. The separation of the general office from operations provides general office executives with the psychological commitment to

be concerned with the overall performance of the organization rather than to become absorbed in the affairs of the functional parts.

5. The resulting structure displays both rationality and synergy: the whole is greater (more effective, more efficient) than the sum of the parts.

These are, by almost any standard, important observations concerning business behavior. That they have not had a noticeable impact on the modern theory of the firm is, probably, attributable to a failure to regard organization form seriously. This neglect of organization form is partly to be accounted for by a common tendency to invoke the standard behavioral assumption (profit maximization) without regard for circumstances.

The view taken here is that business behavior is jointly determined by market circumstances and internal organization—including the strategic decision-making and internal incentive and compliance processes. Organization form has an immediate effect on operations and an eventual effect on market circumstances. Consider its immediate effects first. Thus we inquire in what respects the M-form structure helps to overcome the internal efficiency and strategic decision-making "problems" that the large U-form enterprise is subject to. Also, and related, what internal incentive and compliance processes does the M-form management have access to that the U-form management is either unable or disinclined to employ and with what effects?

The comparison here is strictly between M-form and U-form structures. To place the comparison on common grounds, it will be assumed that the two organizations in question are engaged in identical activities (same product lines and geographic spread) and are similar in size. A comparison of the internal control processes of the M-form enterprise with the controls exercised by the capital market is undertaken in the following chapter. A comparison of the M-form enterprise with a series of independently constituted U-form firms is given in Chapter 10.

1
INTERNAL EFFICIENCY

Assume here (as was done in Chapter 2, where the control loss phenomenon was first examined) that the behavior of every member of the firm is functionally oriented to advance the goals of the peak coordinator. Noncompliance and active subgoal pursuit are, for the purposes of this section, placed in abeyance. Also assume (this will be relaxed shortly) that each of the operating divisions in the M-form enterprise satisfies technical scale economies with respect to production and marketing and that there is an absence of market interdependencies and production externalities among these divisions. What, given these assumptions, are the simple control loss consequences of the M-form organization in relation to an equivalent (in the sense described above) U-form structure?

It will be useful for the purposes of making this comparison to extend the concept of control loss introduced in Chapter 2. There, it will be recalled, only U-form organizations that differed with respect to size (and, hence, hierarchical level) were under examination. Cumulative control loss could thus be expressed as a function of the number of hierarchical levels; namely, as $1 - \alpha^n$. Here, however, size and the number of hierarchical levels are approximately constant; the comparison involves alternative organization forms with respect to internal efficiency. Thus it is interorganizational differences in the value of α (interpreted as a productivity parameter) rather than variations in the number of levels (for a common α) that is critical.

Assume, for purposes of standardizing the comparison, that the span of control in both U- and M-form organizations is identical. The value of α can then be expressed as a function of the communication load and the ease of achieving coordination: *ceteris paribus*, α will vary inversely with the volume of communication and directly with the ease of arranging a coordinated response. Increasing the volume of communication leads to a decrease in α among operators by occupying (preempting) productive energies that would otherwise be available. It also reduces the value of α among members of the management hierarchy by crowding their capacity to summarize and interpret data flowing up and to operationalize instructions moving down. Increasing the ease of utilizing resources in a coordinated way is manifested as a decrease in the cost of accomplishing integration. Internal productivity is impaired to the extent that resources are incompletely utilized or intrinsic interdependencies, with respect either to marketing or production, go unrecognized or are given allowance for only with difficulty. Incomplete utilization of resources results in excess capacity relative to what could be accomplished with more efficient loading, while unadapted interdependencies have the parts of the organization pulling at cross-purposes.

The process of divisionalizing a U-form enterprise to create an M-form structure can be regarded as a decoupling operation of massive proportions. Ordinalily decoupling has communication saving characteristics to commend it; communication between the parts is reduced by isolating richly-interacting from weakly-interacting parts and/or by introducing relatively high thresholds to suppress sensitivity to connectedness [**16**, p. 66]. While the former is a pure gain (in that it eliminates redundant communications), the latter, involves a tradeoff; a loss in the capacity to arrange an integrated response needs to be balanced against the realized reduction in information transfer costs that higher thresholds afford. The question to be addressed here is what are the net consequences of divisionalization under the conditions described.

In substantial measure, the decomposition postulated above involves the definition of "natural decision units" within an agglomerated structure and giving these independent standing. It thus permits a reduction in communication of the pure gain type. Not only does the firm have less cause to originate information—since, as Jacob Marschak puts it, "in general, . . . more communication is justified when . . . the [perceived] effect on one member's action depends on what his colleague is doing" [**108**, p. 317]—but its internal communication network is more compact. Also, inasmuch as both market and production interdependencies are absent or minimal, integration losses are not experienced on this account. At most a sacrifice in the opportunity to pool resources efficiently against market fluctuations is involved. Assuming that the potential economies of such pooling are unimportant or can be realized for the most part at slight compromise to the divisionalized structure, integration losses in the M-form enterprise should be negligible. Altogether, therefore, the M-form enterprise that meets the idealized conditions described should enjoy superior control loss (internal efficiency) experience to that of its U-form counterpart. In other words, the richly interconnected U-form firm can in these circumstances be regarded as one which fails to recognize essential decomposability and attempts excessive integration instead.[1]

If the operating divisions are not fully decomposable in this sense but experience some modest degree of technical or market interdependency, the decoupling described cannot be accomplished without cost. Certain of these costs can be attenuated by specification of appropriate interdivisional rules regarding internal pricing [**13**] [**25**] [**44**], non-interference in market test stipulations, and the like.[2] If these interactions are extensive, however, the information exchange needs of the resulting M-form organization may be merely different from but not significantly less than its U-form equivalent. Its control loss experience need not be better and could easily be worse. From a simple control loss point of view, therefore, the M-form structure is to be preferred over its U- form counterpart in the degree to which decomposability (quasi-autonomy) into operating divisions is feasible or, at low cost, can be arranged. Even if, however, judged with respect to its simple control loss properties, the M-form structure experiences net negative productivity effects, divisionalization of a large U-form firm may still be warranted because of the advantages that the M-form firm offers in other respects.

2
STRATEGIC
DECISION MAKING

In substantial measure, enterprise objectives can be imputed from the goal pursuit activities of the top hierarchical level, which is the locus of strategic decision-making in the firm. It is therefore appropriate to inquire how different organization forms solve the capacity problem at the top and with what consequences.

2.1
The Capacity Problem

The M-form enterprise solves the problem of supplying requisite capacity at the top not by bringing operating executives into this activity but by creating a team of general executives and providing them with an elite staff. The general executives have no direct operating responsibilities. Indeed they have no direct access to the functional parts of the organization. Responsibility for achieving performance goals is fixed on the division managers: each division manager is expected to provide appropriate coordination among the functional parts within his respective operating division. Thus the general executives, having delegated this responsibility and lacking direct access to the functional parts, are able to become fully absorbed in enterprise-wide strategic considerations instead.

Attachment of an elite staff to the general office is a vital adjunct in supplying the peak coordinating function with requisite capacity. As already noted, this staff provides advisory functions to the operating divisions, acting in this respect as in-house management consultants, to help them set up procedures to execute their respective programs more effectively. It also serves an important planning and control function, undertaking ex ante studies of both general market conditions and new enterprise opportunities and making ex post evaluations of the performance of the operating divisions. This provides the general office with important informational inputs for its own planning purposes, inputs that are less subject to the data distortion that occurs when information is processed up through the organizational hierarchy. It also permits the general office to audit divisional performance in a way which, left to its own resources, would be impracticable. Thus the strategic decision-making function can be said to have been solved in the M-form by (1) assigning this function to a team[3] of top executive specialists who are removed from operating responsibilities, and (2) supporting this group of general officers with an elite staff capable of performing the depth analyses necessary to discharge the strategic overseer task effectively.

2.2
Goal Pursuit

The discussion of goal pursuit consequences of the M-form organization will consider first the goal pursuit characteristics of the general office, next those of the elite staff, and finally those of the operating divisions.

2.2.1. General office. As indicated, the general office is created as a means for overcoming the capacity problem at the top. The creation of such a general office does more, however, than relieve bounded capacity constraints. It also, as Chandler points out, alters the "psychological commitment" of the strategic decision-makers. The subgoals associated with the separate functional divisions are no longer natural objects of pursuit.

The most important reason for this commitment shift is that the general executive position is defined in a way which not only frees it but removes it from narrow functional responsibilities. This is accomplished by reorganizing the firm so as to make the operating division rather than the functional division the principal operating unit. Strictly functional issues are therefore resolved intradivisionally with the result that partisan functional input can be greatly reduced, if not eliminated, from the strategic decision-making process. Natural incentives to promote subgoals are in this way attenuated. The general executive is able to focus on genuine enterprise viability considerations and can consider the effect on the individual parts dispassionately. The disposition to expand staff and tolerate slack is supplanted instead by a tendency to regard costs in a strictly instrumental fashion. If, as indicated earlier, profit maximization is an effective proxy for the enterprise viability objective, the M-form organization, at least at the level of the general office, can be expected to give greater weight to this organizational objective.

2.2.2. Elite staff. Inasmuch as the staff attached to the general office has an important role in both formulating and executing strategic decisions, it is relevant to consider whether this group has own-preferences that run contrary to those of the general office, and if so whether these are apt to be important to an assessment of M-form performance. With respect to own-preferences, this group, like most professional staffs, may be anxious to extend the scope and quality of its services. Quantitatively, however, the elite staff is not apt to be sufficiently large, in relation to overall enterprise activity and employment, to have a substantial immediate effect on cost even if it is successful in realizing own-staff expansionary aspirations. More worrisome are its indirect cost consequences and its choice of evaluative criteria.

Since the relation of this staff to the operating divisions is mainly instrumental, identification with the operating divisions in a partisan sense is missing. Excellence is thus apt to be measured in terms of the criteria specified by the general office, i.e., principally revenues in relation to costs (profit), rather than by the size or prominence of the functional divisions. The elite staff serves to reinforce the preferences of the general office in this respect.

The indirect cost consequences of elite staff initiatives are more troublesome, however. Thus, although zealousness of the elite staff may have insubstantial own-cost effects, these may cumulatively become great when their operating division consequences are assessed. Special precautions may therefore be needed lest the elite staff require the operating divisions to undertake planning and control activities (records, reports, etc.) the net benefits of which, while positive in terms of an elite staff calculus, are negative when expressed in terms of profits.

Note that no special moral superiority is assigned to either the general office or the elite staff. The reason why strategic decisions favor profitability is because this is the natural outcome of the way in which the M-form organization is structured. Organizational design thus involves more than technical efficiency considerations. It is also a means of defining roles which in turn elicit characteristic behavior. With a few exceptions, notably Chandler [42], the latter is a relatively neglected aspect of the organizational design literature.

2.2.3. Operating divisions.   As indicated earlier, the operating divisions in the M-form organization have many of the attributes of independent firms and might be described as "quasi-firms." Each of these quasi-firms has a U-form structure. One might then reasonably expect them to display U-form preferences—which may or may not place these units in goal conflict with the general office. Whether it does depends jointly on organization form, size, and internal role expectations and incentive processes. If each of the operating divisions is individually small enough that the division manager's office possesses requisite capacity for peak (divisional) coordination, preferences characteristic of the large U-form structure (and attributable to the extensive participation in the strategic decision-making process of partisan functional executives and to control loss experience) need not obtain. Medium-sized, U-form operating divisions (like independent, medium-sized, U-form firms) may display profit-maximizing preferences instead. Moreover, in consideration of the separable profit performance assignable to each of these divisions, deviant tendencies can presumably be checked, if not eliminated, through judicious use by the general office of incentive awards.

Although the argument has a certain a priori plausibility, it disposes too easily of the potential goal conflict between the operating divisions and the general office. For one thing, overcoming partisan functional representations does not necessarily dispose of partisanship altogether. An advocacy posture is still natural for division managers— only now, presumably, expense biases are supplanted by general size aspirations (which correspond, approximately, to the revenue-profits model of Chapter 4, section 3). Thus whereas the heads of the functional divisions in the large U-form firm are observed to expend efforts to extend the size and prominence of their respective functional activities, the operating division chiefs in the M-form firm are engaged instead in efforts to expand the size and prominence of their respective operating divisions. Although, for a given expansion of expenditures, the latter are apt to have a less pernicious profit impact, the potential for conflict needs to be recognized. Moreover, if in addition either scale economies or design error has produced operating divisions of sufficient size that large, U-form goal consequences are induced at the divisional level, the conflict potential is compounded. Any claims, therefore, that the general office preference for profit will be prevailing requires that the efficacy of the internal compliance processes be examined; merely to establish that a decisive preference for profit in relation to hierarchical expense prevails at the top of the M-form organization is not sufficient. Whether and for what reasons the general office can be expected to be successful in constraining the operating divisions to perform "appropriately" is considered in section 3 below and in the following chapter.

2.3
Contrasts with the U-form Structure

The different solutions to the capacity problem in the U- and M-form structures manifest themselves as different inputs to and, as a result, different outputs of the strategic decision-making process. Thus, whereas the U-form organization responds to the capacity problem by bringing operating executives with their partisan interests into the strategic decision-making process, the M-form enterprise

converts the task of peak coordination into a team function and supports this group of general executives with an elite staff. Partisan
identifications are missing under this M-form structure (or at least
are greatly attenuated) with the result that the staff-favoring preferences characteristic of the U-form structure (and possible slack-
favoring tendencies as well) will be suppressed. Selection on profit is
favored instead.

If, provisionally, the elite staff is absorbed into the general office,
the M-form organization can be represented as a somewhat "cleaner"
solution to the ultrastable system assignment problem than does the
U-form structure. Table 8-1 shows the three basic components of the
ultrastable system and corresponding hierarchical parts in the U- and
M-form organizations respectively. Whereas the functional vice-
presidents of the U-form structure are represented at both the essential
variables and step functions, and thus the mapping of the U-form
hierarchy to the ultrastable system is many-one, the mapping of the
M-form structure to the ultrastable system is one-to-one. (Actually,
in the *small* U-form structure the one-to-one mapping also prevails;
it is only when the U-form enterprise becomes large that the capacity
problem at the top requires that the functional vice-presidents be
brought in. Expansion of the U-form enterprise is what causes "imperfect" correspondence with the ultrastable system.) The M-form innovation can thus be viewed as a means of restoring isomorphic large-firm
correspondence between hierarchical levels and ultrastable system
components.

TABLE 8-1

Ultrastable system component	Hierarchical part	
	U-form	*M-form*
Essential Variables	Chief Executive and Assistants plus Functional Vice-Presidents	General Office and Elite Staff
Step Functions	Functional Vice-Presidents and Staff	Operating Division Chiefs and Staff
Reacting Part	Operations	Operations

3
INTERNAL CONTROL

Aspects of the administrative process of exercising constraint can
be tied into the discussion of the ultrastable system in Chapter 3.
These include specification of the performance goals at the essential

variables, stipulation of parameter values and decision rules at the step functions, control over personnel through remuneration and by the selection-training-promotion process at the reacting part, and auditing. Related to this last is the possibility of using the resource allocation process as a control activity. In combination, these two make a powerful pair. Before comparing U- and M-form structures with respect to control techniques, therefore, consider first the importance of resource allocation and auditing.

3.1
Internal Resource Allocation and Auditing

Internal resource allocation can be regarded both as a market substitute and an internal control technique. The market substitute aspect was originally considered in Chapter 2 and is discussed further in Chapter 9. Here we examine resource allocation as an indirect control over personnel. The argument turns on the proposition that the renewal of resource commitments is vital to the continuation of each organizational subdivision. To the extent that performance and subsequent resource assignments can be connected in rational ways, the resource allocation process can be made responsive to differential performance. *Ceteris paribus*, those parts of the organization that are realizing superior performance will increase in relative size and importance, with all of the beneficial local gains associated with expansion. Moreover, recalcitrant parts of an organization might further be pressed to fall into line by using the resource allocation process to bring pressure from lower-level participants on otherwise unresponsive middle-range executives to comply with higher-level objectives: inasmuch as lower-level participants are among the first to feel the effects of a reduction in resources allocated to a particular task or function, and as lower-level support is usually essential to the effectiveness of a middle-range executive, the ability to manipulate resources in semipunitive ways enhances the control of the higher-level group.

Auditing naturally plays an important role in any such efforts. Performance checks of three types should be distinguished. The first involves advance, the second contemporaneous, and the third ex post evaluation. An advance evaluation would entail reviewing proposed programs with respect to their intrinsic merits, balance between the parts, and general level of expense. Contemporaneous evaluation would entail checking current performance against projections, examining sources of variance, and possibly comparing performance with that of the firm's principal rivals. Frequently more important than either of these, but an often neglected aspect of the control program, is the

possibility of conducting *repeated* ex post evaluations. Current variation may well be "excused" in plausible ways, but where a persistent
pattern of performance failures is identified, explaining variance becomes more difficult.

A distinction between the one-time and the persistent power of
lower-level participants is relevant in this connection. It is invariably
true that the one-time power of lower-level participants exceeds that
which they can expect to exercise in a continuing way. Despite expertise in substantial amounts at the top, lower-level participants in the
business firm can sometimes distort the data or execute directives in
lackadaisical ways, either of which can effectively frustrate the objectives of the general office—on a one-time basis. But they cannot ordinarily expect to do this repeatedly. The cumulative evidence becomes
too strong, and their dismissal is too easily effected. Since indeed the
usual employment relation is a continuing rather than one-time sort,
the evident "instantaneous" powers to which lower-level participants
have access should not be uncritically generalized. Their persistent
power is much less. Neglect of this possibility of developing a performance history has led some observers to overstate the power of lower-
level participants. By focusing on the short run and the uncertainty
associated with individual programs, they have failed to appreciate
that inference techniques applied to a series of (individually) uncertain programs permit the surveillance agency to sharpen its evaluations significantly.[4]

3.2
U- and M-form Comparisons

The questions to be considered now are to what extent, if any,
and for what reasons the M-form structure can be expected to exercise the compliance machinery with greater effectiveness than its
U-form counterpart. Can the general office realistically expect that its
preferences will prevail?

3.2.1. Step-function intervention. Recall that the middle level in
Simon's three-tiered hierarchy is represented in the ultrastable system
by the step functions. This corresponds in the U-form organization to
the heads of the functional divisions and their staffs, while in the
M-form enterprise the heads of the operating divisions are assigned
this task. Extensive intervention by the peak coordinator in the
detailed affairs of the functional divisions is not feasible in the large
U-form structure; the chief executive is apt to have neither the time
nor the expertise to engage in such activities. The greater capacity
of the general office together with the elite staff to which it has access

potentially permit more extensive intervention by the M-form organization. Yet this needs to be done with care lest the quasi-autonomous standing of the operating divisions be upset, which would violate the structural integrity of this organization form. The operating divisions could not really be held accountable if operating decisions were commonly prescribed.

To the extent, therefore, that the general office intervenes at the step mechanisms, this is apt either to involve policy matters (planning and rule making) or the provision of "consulting" services for special projects or problem situations. Albeit limited, these are relatively powerful control techniques and indeed distinguish the M-form from the U-form organization in this respect. It nevertheless bears repeating that, on a routine basis, neither the U- nor the M-form structure invites extensive intervention from the top at the step functions.

3.2.2. Reacting part (personnel). The screening-selection-promotion process is an important means of securing consensus within both the U- and M-form organiations. For all practical purposes, direct control over personnel rarely reaches down more than one level. Employment policies, however, can have pervasive consequences, and personnel changes at a high level are apt to have secondary effects across several successive hierarchical levels. Thus control over personnel at the top together with the disposition to exercise it is a potentially significant compliance measure.

For purposes of making U- and M-form comparisons, consider the problem of replacing the chief *operating* executives where malperformance or noncompliance is detected. This should prove easier in the M-form than in the U-form organization. The reason is related in an essential way to the manner in which the capacity problem is solved in each type of organization form. Recall that in the M-form organization, strategic and operating decisions are made by different personnel, while in the U-form organization the heads of each of the functional divisions (who are the principal operating executives) also share the strategic decision-making load. Thus for the senior executives responsible for strategic decision-making in the U-form organization to replace the head of a functional division requires that they reject one of their own kind. No such delicate choice is experienced in the M-form organization. Here the relation between the heads of the operating divisions and the general office can be addressed on mainly professional grounds. One might therefore expect that, to the extent that operating executives attempt to deviate from strategic directives, their replacement can be effectuated more easily in the M-form organization.

3.2.3. Auditing and resource allocation. Probably the most important differences between the U- and M-form structures with respect to their compliance properties are those which are attributable to the auditing and resource allocation processes in each. The differences are both attitudinal and structural. The attitudinal argument follows that developed above in examining the problems of replacing the chief operating executives: the U-form executives who participate in the strategic decision-making process are simply disinclined to audit themselves. The structural reasons can be treated in three parts: commensurability, decomposability, and expertise.

Consider the commensurability aspect first. The essential difference to note between the U- and M-form organization structures in this respect is that comparative performance evaluations between the functional divisions in the U-form organization involve intrinsically different characteristics (the intractible apples and oranges comparison), while in the M-form organization, in which each operating division represents a "profit center," a common denominator exists.

Decomposability permits resources to be meaningfully redirected in response to ex post evaluations in the M-form organization. In the U-form organization, however, implementing recommendations to shift resources around in a fully interconnected system in semipunitive ways may be dysfunctional. Spillovers from intended rewards and punishments would, by reason of intrinsic interdependencies, almost certainly be extensive.

The differential expertise which these two organization forms are able to bring to bear in securing compliance is due to differences in the quality, commitment, and size of the staffs on which the senior executives can call. The staff attached to the general office is an elite one that is able to make depth evaluations of both the prospects and past performance of each of the operating divisions.[5] A similar capability is missing (and indeed might threaten organization chaos) in the U-form organization: staff analyses of this sort here are made difficult by the lack of decomposability among the operating parts and may entail extensive second-guessing of the functional division heads—both in their capacities as operating officers and as strategic decision-makers. Such an undertaking, even if it were feasible, is not obviously functional. Altogether, the technical capability, incentives, and constitutional authority of the M-form staff must be regarded as superior to that of the staff attached to the chief executive's office in the U-form enterprise.

One concludes, therefore, that not only does the structure of the M-form organization yield internal efficiency and high-level goal pursuit outcomes different from those which an equivalent U-form enterprise would display, but, in addition, the M-form structure facilitates the exercise of the internal compliance machinery in especially effective ways. That the preferences of an assertive general office in an M-form corporation should (up to a first approximation) prevail seems at least plausible.

4
THE MULTIDIVISION FORM
HYPOTHESIS

To the extent that economists have been concerned with a rationale for the firm it has mainly been in connection with such matters as scale economies, externalities, and uncertainty. The bureaucratic theory literature, by contrast, has been concerned with such matters as goal formation, subgoal pursuit, communication processes, and compliance machinery. The implications of the latter have sometimes been brought to bear on the former [49] [117], but this has been incomplete. That the argument has not been carried to completion is perhaps attributable to the failure to express it in organization form terms. This provides the linkage that permits the theory of the firm literature and bureaucratic theory literature to be more fully joined.

Ashby, with quite different interests in mind, has put the argument this way [16, p. 53]:

> That a whole machine should be built of parts of given behavior is not sufficient to determine its behavior as a whole: only when the details of coupling are added does the whole's behavior become determinate.

In part, at least, the M-form organization can be regarded as a different solution to the coupling problem than that provided by the U-form structure—one that takes advantage of essential decomposability. In the process it gives rise to, because of the natural incentives it sets up, different goal pursuit tendencies.

The argument can be summarized in the following way: the transformation of large a business firm for which divisionalization is feasible from a unitary to a multidivision form organization contributes to (but does not assure) an attenuation of both the control loss experience and subgoal pursuit (mainly staff-biased expansion) that are characteristic of the unitary form. Realization of these attenuation effects, however, requires that the general office be aggressively constituted to perform its strategic planning, resource allocation, and control functions. Both the form and substance of multidivision organization are required for this transformation to be effective. Expressed in conventional goal pursuit and efficiency terms, the argument comes down to this: *the organization and operation of the large enterprise along the lines of the M-form favors goal pursuit and least-cost behavior more nearly associated with the neoclassical profit maximization hypothesis than does the U-form organizational alternative.*

It will be noted that the argument has been developed in comparative terms. It could, therefore, as easily be expressed instead as a U-form hypothesis; namely, the organization and operation of the large enterprise along the lines of the U-form favors goal pursuit and cost behavior more nearly associated with the managerial discretion hypothesis than does the M-form organizational alternative. This equivalent statement makes evident an underlying symmetry that some may find disconcerting: if one accepts the affirmative argument on behalf of the M-form organization advanced above, a tacit acceptance of managerial discretion theory (in the context of U-form organization) may also be implied. That is, if the M-form organization has, for the reasons given, the superior efficiency, motivational and control properties that have been imputed to it, then presumably the organization and operation of the large enterprise along the lines of the traditional (U-form) structure contributes to control loss and utility-maximizing behavior of the sort described in Chapters 2-5. To the extent therefore that the coincidence of large, unitary form structures and nontrivial opportunity sets (mainly by reason of favorable product market conditions) is observed in the economy, utility-maximizing behavior (and its attendant consequences) is to be expected.

It is important to note that the M-form enterprise does not abandon the U-form structure; rather, it attempts to harness the U-form solution to the division of labor problem within a larger organizing framework. The technical benefits of the U-form organization are thereby preserved, while its undesirable control loss and goal pursuit properties are restrained. Expressed in opportunity set and utility function terms, the M-form enterprise is able, because of its superior efficiency properties, to operate on a larger opportunity set than a comparable U-form structure. Also, because of the separation of strategic from operating decision-making, the M-form enterprise favors goal pursuit more nearly characteristic of the neoclassical firm. Finally, the decomposability and commensurability properties of this structure and the creation of an elite staff permit this organization form to secure a high order of compliance from its operating divisions. Altogether, the M-form enterprise tends, through *internal* organization, to provide institutional underpinning for the *prima facie* standing ordinarily accorded to the profit maximization assumption— support which, in large organizations that have access to market insularity, has hitherto been lacking.

The argument, it will be noted, is advanced at the level of the firm rather than the operating division. It does not preclude the possibility that it may be more instructive, frequently, to employ managerial discretion models to study the *short-run* behavior of the individual operating divisions (quasi-firms).[6]

FOOTNOTES

[1] Simon's parable of the two watch manufacturers, Hora and Tempus [**142**, p. 472] illustrates what is meant by "excessive" integration. Each is assembling an identical watch of 1,000 parts. Tempus Co. has designed the work in such a way that all 1,000 parts form a single, indecomposable whole. Hora Inc., however, has a design that provides for 10 major subassemblies of about 100 parts, each of which is turn is decomposable into 10 subassemblies of about 10 parts each. An interruption at any phase of the work means that the entire assembly stage at which the interruption occurs must be repeated, although all previously completed subassemblies are unaffected.

An interruption for Tempus means that the entire watch must be started anew, while Hora loses only the work at the most recent stage of subassembly operations. If the probability of interruption is .01 per assembly operation (of which there are 1,000 in Tempus Co. and 1,111 in Hora Inc.), it can be shown that it will take Tempus about four thousand times as long to complete a watch as Hora.

Although the parable does not raise U-form versus M-form comparisons *per se*, the spirit is clearly similar.

[2] Deliberate efforts to interfere with the market tests of rivals are alleged to be common in the home soap and dentifrice markets [**85**].

[3] The team will be treated "as if" it were a group of equals, although in fact the differential formal rank and capabilities of these executives will be manifest on close issues.

Multi-headedness by itself is not a sufficient response to the capacity problem in the general office. Clarity of objectives, unity of purpose, and a common language by which to evaluate alternatives are also needed. Lacking these (as is characteristic, for example, of the independent regulatory commissions), multi-headeness may induce conflict or otherwise cause the organization to founder—reducing rather than enhancing effective capacity at the top.

[4] The problem can be likened to that of estimating the mean of a population with varying sample size. The standard error of the sample varies inversely with the square root of the sample size. Thus, although any single observation may deviate substantially from the population mean if the variance is great, the sample mean for large sample size can be expected to converge to the true mean. I discuss this "repeated-exposure" phenomenon elsewhere in connection with military procurement [**162**]. Note in this connection the "moral hazard" problem discussed in Chapter 2 is more serious when regarded in one-time rather than repeated-exposure terms. Cost-plus contracts have less debilitating properties if repeated business is contemplated and ex post evaluations are feasible. Also, the "reputation" of a contractor, based on the pooled experience of many one-time users, can be made to serve as a protection against one-time abuse.

[5] As Churchill, Cooper, and Sainsbury observe, and as their experimental evidence confirms, "to be effective, an audit of historical actions should have, or at least be perceived as having, the power to go beneath the apparent evidence to determine what in fact did happen" [**47**, p. 258].

[6] This appears to correspond with Armen Alchian's view that "The wealth maximizing postulate is usually appropriate (or least inappropriate) when applied to the (M-form) 'firm' as a unit of analysis. But in seeking to explain individual behavior *within* the firm, utility maximizing criteria are more general and powerful than wealth maximizing criteria" [**6**, p. 350].

9

applications
of the
multidivision form
hypothesis

Although some may express misgivings, let us assume, arguendo, that a plausible a priori case had been made on behalf of the M-form hypothesis. The evidence now needs to be examined. Except for Chandler's study [**42**], this is mainly fragmentary. Ordinary prudence might, in these circumstances, favor a systematic development of the data prior to any effort to take the argument further. At the very least, efforts that are made to advance the argument might be regarded with cautious skepticism.

Bearing this admonition in mind, there are nevertheless three reasons for wishing to push ahead at this time. For one thing, sharper tests of the basic hypothesis may be possible if certain applications of the argument are first developed, which is the purpose of this chapter. For another, lest inappropriate tests be performed, the hypothesis needs to be delimited. This is attempted in Chapter 10. Finally, certain policy implications of the argument are too important to hold in abeyance until the evidence is wholly conclusive; the antitrust agencies [171] [88] and the Congress [40] have been contemplating or attempting to enforce limitations on conglomerate corporations based on theories and evidence that, at best, are incomplete. Presumably the potentially beneficial consequences of conglomeration deserve to be exposed.

Tracing out the importance of the M-form innovation goes beyond the comparisons of U- and M-form enterprises of equivalent size and variety such as were developed in the previous chapter. Also relevant are its systems consequences. Of special significance in this regard are its eventual (as distinguished from its immediate) effects on product market competition and its properties as a capital market substitute and complement. A brief statement of its product market properties is given in section 1. A somewhat more extensive statement of its capital market consequences is developed in section 2. The implications of this argument for conglomerate organization—assuming that the conglomerates in question preserve the M-form structure, which by no means holds by definition—are considered in section 3. The significance of the M-form structure for European economic development is treated briefly in section 4. The matter of executive compensation practices in relation to organization form is examined in Section 5.[1]

1
COMPETITION
IN THE PRODUCT MARKET

A proposition for which general assent can be presumed is that any significant efficiency change that is adopted by a set of firms (possibly only one) having a nontrivial market share can be expected eventually to place rivals under pressure to imitate. In the absence of countervailing advantages (patents, resources, etc.) among rivals or excesses of slack among the innovating firms, the natural selection process can be expected to operate: those who propose the innovation and realize the economies which it permits "will prosper and acquire resources with which to expand" [61, p. 22]. Although innovators may be anxious to take their rewards in nonobstreperous ways (possibly initially holding prices unchanged but increasing margins), over time the competitive advantage can be expected to manifest itself through shifting market shares. Aggressive price competition is not essential: product quality, variety, or service might be increased without corresponding price increases; factor price increases might be absorbed. For these or similar reasons, the profit and market positions of nonadapting rivals are apt to deteriorate.

The eventual system consequences of a successful organizational innovation therefore will, because of the product market pressures to imitate and subsequent performance consequences that obtain, tend vastly to exceed in economic importance the immediate effects experienced by the innovating firm. Inasmuch as innovations of this type are not patentable, the private returns that the innovating firm can appropriate are only a small fraction of the social returns. A tendency to underestimate the importance of organizational innovations may for this reason be common [48]—if indeed they are not neglected altogether.

2
COMPETITION
IN THE CAPITAL MARKET

The relation of competition in the capital market to organization form will be developed in three stages. First, the effect of the large U-form organization on the separation of ownership from control is considered. Second, the effect of the M-form firm on displacement costs and its properties as a capital market substitute are developed. Third, the relation of the argument to conglomerate organization is assessed. This last is deferred to section 3. The first two parts are treated here.

2.1
The Separation of Ownership from Control

Although the emergence in the late 1800s of large, single-product, multifunction enterprises organized along U-form lines (in steel, meat-packing, tobacco, oil, etc. [42, Chap. 1]) presumably permitted the realization of scale economies (and perhaps monopoly power), it probably contributed to an eventual weakening of the ability of both product and capital markets to enforce selection on profits. Concern over this condition was expressed in the early 1930s by Berle and Means when they observed that the development of the large corporation had resulted in a separation of ownership from control with uncertain performance consequences [31].

The multifunction operations of the U-form organization represented a substitution of administrative integration for integration that had previously been accomplished through product market exchange. If, ordinarily, an integrated firm is, both for size and complexity reasons, more difficult for an outside surveillance agency to monitor than a series of nonintegrated firms, administrative integration of this sort may simultaneously impair the capital market's policing capabilities.[2] However favorable its operating efficiency consequences, the U-form innovation may have expanded the management's opportunity set (in relation to that of the enterprise) and in this way contributed to opportunities for discretionary behavior.

The concern over this condition expressed by Berle and Means has since been repeated by numerous other students of the modern corporation. A common finding is that the separation of ownership from control is extensive and that it is merely a matter of good fortune that the corporate sector performs as well as it does. In the background lurks the suspicion that one day these enclaves of private power will run amok [112, pp. 7–9], and a search for substitute external controls has been set in motion on this account.

2.2
The M-form Innovation

As indicated earlier, the M-form innovation was first "discovered" in the 1920s. By the 1930s its effects on selected industries were beginning to be felt quite generally, foreshadowing its eventually pervasive transformation of the enterprise system. It is perhaps ironic that at the very time the M-form innovation was beginning to take hold, widespread concern over the failure of the modern corporation to satisfy legitimacy tests was first expressed. It is the burden of the argument here that the perceived separation of ownership from control was mainly attributable to conditions observed in the large U-form firm and that, while the M-form innovation was designed mainly in response to the control loss experience of the large, diversified U-form enterprise, this innovation has also had the effect of restoring integrity to the goal specification and policing processes. Prior failure to distinguish clearly between internal and external control processes, including the relations between internal control and organization form, is responsible for the uncritical application of the early U-form argument to the M-form condition.

Recall that the capital market was regarded as a less than wholly efficacious surveillance and correction mechanism for three reasons: its external relation to the firm places it at a serious information disadvantage; it is restricted to nonmarginal adjustments; it experiences nontrivial displacement costs. The general office of the M-form organization has superior properties in each of these respects. First, it is an internal rather than external control mechanism with the constitutional authority, expertise and low-cost access to the requisite data which permit it to make detailed, contemporaneous evaluations of the performance of each of its operating parts. Second, it can make fine-tuning as well as discrete adjustments. Taken together, these permit the general office to intervene early in a selective, preventative way—a capability which is lacking in external control mechanisms in general [29, p. 263] and the capital market in particular. Also, it can make ex post corrective adjustments, in response to evidence of performance failure, with a surgical precision that the capital market lacks (the scalpel versus the ax is not a wholly inappropriate analogy). Finally, the costs of intervention by the general office are relatively low. Altogether, therefore, a profit-oriented general office in an M-form enterprise might be expected easily to secure superior performance to that which the capital market can enforce.

The argument can be expressed in opportunity set terms by resorting again to the quasi-firm construction employed earlier. The relevant question is: does the general office act simply as a transmission agent to distribute the profit constraint ($\overline{\overline{\Pi}}$) which the firm experiences on a pro-rata basis to each of the operating divisions, or does it demand more? Put differently, letting $\overline{\Pi}_i$ be the profit constraint assigned to the ith division by the general office, is $\sum_i \overline{\Pi}_i$ greater than or just equal to $\overline{\overline{\Pi}}$?

In capacity terms (that is, setting volitional considerations aside), the answer would appear to be quite unambiguous: the $\sum_i \overline{\Pi}_i$ should easily exceed the $\overline{\overline{\Pi}}$ requirement to which the firm as a whole is subject. The M-form organization can thus be viewed as capitalism's creative response to the evident limits which the capital market experiences in its relations to the firm as well as a means for overcoming the organizational problems which develop in the large U-form enterprise when variety becomes great. The conjunction of these two consequences in a single organizational innovation should probably be regarded as fortuitous.

The argument can be carried yet a step further by considering the effects of the M-form innovation on capital market displacement efforts. *Ceteris paribus*, displacement is more likely the greater the unavailed profit opportunities in the target firm and the lower the costs of effecting displacement. In relation to the U-form enterprise, the M-form innovation enhances the attractiveness of making a displacement effort in both respects.

The realization of operating economies by reconstituting a large U-form enterprise along M-form lines represents a source of potential profit gain which, in the absence of reorganization, is unavailable. The resulting economies are due to more effective resource allocation (between divisions and in the aggregate), better internal organization (a reduction in technical control loss), and the attenuation of subgoal pursuit. Unitary form organizations for which either divisionalization is difficult (the natural unit is the integrated form) or the management is otherwise disinclined to reorganize thus offer an opportunity to realize economies by a displacement agency which can effectively produce the change. *Ceteris paribus*, the potential profits are greater if the incumbent management is actively engaged in subgoal pursuit —although, it should be noted, the existence of subgoal pursuit is not essential for structural economies to be realized.

Existing M-form enterprises are probably the least-cost instruments for achieving displacement. For one thing they are apt to have superior inference capabilities; the elite staff of the M-form structure may have as one of its principal assignments the discovery of potential takeover candidates. In addition, such firms are already experienced in the organizational advantages which this structure offers.[3]

Unitary form enterprises that anticipate such takeover efforts may attempt to shrink the potential displacement gain by making appropriate internal changes: subgoal pursuit may be reduced or, possibly, self-reorganization along M-form lines may be initiated. Such forestalling efforts are not apt to be common, however, until the probability of a takeover attempt has reached a nontrivial value. Except in U-form enterprises which have been specifically targeted for takeover, this may require that there be a relatively large number of multidivision enterprises actively surveying takeover opportunities. With only a few multidivision firms performing this function, the probability that any one unitary form enterprise will be the object of a takeover attempt is too small to warrant ex ante adaptation. Once the number of multidivision firms becomes sufficiently large, however, the effect on unitary form enterprises that are otherwise shielded from product market pressures is equivalent to an increase in competition insofar as subgoal pursuit is concerned. Selection on profit is thereby enhanced; the effects indeed may be pervasive. The argument thus reduces to the following proposition: internal organization and conventional capital market forces are complements as well as substitutes; the two coexist in a symbiotic relationship to each other.

3
"CONGLOMERATE" ORGANIZATION

3.1
Conglomerate Organization Conventionally Regarded

The efficiency and market power consequences of the so-called "conglomerate" corporation have been a source of long-standing puzzlement. Mainly, the opinions of academics who have considered this phenomenon have been negative. Policy statements such as the following are common: "Of all types of merger activity conglomerate acquisitions have the least claim to promoting efficiency in the economic sense" [**33**, p. 679]. "Doubtless some conglomerate mergers are harmless; some may even be useful. But the merger of unrelated activities seldom offers much prospect of efficiency" [**58**, p. 46]. Perhaps the most explicit treatment of this argument is that offered by Igor Ansoff and Fred Weston [**9**]. They contrast vertical and horizontal mergers with conglomerate mergers. The complementarities (economies, market power) available from mergers of the first type give rise to what they regard as synergistic effects, while the conglomerate merger yields no such combinatorial gains [**9**, pp. 51–52]. They then go on to examine the appropriate control arrangements for each type of merger and indicate that while comprehensive controls are essential to realize the benefits of horizontal or vertical combination, "financial targets" may be all that can usefully be employed in the conglomerate organization [**9**, pp. 57–58].

Others who have viewed the conglomerate form have been somewhat more sanguine regarding its efficiency properties, but it has virtually no vigorous supporters among academics. Even in the business community there are numerous skeptics (as is evident in the January 1, 1969 issue of *Forbes*, for example).

The usual efficiency arguments on behalf of conglomerate organization rely either on risk pooling or operating economies. Morris Adelman has identified investment economies that are distinctively conglomerate in the portfolio diversification (risk) consequences which such a combination affords [**1**]. The typical static efficiency arguments in favor of conglomerate merger have been identified by Donald Turner as those which are attributable to commonalities in marketing, manufacturing, or administration [**155**, pp. 1323–39]. He goes on to observe that the possibility of such economies is naturally "slight" in a "pure" conglomerate merger [**155**, p. 1330]. If these exhaust the favorable arguments that can be marshaled on behalf of this organization form, the beneficial effects of conglomeration might well be dismissed as *de minimis*.

3.2
An Alternative View

One of the principal difficulties in dealing with the conglomerate phenomenon is that it is so ill-specified. To say that the conglomerate corporation is a collection of dissimilar business activities is not very useful until degrees of dissimilarity are established and the relative importance of the parts is determined. Even this may not be sufficient, however; it is also essential that the control processes be considered. As indicated in Chapter 10, the free-form corporation needs to be distinguished from the M-form structure, even though they may be identical in terms of markets and technology. The argument here is restricted to the M-form version of the conglomerate; no special efficiency claims are either made or intended for conglomerate merger (or expansion) activity for which the M-form structure does not prevail.

The question to be asked, therefore, is whether risk pooling and/or slight commonalities adequately reflect the investment advantages and operating efficiency properties of an M-form firm that is diversified in sufficient degree to warrant the conglomerate appellation. Consider the investment efficiency aspect first. It will be useful for this purpose to consider two alternative economies that differ only in the way that production is organized. Assume that the M-form structure prevails in both, but that in one economy the firms are specialized (division-alized, say, according to brand or geographic lines) while in the other the firms are multi-market organizations. Will the latter (conglomerate) economy out-perform the former and why?

An answer to this turns in large measure on earnings retention proclivities. Assume that the retention of earnings by firms of both types is favored by either or both of the following conditions: (1) the differential tax treatment of dividends together with non-trivial trans-action costs associated with stockholder reinvestment; (2) positive ploughback preferences of the managements in conjunction with signifi-cant takeover frictions in the capital market.

If, for either of these reasons, an earnings retention bias exists, and since assigning cash flows to their sources constitutes what may often be a serious investment restraint, the economy organized along conglomerate lines might well enjoy an advantage over the specialized firm economy. The ear-marking of funds in the latter would result in what would frequently be delayed responses to market signals and otherwise arbitrary allocations of investment. In the conglomerate firm economy, by contrast, cash flows, from whatever source, are not automatically retained by the sectors from which these funds originate but are (ideally) assigned on the basis of prospective yields instead.[4] The conglomerate acts in this respect as a miniature capital market; it internalizes the funds metering function normally imputed to the capital market—a function which Baumol's analysis of the traditional mechanisms found to be defective [27].[5]

It could of course be argued that these investment efficiencies are attributable to remedial system defects, and that these should be corrected. The position has merit, but it should be pointed out that the argument against conglomeration has been shifted. Until such time, therefore, as the necessary remedies have been proposed and put into effect, investment efficiency presumably warrants consideration in evaluating the consequences of M-form conglomeration for which resource shifts into high yield activities can be expected.

The diversification argument is, however, subject to diminishing returns qualifications. First, for a fixed size firm (and assuming that all technical scale economy conditions are satisfied), increasing the degree of diversification eventually encounters control loss conditions. Prescribing the optimal degree of diversification thus requires sensitivity to the trade-offs between static operating efficiencies and investment alternatives. Second, as firm size increases for a fixed degree of diversification, the control loss consequences of hierarchical organization cumulatively become great (see Chapter 10). Lest proliferating variety become unmanageable, very large firms may need to maintain relatively high product specialization ratios or disperse some of the control which in the M-form structure is concentrated at the top and is fundamentally responsible for its special performance characteristics.

Whereas claims of investment efficiencies involve an extension of the M-form argument to include multimarket occupancy, operating economies obtain by a straightforward application of the standard M-form economies analysis given earlier. Multidivisionalization without multimarket occupancy is sufficient for these to be realized. In consideration, however, of current antimerger policies, which bear down hard on horizontal and vertical mergers, a vital route by which small U-form firms can quickly obtain the requisite size to support the M-form structure and thereby realize the economies which it affords is by conglomerate merger.[6] If, therefore, the operating economies arguments of preceding chapters are correct, if M-form organization requires that large (but not necessarily giant) size be reached, and if alternative merger possibilities are barred, then, lacking countervailing considerations, operating economies grounds for conglomerate merger would appear to be more substantial than have previously been indicated.

A similar argument applies to the transfer process by which many technical innovations are brought efficiently to completion (see Chapter 10, section 2). If, often, efficient final supply (production, distribution) is facilitated by permitting large, multidivision enterprises to acquire the successful inventions of small firms, and if enforcement of the antimerger statutes against horizontal and vertical mergers is to remain tough, conglomerate acquisition may be a vital means by which to maintain transfer process viability.[7]

One possible countervailing consideration to these arguments is that, despite the prospect of immediate economies through merger, the time horizon employed is too short: if one is patient, the requisite size needed to support M-form organization, with its superior operating efficiency consequences, can be realized by internal expansion. The point is not contested but it is relevant to note that the argument is now shifted: it is not whether managerial economies are available by merging unrelated firms (which otherwise lack requisite size to support the M-form structure), but rather rests on what adjustment path is to be preferred. To delay the realization of these economies by prohibiting such mergers presumably requires that offsetting eventual benefits be shown.

A further operating economies argument favorable to conglomeration that is not subject to this last qualification concerns the takeover issue. If the M-form firm is to perform the capital market policing function described in section 2 above while present antimerger policies with respect to horizontal and vertical acquisitions are to remain in effect, preserving the conglomerate option may be essential. Otherwise the threat of takeover to firms operated by moribund managements will be rendered effete: bringing every form of market organization— including the conglomerate—under antitrust attack would have the unfortunate and presumably unintended consequence of impairing what Manne refers to as the "market for corporate control" [**99**].

3.3
Social Costs of Conglomeration

The above is an essentially affirmative statement on behalf of the conglomerate form of organization. However, dealing as it does mainly with potential rather than actuality, neither the frequency nor extent of the indicated effects can be said to have been established. This awaits the development of the data. It is sufficient for our purposes here if the relevant dimensions of the issue have been more fully exposed and it is evident that the *a priori* case on conglomeration is not wholly negative.

That there may be social costs which the conglomerate generates in particular instances is, nevertheless, freely conceded. Consider in this connection the Federal Trade Commission Staff Study on conglomerates [**171**]. It concludes that reciprocity, cross-subsidization, and conglomerate interdependence are common anticompetitive consequences of conglomerate merger (or expansion) [**171**, Chap. 6] and recommends that conglomerate mergers which satisfy the following criteria be regarded as potentially offensive and within the reach of current antitrust laws [**171**, p. 17]:

1. When the acquiring corporation is a large enterprise having a substantial volume of sales in one or more concentrated industries. (For this purpose a large firm is defined as having annual sales or assets in excess of $250 million.)

2. When the acquired company is one of the leading firms in at least one concentrated industry. (A concentrated industry is defined as one in which the 4 leading firms account for 40 percent or more of sales. A leading firm is one included among the 4 to 6 largest sellers in an industry.)

The staff report also goes on to observe that *"any* merger or acquisition in which each of the parties has assets exceeding $250 million is likely to be anticompetitive within the meaning of section 7" [171, p. 18]—a position that is, apparently, shared in large measure by the Justice Department [88].

Expressed in terms of *Fortune's* 1969 ranking, the suspect conglomerate mergers in these circumstances would involve, mainly, (1) mergers in which both firms were included among the 250 largest industrials, the 25 largest merchandising firms, the 25 largest transportation companies, and an indeterminate number of financial corporations (the size of which is difficult to specify in comparable terms), or (2) mergers in which one firm was among the 300 largest industrials, 50 largest merchandising firms, 25 largest transportation companies, or an indeterminate number of financial corporations, and the other firm had a market share as large as 10 percent in a market where the industry concentration ratio exceeded 40 percent.[8] These are hardly narrowly drawn criteria. It is all the more essential in these circumstances that the alleged conglomerate dangers be evaluated.

The reciprocity complaint seems wholly inappropriate. For one thing, reciprocity is a conduct offense that itself can be (and indeed has been [171, p. 337]) made the object of an antitrust suit. For another, the effects of reciprocity on competition are not wholly adverse and may not even be net negative [171, p. 328, fn. 2]. Until it is clear that enforcement efforts against reciprocity taken by itself cannot hope to be effective and that overall effects are undesirable, a structural attack against conglomerates on grounds of reciprocity seems hasty and ill-advised.

The claim that conglomerate organization favors cross-subsidization also requires scrutiny. The staff report alleges that predatory price cutting may be common among conglomerates and illustrates this by reference to Safeway, Anheuser-Busch, and National Dairy Products [171, pp. 406–43]. But both Safeway and Anheuser-Busch are highly specialized organizations and National Dairy is diversified on a relatively narrow basis. Also, as with reciprocity, predatory price cutting is an antitrust offense that itself can be made the object of an antitrust suit. Unless it is evident that the behavior complained of is really (1) anticompetitive, (2) quantitatively significant, and (3) beyond the reach of more conventional relief, a structural rule seems ill-advised.

An aspect of cross-subsidization that, nevertheless, raises real social cost (if not antitrust) issues is the possibility of diseconomies due to ineffective or misdirected control activities—including internal subsidization of weakly performing operating divisions which, objectively, should be cut back or discontinued. Such effects are perhaps most likely if the acquiring firm has reached "excessive" size or if the requisite control apparatus of the M-form structure is not employed. If neither of these conditions is satisfied, the argument would, unless otherwise buttressed, appear to be too thin to warrant serious consideration.

Conglomerate interdependence is the most serious of the alleged conglomerate dangers identified in the staff study. The mechanics of this attenuation process, if it exists, is, presumably, not unlike that of traditional oligopoly: competition is restrained out of mutual dependence recognized. This may take the form of either less aggressive competition in markets where interfaces exist or, as indicated below, a reduction in potential competition in markets where entry might otherwise occur. The argument, essentially, reduces to a proposition that the mutual deference displayed among 20 super-giants is detectably different from that which would obtain among, say, 50 "equivalent" firms (which, in the aggregate, have identical product mixes and, in individual markets, identical concentration) and assumes that entry by firms of much smaller size is not easy. It thus crucially assumes that a group of super-giants somehow acquires a more refined sensitivity to interfirm relations than would otherwise prevail—which result, were super-conglomeration to proceed apace, is at some stage reasonably to be expected. At the same time, however, it should be noted that the argument loses credibility as the number of firms to be included in the objectionable category is progressively extended.

To the extent that attenuation occurs in this way, it is due not so much to any single merger as it is to a general transformation of interfirm relations in which a number of large combinations are involved. Thus, although case-by-case review may ordinarily be sufficient to reveal anticompetitive effects where large horizontal combinations are involved, such a procedure would be much less satisfactory in this instance. A case-by-case examination of very large conglomerate acquisitions on their individual merits would tend to miss the overall systems consequences.

Attenuation does not exhaust the case against conglomeration. Other possible objections include the possibility that such combinations impair potential competition, that wealth concentration generates secondary productivity losses, and that giant size poses extra-economic socio-political problems. Only the first of these is discussed by the staff report. Unfortunately it is described in such sweeping terms as to render the enforcement significance of potential competition suspect. Thus the report observes that [171, p. 15]:

> It is difficult, often impossible, to determine the precise identity, or even the number and relative importance of an industry's potential competitors, except to note that the most imminent potential competitors are those (a) engaging in the same industry but serving different geographic markets, (b) bearing a vertical relationship to the industry, or (c) operating in industries that may be currently or potentially related technologically in production or marketing. In the light of American industrial history, the long view of the competitive process argues persuasively for a broad definition of potential competitors; technological and other developments have brought quite unrelated companies into competition at later times.

Roughly, potential competition may have behavioral significance on account of the perceived threat of entry in one of more of the following three respects: (1) a firm-specific prospect of entry; (2) a group-specific effect on entry; or (3) a general background threat of entry. Elimination of a firm-specific potential entrant has clear competitive significance and consequently raises legitimate antitrust concern. This is well within the purview of current enforcement efforts. A group-specific effect on entry is described above in conjunction with the systems consequences of super-giant combinations. This is somewhat more conjectural but perhaps is not so wholly speculative as to be beyond antitrust concern. The general background threat of entry that the staff study describes, however, is so vague as to raise serious doubts over its competitive significance. Inability to identify either the number or relative importance of the firms in this group stands as an invitation to open-ended enforcement with dubious performance consequences. For one thing, even if the perceived threat of entry rises monotonically with the number of large firms, this relation almost certainly experiences diminishing returns. To include (as the staff study appears to) several hundreds of large firms as the relevant subset seems extreme. For another, the competitive implications of conglomerate changes in the composition of these large firms are not obvious a priori. Especially if consideration is given to the goal seeking and least cost consequences of shielding some 300 or more firms from the threat of mutual takeovers, the net competitive impact of such a policy could easily be negative.[9]

The possibility that giant size conglomeration has unfavorable secondary productivity consequences may obtain in either or both of two ways.[10] The first turns on differences between the private and social discount rate. Thus, assume that there are immediate efficiency benefits to be realized when an aggressive M-form firm takes over a moribund giant but, predictably, the reconstituted firm faces eventual control loss problems which are more severe than would otherwise obtain and that the private exceeds the social discount rate. Future control losses will not then be given sufficient weight by the private decision calculus and social productivity losses may commonly result.

The second type of secondary productivity loss that giant size conglomeration potentially poses is that "outsiders" may regard, for rational reasons or otherwise, concentrations of wealth for which no clear social gain is evident to be an indication that the system lacks sensitivity to the concerns and aspirations of individual participant-observers (employees, small businessmen, students, housewives, etc.). They may at some stage boggle, restricting their participation to a minimum and insisting, for example, that work rules be narrowly drawn and precisely observed. Alternatively, political redress that does not limit itself to the offensive subset may be sought. In either case, unfavorable productivity consequences would easily obtain. Although conjectural, the argument is perhaps not so wholly speculative as to be dismissed altogether when size on super-giant dimensions comes under review. If, by general consent, the affirmative case for super-giants is thin, even speculative counter-arguments deserve standing.

All of the above is concerned, directly or indirectly, with allocative efficiency effects that, in principle, can be brought within the ambit of antitrust. The socio-political objection to giant size shifts the terms of reference to consider size *per se* effects. Economists here have no special claims to expertise (although, presumably, they can be of assistance in helping to assess the economic consequences of a program designed to restrict giant size enterprise); antitrust, to be responsive, stands in need of additional authority. If, as indicated, the affirmative economic case in support of giant size conglomeration is weak or lacking, it is only charitable that other preferences and value considerations should prevail. The problem then is merely to supply the necessary legislative mandate. This, however, may be easy neither to design nor, in the light of changing circumstances, subsequently to amend.

Possibly, however, the felt-need for new legislation could be overcome if antitrust were to address the size *per se* question indirectly— which is to say in terms of the competitive attenuation effects of conglomeration and the secondary productivity losses that giant size (in whatever form) potentially presents. An effective basis by which to deal with acquisitions by giant sized firms that avoids the difficulties which new legislation presents, but nevertheless reaches the policy relevant subset, may in this way be realized. Such a program, especially at its inception, should be carefully delimited. It should not be made to apply exclusively to conglomerates but would also embrace conventional combinations. Thus mergers which fall in the giant size subset but, despite their mainly horizontal and/or vertical features, have in the past secured Justice Department approval would now be less favorably regarded. (Humble-Signal and McDonnell-Douglas are examples.)

4
THE "AMERICAN CHALLENGE"

J. J. Servan-Schreiber, in an interesting analysis of recent economic developments in Europe, regards the modern American corporation as displaying superlative organizational properties. He acknowledges "the ease with which American firms reorganize themselves to tap the full potential of the new market" [**136**, pp. 7–8]. The American way is distinguished from the European by citing the experience of an American executive in Frankfort: Americans "know not only *how* to produce, but how to produce the desired quantity at the lowest cost. What interests me is my profit margin. What interests my European competition is a factory that produces. *It isn't the same thing*" [**136**, p. 81]. He goes on to observe that the effective control over strategic decisions by the home office provides the essential coordination demanded by an opportunistic enterprise [**136**, p. 43]. The American challenge is not so much one of industry or finance as it is one of "organizing production . . . and social relations" [**136**, p. 203]. The key to his plan for revitalizing and assuring the independence of the European economies is a reconstitution of European methods of organization [**136**, p. 154].

Although the differences between the traditional U-form and the modern M-form structure with respect to subgoal pursuit, profit motivation, resource allocation, etc, may be implicit (Servan-Schreiber clearly perceives that American corporations have somehow "solved" the rational resource allocation problem in a way which presents an enormous challenge to their economic counterparts), the reasons for these differences are nowhere made explicit. The advantage of laying out, as we have here, the causes for the success of the new form is that European imitation is apt to be quicker and more successful if it proceeds in a self-conscious way using the correct model. Consider Servan-Schreiber's quotation of Cambien to the effect that "size is a means, not an end. The problem is not to change a brontosaurus into a dinosaur by doubling its size, but to form biological units adapted to new conditions of growth" [**136**, p. 160]. This is all well and good, but operationally it is incomplete. If the basic argument here is correct, one concludes that the "biological adaptation" needed is that M-form structures—in each of which a series of quasi-firms are mediated centrally by a general office that discharges the strategic planning, evaluation, and resource allocation functions and in which the firm is imbued with a profit dynamic—replace U-form firms.

The diffusion of technological innovations from one culture to another often presents unanticipated difficulties. This may be all the more true of organizational innovation. Although one does not detect in the M-form structure anything that should uniquely suit it to the American experience, the quickest way, probably, to achieve such a transformation is to bring in experienced M-form managers. Initially, therefore, European firms may wish to attract human capital which experienced M-form executives embody (perhaps from the European offices of American M-form firms) as a means of setting the reorganization in motion.[11]

5
EXECUTIVE COMPENSATION

Indecomposability in the U-form organization makes for difficulty in tracing out intrafirm causality in any but the crudest way. Even to distinguish superior performance among groups or individuals in a complex, interconnected system may be hard; what appears at first to be superior local achievement may on further examination be aggressive suboptimization with serious spillover consequences. Moreover, even where superior performance can be recognized, assigning quantitative importance to it in terms of profit may be virtually impossible. As a result, meaningful incentive compensation in the U-form enterprise is difficult to provide.

The division of effort in the M-form organization helps to overcome these difficulties. First, the general office bears the responsibility for and possesses the means decisively to influence overall enterprise performance. Second, decomposability between the operating divisions makes it possible, over a period of time, to distinguish superior from inferior operating performance—at least at the level of the division, although intradivisional causality assignment may continue to be difficult. Given appropriate divisionalization, spillovers between divisions can be presumed to be of second-order significance.

Incentive compensation to the general office should presumably encourage and reflect superior enterprise-wide achievement, while the operating divisions should be evaluated and rewarded on the basis of own, local accomplishments. Awarding stock options to general executives would be consistent with the objective of rewarding overall performance. Although stock options are incredibly crude incentive instruments (short-run performance may frequently be swamped by environmental considerations) and are subject to abuse [92], their broadly based contingent reward characteristics and their advantageous tax features make them attractive incentive devices for general officers by comparison with the available alternatives. Stock options are less clearly suited for division managers, however. Bonuses that reflect local achievement would seem to be more appropriate here instead. As one moves below the division manager level, increasingly difficult imputation problems are apt to be encountered. But this is merely to say that the efficacy of incentive compensation is limited at the lower levels; the rational use of stock options at the top and of bonuses at the division manager level is not upset.

FOOTNOTES

[1] For those who may be interested in the relationship between Galbraith's techno-structure theory of the firm [64] and the M-form structure, I offer the following summary observations: (1) The technostructure theory is not concerned so much with organization form as with the locus of power. It is a strategic factor model, somewhat along lines earlier sketched out by Veblen [157], and can be regarded, more generally, as one of a family of lower-level participant theories of organization [115]. (2) The top management in this theory is relegated to a limited and sometimes mainly cere-monial role [64, pp. 69, 70, 116]. (3) To the extent that it has a bearing on the U- and M-form structures discussed here, it is probably a more accurate characterization of the conditions that prevail in the U-form firm.

For a critical discussion of technostructure theory in other respects, see [107] [114] [146] [151].

[2] This is almost certainly true when expressed in absolute terms, but may not be when regarded as a percentage. Thus, although surveillance and displacement costs will vary directly with the size and complexity of the corporation, the ratio of these costs to any of a variety of size measures (e.g., sales) may, over some range, decline.

[3] Conceivably, however, this experience can be obtained by inducing M-form managers to join U-form firms which then take on the M-form structure by either self-divisionalization or themselves undertaking an acquisition effort.

[4] Consider in this connection Robert Hansberger's explanation of Boise Cascade's acquisition of Ebasco:

> [Ebasco] didn't have the opportunity to invest their cash resources at the good rate of return we have. This is what provided the motivation for putting the two companies together. We have a large inventory of projects that involve the prospect of high return —and that require large amounts of cash. We can use that money . . . at returns well above what they can achieve.

(*Fortune*, October 1969, *80*, p. 136)

[5] In a research memorandum that has only recently become available (W. J. Baumol, Peggy Heim, B. G. Malkiel, and R. E. Quandt, "Earnings Retention, New Capital, and the Growth of the Firm," Research Memorandum No. 2 [revised], Princeton Financial Research Center, 1969), the rate of return on ploughback is reported to fall in the range from 3.0 to 4.6 percent, while that associated with new debt financing ranges from 4.2 to 14 percent and the rate of return on new equity ranges from 14.5 to 20.8 percent. The authors conclude that the rate of return on ploughback is "sur-prisingly small" (p. 27); some might even regard it as distressingly small. No effort was made in this study to distinguish between alternative types of organization struc-tures and degrees of diversification. If the argument advanced here is correct, the M-form conglomerate should experience greater rates of return on ploughback than the average levels reported above.

[6] Consider in this connection the following observations of Tinkham Veale (reported in the *New York Times*, July 8, 1969, Sec. F, p. 3)

> . . . all too often owner-managers of small companies hit a plateau when sales reach the $5-million mark. At that point they can't seem to expand further.
> The company's head finds himself devoting too much time to legal, accounting, administrative and financial problems that he simply is not equipped to handle, and neglecting the production and engineering problems at which he is an expert in solving.

Veale accordingly regards conglomeration (albeit of a mixed M- and free-form variety) as a means of permitting these firms to move off of this plateau.

A similar position is taken by James Pandapas, a former Litton Division chief. He is of the opinion that

> Without the merger as an escape hatch . . . many new companies would never be born, and many young ones would never survive. Probably a third of Litton-acquired companies wouldn't have made it on their own . . . and financial problems aside, one reason is simply that many men who start a company simply haven't the skill or taste for the kind of management needed to bring a company to maturity.

(As reported by Robert C. Alworth, "The Frustrations of the Acquired Executive," *Fortune*, November 1969, *80*, p. 156.)

J. Keith Butters, John Lintner, and William Cary, in a much earlier study (*Effects of Taxation: Corporate Mergers*, Harvard Graduate School of Business Administration, Boston, 1951), found that while management considerations were an important motive for merger in companies of every size, they were the major reason for merger in half of the mergers in all size classes for which the acquired firm had assets as large as $15 million (pp. 214–18). Some of these management related mergers were induced by imminent retirement. Inasmuch as the tax incentives for merger among owners of closely held corporations have since been reduced (pp. 28–35), management considerations may well bulk larger—at least in relation to tax incentives—as a reason for the merger of small enterprises in more recent years.

[7] A somewhat different argument is sometimes made that the conglomerate favors investment in R&D because of its superior appropriability characteristics: unanticipated spillovers from R&D can be more easily utilized. In relation to smaller firms, however, the R&D commonalities enjoyed by large conglomerates may be more than offset by the disabilities common to large firms quite generally in the performance of early stage inventive activity [**156**].

[8] Rarely, even in industries where the concentration ratio is as high as 80 percent, does the fourth or sixth largest firm have as much as a 10 percent market share. Effectively, the criteria will sweep up most 5 percent acquisitions by any large firm in the circumscribed subset if the acquired firm is in an industry where the concentration ratio exceeds 40.

[9] If, however, a broad standard of potential competition were to be adopted, attention ought simultaneously be given to ways by which firms or groups outside this subset might more effectively exercise indirect capital market controls over firms in the circumscribed region.

[10] Actually, there is a third possibility: a conglomerate merger may experience real cost losses that are more than offset, in a private returns sense, by pecuniary gains. Claims of opportunistic takeovers supported by dubious financial arrangements are common. (These are often self-serving, however. The corporation that, because of the risk averse preferences of its management, maintains unusually high liquidity balances and avoids debt financing does not obviously serve either the stockholders' or the social interest.) While the closure of hitherto latent loopholes that are now exploited with net negative social consequences is clearly indicated, it is doubtful that any such changes should be made to apply to conglomerates exclusively.

[11] See in this connection Arrow's observations on the problems associated with the international transmission of knowledge and the importance of interpersonal contact [**15**, pp. 33–34]. The international market in management consultants appears in part to be a response to these conditions [**3**].

10

qualifications to the multidivision form hypothesis

The preceding chapters have been focused in an essentially affirmative way on the properties of the M-form organization. Problems of the U-form enterprise were noted, and the respects in which the M-form innovation was responsive to them were assessed. The systems consequences of the M-form innovation regarding competition in the product and capital markets were also examined.

There is, however, no special reason to believe that the M-form structure represents a final stage in the evolutionary development of the corporation. If one were to predict what subsequent changes are to be expected, he would, presumably, attempt to discover what problems the M-form organization experiences. Some of these are noted here, but many of the limits of the M-form structure may be evident only with additional experience.

Although the qualifications to the M-form hypothesis offered are somewhat conjectural, it seems better that they be considered, however tenuous the argument, than omitted altogether. The following qualifications are registered: the M-form organization in relation to a series of independent U-form firms; technical innovation in a systems context; limits to firm size; the "free-form" distinction; "exempted" industries; management default regarding the discretionary remainder; and stipulation of the objective function. Consider these seriatim.

1
U-FORM INDEPENDENTS

Although the M-form enterprise appears to have better control loss experience and goal pursuit properties than a comparable, large U-form firm for which divisionalization is feasible, its superiority over a series of independent, market-mediated, U-form firms that perform the same functions remains to be established. The technical innovation side of this question, which can be treated in a systems context, is considered in section 2. Here we focus on static and dynamic properties of these alternative organizing strategies and regard technical innovation as exogenous.

1.1
Static Aspects

To place the comparison on a "fair" basis it will be assumed that each of the independent U-form firms realizes essential scale economies with respect to production and distribution and that other conventional economies (e.g., capital, management) are strictly *de minimis* in importance. What, then, are the advantages (or disadvantages) of making each of these independent U-form firms an operating division of an M-form enterprise?

On the above assumptions, and focusing strictly on static aspects, the series of independent U-form firms would appear to be at little disadvantage and may have a slight edge. Their simple control loss experience would appear to be at least as good as the M-form enterprise and possibly better. Temptations to substitute administrative for market integration when the latter would suffice can be avoided. Their goal pursuit properties are less clear. On the one hand they have the esprit that only small organizations are able to engender and are each subject to product market survival pressures of a more severe sort than the discipline of the M-form enterprise is ordinarily apt to afford. The former has the effect of attenuating subgoal pursuit while the latter tends to shrink the perceived opportunity set, and thereby discourage discretionary behavior, in these independent U-form firms. On the other hand, the operating divisions of the M-form enterprise are subject to a number of internal controls that the capital market lacks access to. If, therefore, some of these U-form firms are individually large, so that the strategic decision-making process is compromised by the inclusion of functional division chiefs, subgoal pursuit may proceed apace.

Goal pursuit tension of this sort, however, is apt to be a problem only if technical scale economies require the U-form firm (operating division) to be quite large. If requisite size is reached at moderate scale, the series of independent U-form firms is apt to have superior static control loss and goal pursuit properties in relation to their M-form counterpart.

1.2
Dynamic Aspects

The series of independent U-form firms comes off less well when attention is shifted to consider problems of maintaining internal vitality and allocating funds to high-yield investment activities. Independent, specialized U-form firms are apt to experience growth limitations both by reason of their organization structure and their markets. For these firms to continue to expand will eventually move them into a size class which, for all the reasons given earlier, has disabling control consequences. Conceivably the firms in question could suspend growth, but this runs counter to managerial aspirations and may result in the loss of the talents of the more competent upward-mobile managers [55, p. 21].

Their specialized market position also impairs the ability of these firms to direct resources to high-yield investments. Considering that managerial own-preferences for retention are reinforced by the practice of subjecting dividends to double taxation, the independent U-form firm may be a distinctly inferior investment medium. Diversification is a possible remedy, but if carried very far the M-form structure is apt to become the superior organization form.

Of course M-form firms are themselves subject to size limitations (see below), but their internal variety better affords opportunities for high-performance managers to get ahead. In addition, the M-form firm has the option of selling off or closing down components as new activities are taken on, and in this respect has a greater capacity for self-renewal. Failure, of course, of large M-form firms to recognize and implement self-renewal strategies makes this an idle argument. In principle, however, and at least occasionally in fact, the M-form enterprise has superior properties in this respect.

Altogether, therefore, insofar as the management of proven resources is concerned, the dynamic properties of the M-form structure tend to compensate for the deficiencies it experiences in the static comparison. The argument requires further qualification, however, when the technical innovation question is considered.

2
TECHNICAL INNOVATION

As indicated earlier, the U-form structure is the natural organization form for a small enterprise to adopt. Hence, at any stage of productive activity (invention, development, mass production, or distribution) for which the small firm enjoys (perhaps transitory) advantages, the unitary form can be expected to prevail. Although a number of such advantages have been adduced to explain the continuing presence of small firms and U-form structures on this account [153], a somewhat neglected aspect of the argument is the importance of small firms to the technical innovation process.[1]

What is proposed here is that innovation should be conceived of not as an indivisible but as a sequential process and that, contrary to prevailing practices, the relevant unit of analysis may be larger than the firm. Consider in this connection the following hypothesis: an efficient procedure by which to introduce new products is for the initial development and market testing to be performed by small firms (perhaps new entrants) in an industry, the successful developments then to be acquired, possibly through merger, for subsequent marketing by a large M-form enterprise.

The argument is a simple extension of classical specialization arguments to include technical progress within the framework of organization form analysis. The reasoning is this: although the M-form enterprise has, for the reasons given earlier, control advantages for dealing with ongoing activities for which large size and hierarchical organization are essential, it may be ill-suited, in relation to smaller firms, to handle high-risk inventive activity. We focus on the latter part of the argument here.

The large corporation experiences what may be referred to as aptitudinal or organizational failures in the support of inventive activity. It may also suffer structural limitations in the venture capital market. The aptitudinal disabilities are attributable to its attitude toward risk and its error admission properties. As Daniel Hamberg observes and documents [70], the large corporation often displays risk averse tendencies with respect to its selection of research projects. Although he makes no organization form distinctions, at least some of his cases seem to be M-form firms, and Norman Berg specifically detects M-form (or at least divisionalized) weaknesses in this respect [30]. The aging process and reward structure in the large bureaucracy apparently tends to suppress spontaneity or other "irregularities" [55, pp. 18–20, 96–101]. A preference for programmed activities drives unprogrammed activities out of existence [104, p. 185]. Untidy, poorly structured, high-risk activities may not be ones which the large bureaucracy is constitutionally well suited to handle.

Related to, and (possibly in a policy sense) accounting for, these risk attitudes are the error admission properties of the large corporation. By comparison with the large U-form organization, the M-form structure (in which decomposability and commensurability have been provided) should display superior adaptability characteristics in this respect. But this is not the only relevant comparison. What are the error admission properties of the large M-form structure in relation to small enterprises? Organization form may be less decisive here than mere size. The difficulties which the M-form structure experiences are endemic to large organizations quite generally: bureaucratic commitment compounded by ex post access to large resources commonly results in a tendency to persist beyond judicious cutoff limits. A decision to proceed easily becomes a commitment to succeed, whatever the costs. Although error admission may also be difficult in the small firm, its inertial qualities are fewer and the latitude needed to delay response is apt to be lacking.

Consider now the funding limitations of the large firm in support of inventive activity. That one should identify funding as a weakness is perhaps too strong; this is, after all, commonly regarded as one of the strengths (sometimes referred to as competitive "advantages") of the large corporation. Indeed, with respect to ease of access to internal funds and debt financing, the conventional assessment is surely correct. But the standard arguments invariably overlook the fact that *venture* capital may be earmarked specifically for investment in small organizations for which appropriability is greater. Investor inability to select among the investment projects in a large firm and thus appropriate the undiluted gains (or losses) of high-risk activities is responsible for this condition. Where, *ceteris paribus*, high variance outcomes are favored (say on account of gambling instincts or the tax laws), the risk pooling which the large (and particularly the large, diversified) corporation provides [1, pp. 241–42] can simultaneously impair the attractiveness to venture capital suppliers of investment in these firms.

Conceivably, therefore, small specialized organizations that do not suffer these nonappropriability and bureaucratic disabilities may be better fitted (or less unsuited) to new product development and market testing than is often claimed. The vitality of these small organizations may indeed continue to stand them to advantage during the introductory period when the product (or service) experiences rapid growth. But once market success is reasonably assured and routines begin to develop or become feasible, the scale and control economies of operating within a large M-form structure may dictate a transfer. The innovating firm can thus have the option either of attempting to make the divisionalization transition itself (possibly through diversification) or of permitting itself to be acquired by a successful M-form enterprise that seeks such associations. Since to make the transition unassisted may be both economically and temperamentally difficult, merger with an established M-form firm may often have beneficial net consequences.

The established M-form enterprise can in this way become the means for ensuring continuing success of a product line by acting to limit the subgoal pursuit and control losses that predictably develop as the unitary form organization reaches maturity. The established M-form organization that follows *a conscious policy of imitation or acquisition* as an important part of its new product strategy (supplemented, perhaps, by a set of internal operating rules designed to check its worst tendencies to persist with own-projects for which merit is objectively lacking) may thus be judged to display rationality of a high order in its allocation of resources to R & D. Put differently, a division of effort between the new product innovation process on the one hand and the management of proven resources on the other may well be efficient. The observed tendency for this division of effort actually to occur is, presumably, evidence of the enterprise system's adaptive capability. It is a reflection of Simon's dictum that "Organizational form . . . [is] a joint function of the characteristics of humans and their tools and the nature of the task environment" [**140**, p. 104]. If indeed the hypothesis has merit, it becomes necessary to view the innovation process in system rather than (exclusively in) individual firm terms. Conceivably the optimum system will not include among its parts any firms which, when the R&D process is regarded in strictly intrafirm terms, would be considered individually "optimal." Parts of the recent discourse on innovation in relation to firm size might thus require reworking.

The argument requires qualification in at least two respects. First, to suggest that the large firm is ill-suited to perform high-risk inventive or product development activities should not be regarded as a wholly negative estimate of the R & D potential or performance of the large firm.[2] Second, the argument (if correct) makes evident the need to express "optimum" industry structure not in static but in moving equilibrium terms. Especially important in this regard is that the requisite ease of entry for new product innovators be provided. Goal tension among existing firms with respect to this objective may be expected: they face a tradeoff between the gains of inhibiting entry, so as to increase current profits and maintain their respective market positions, and the advantages of participating (in a systems sense) in new product development. Inasmuch as the latter involves both uncertain and future rather than immediate returns, established firms may frequently opt for an entry-inhibiting policy. The social interest, however, would appear generally to be served by preserving easy access.[3]

3
LIMITS
TO FIRM SIZE

The discussion of optimum firm size in Chapter 2 assumed that expansion took the form of amplifying the U-form enterprise rather than of multidivisionalization. We consider now the latter alternative. What is responsible for limitations to firm size in the M-form corporation?

One might take the point of view that, if the M-form structure is careful to assemble U-form divisions none of which exceeds optimal scale, this assembly process could continue indefinitely. This overlooks the important control function that is imputed to the general office and elite staff, however. Increasing the number of U-form divisions by lateral expansion eventually exhausts the capacity to supply requisite control at the top. To overcome this condition requires that the general office and elite staff themselves take on hierarchical structure. For example, operating divisions may be clustered according to product or other similarities, with a group vice-president assigned to each. The general office then overlays the group vice-presidents rather than the operating divisions. More complex structures can also be envisaged as the size and variety of activities in the firm proliferate.[4]

Successively building up the administrative hierarchy in this way is subject to two problems. One of these is simple control loss: intrafirm communications are extended with predictable control loss consequences. The other is that the identity of purpose characteristic of the M-form structure becomes increasingly difficult to sustain as its size and variety is progressively extended and the relation of the general office to operations becomes more remote. Discretionary objectives may tend again to surface among the upper echelons—although the effects may be less severe than in the U-form organization, since narrow functional identification is not involved.

Thus, despite the expansionary consequences of changes in

organization form and in communication technology, the control loss phenomenon is not eliminated or even shrunk to insignificance; although the M-form organization has had the effect of increasing feasible firm size, perhaps by an order of magnitude over what the unitary form could support, it is still subject to firm size limitations of the sort described in Chapter 2. To recapitulate, these are bounded rationality at the top and control loss in the communication process: the dyad is robust; its consequences on firm size are constraining. This is not to suggest that organizational and technological innovations will not permit the boundary to be progressively moved out over time, but the "elementary laws of matter" on which the optimum firm size issue rests are not easily subject to repeal.[5] Considering the cumulative nature of the losses experienced as firm size is scaled up, there appears to be little basis for arguing that industry should be reconstituted into giant-sized units. The significant economies associated with M-form organization are available for most technologies when moderate firm size and variety have been reached.

Indeed, one might hope for this reason that an organizational innovation would be forthcoming that would make mitosis attractive once the firm begins to take on giant-size proportions. Voluntary decisions to split off viable, independent M-form organizations from an overextended giant could have beneficial economic consequences, and many would regard structural change of this sort as productive of social and political gains as well. The problem is to supply the requisite incentives to bring this about. Possibly, as with the M-form innovation itself, the accumulating problems of control in conjunction with adversity will induce the change. But the possibility of changing the institutional environment—at a minimum, to remove existing tax disincentives to make this more attractive—should not be neglected. Devising punitive measures against giant-sized corporations is one possibility, but these are typically crude and induce elaborate (and often costly) adaptive responses. One would hope that the corporation would be susceptible to the design of affirmative incentives instead. Since incumbent managements may be less inclined to respond to such incentives than opportunistic outsiders, simultaneous attention to the displacement mechanism may also be required.

4
FREE-FORM
STRUCTURES

Lest the argument be incorrectly generalized to include all divisionalized structures, we take this opportunity to distinguish between M-form and federated (or free-form) organizations. The latter corresponds roughly to what is commonly regarded as a holding company. Thus, although in organization chart terms the apparent (gross) differences between M- and free-form structures may be negligible, operationally they are considerable: whereas both provide for the creation of largely self-contained and autonomous operating divisions, the direction and control provided by the general office differ significantly. The free-form enterprise is, as the name suggests, much more permissive in its control relations with the operating parts. Hence, few of the special control or performance superiority properties attributed here to the M-form organization can be similarly claimed for the free-form enterprise. (If they obtain, this must be due mainly to other factors.[6]) Care should therefore be taken lest the above argument, which applies strictly to M-form structures, be inappropriately extended to include free-form as well.

If ever a counterexample were needed to dispute the proposition that divisionalization by itself leads inexorably to coherent profit maximization, Olin Mathieson is it. The problems which this organization experienced in the late 1950s are picturesquely described by Richard Austin Smith in the following terms [145, pp. 20–21]:

> Rather than bringing its multiform affairs to a burning focus, Olin Mathieson scattered them . . . : its fifty-odd plants and enterprises were never effectively coordinated. . . . The stature it might have achieved as a coherent enterprise with $593 million in sales (1957) was drastically circumscribed by the lack of orientation and central purpose. . . . The company degenerated into a loose confederation of tribal chieftains. Executive vice-presidents proliferated (there were ten in 1957). Division chiefs assumed the power and perquisites of corporation presidents.

Olin Mathieson, apparently, had divisionalized along free-form rather than M-form lines: a strong general executive group had not been provided for. This makes all the more evident the need to go below mere surface manifestations of divisionalization to examine the control relationships among hierarchical levels.

5
"EXEMPTED" INDUSTRIES

The M-form structure may be created in a number of ways. The most common is to divisionalize the activities of the multiproduct enterprise along product lines. A second would be to divisionalize on a geographic basis, where each plant, although producing a common product, was sufficiently autonomous to be evaluated separately. A third would be to set up parallel brand lines within a single product line, where the brands may (but need not) vary in quality. An industry for which the technology of the product makes divisionalization in any of these ways difficult or forced, especially if it were one for which large size was necessary to realize essential scale economies, would not be expected to be among the first to adopt the M-form structure. Integrated metal processing industries come immediately to mind as ones which, for purely technological reasons, could be expected to persist with the unitary form. It is perhaps not surprising, therefore, to find that the copper, aluminum, nickel, and steel industries have been slow to adopt the multidivision form [**42**, pp. 404-23].

Public utilities and common carriers, for both technological and regulatory reasons, may also be slow to adopt the M-form structure. For one thing, the nature of the product may not lend itself easily to meaningful divisionalization along M-form lines. In addition, the regulatory authorities, so as to preserve "clean" regulatory relations, may resist efforts at diversification into nonregulated areas. Finally, the regulatory process itself may impair the incentives to move away from the U-form structure even where this is feasible. Maximum rate of return regulation limits incentives to achieve least-cost results, particularly if the utility has access to an inelastic demand class upon which to lean for revenues.

Another product market area for which an exception to the main argument might be expected is in the defense industries. Although divisionalization may be common among defense-related firms, the performance of those divisions specializing in defense work may not conform to that indicated by the M-form hypothesis. Thus although "competition" at the contract proposal and award stage can indeed be vigorous, the structure of the task, the ex post flexibility of the contract, the unusual incentives which the parties on both sides of the contract experience, and the surveillance system provided all combine to support contract execution that, frequently, exhibits many of the characteristics of the managerial discretion rather than the M-form hypothesis.[7]

6
DISCRETION

Drives for professional excellence are characteristic of most groups which have reached ascendency; for such attitudes to emerge in the large corporation is hardly less natural. That profit should emerge as the principal criterion is broadly consistent with the fiduciary responsibilities of the management. It is, moreover, reinforced by the experience of the firm in the product and capital markets. Inasmuch, however, as the latter pressures are long run, recurrent opportunities for the short run discretionary pursuit of nonprofit goals can be anticipated.

At least occasionally one must expect either that the general executive group will not have made the necessary attitudinal transformation to ensure that resource allocation will be dictated by prospective profitability or that division managers will have secured more than the usual amount of influence over the policy-making process. For either or both of these reasons, aberrations from the profit maximization norm may occur in firms organized along multidivision lines.[8] Whether this is a random or systematic occurrence is problematical. The latter would presumably obtain if the professionalization process is firm-specific in character.

Assuming that we are concerned with central tendencies rather than individual behavior, it seems that both structure (removal of the general executive from operating responsibility) and professional demands for system integrity make the prospects for profit maximization in the multidivision enterprise greater than in the corresponding unitary form organization. Still the volitional element remains: neither form nor "natural" goals are sufficient to ensure that profit maximization will obtain. One should not, therefore, conclude that subgoal pursuit by lower-level participants will continuously be driven to insubstantial amounts. Laxity in the surveillance system, evidence of discretionary behavior at the top, or carelessness in the selection-training system can each permit or induce subgoal pursuit at lower levels of the operating divisions. (Where this is at all extensive, especially if it permeates the upper levels of the division management, the divisionalized organization might more accurately be characterized as a free-form structure. The necessary extension to the unitary form managerial discretion model is straightforward [**160**, p. 161].) Thus, over the short run, especially when dealing with giant-sized corporations, one cannot easily dismiss the possibility that executive discretion is sufficiently great to give rise to behavior that occasionally deviates from the central tendencies imputed to the M-form structure above. Ordinarily, however, this seems unlikely to persist: the management that is disinclined to be assertive is likely, over the long run, to be displaced. Incoherent operations are apt to render the firm non-·viable. Survival pressures will, but for circumstances where the firm possesses substantial market power or the industry is characterized by unaggressive interfirm relations, typically force a restoration of power to the top.

7
THE OBJECTIVE
FUNCTION

The question to be faced here is whether the utility function has been overspecialized by our statement of the M-form hypothesis. Thus, although the M-form organization may effectively concentrate discretionary choice at the top and produce a commitment shift in favor of profit objectives, conceivably the general office executives of the M-form organization also entertain other enterprise-wide objectives. Among these, growth and "enterprise prestige" are probably the most conspicuous candidates.

Operational content is assigned to enterprise prestige only with difficulty. One suspects in any case that growth will often be an adequate proxy for it. Where this is not true, enterprise prestige objectives are apt to be of an *ad hoc* rather than systematic sort. This is hardly stuff from which to build models and will therefore be set aside.[9] Growth, however, is less easy to dismiss.

Growth (or enterprise expansion) might be regarded as the M-form counterpart of the hierarchical expense component that we have associated with the utility function of the U-form enterprise. Not only is this a natural generalization of the argument, but it follows along lines already suggested by William Baumol [23] [24] and Robin Marris [105] [106]—although, it should be noted, neither of them make the organization form distinctions suggested here. Expressing growth in asset or sales terms, as Baumol and Marris do, the favored growth path will display none of the staff-biased properties characteristic of the U-form organization. Such growth aspirations as the firm entertains are apt to be manifested mainly in an aggressive acquisition policy and/or in the amounts of resources allocated to investment (interpreted broadly to include advertising, research and development, etc., as well as plant and equipment).

Although the Baumol-Marris argument is an attractive one, I am reluctant at this stage to complicate a reasonably clean hypothesis by including additional enterprise objectives before it is evident that profits will not do. I therefore merely note that (1) if the M-form hypothesis were to be extended to include multiple goals, a growth goal would be a most natural first extension; but (2) lacking a quantitative basis for assigning special significance to the growth goal, the simpler (profit-maximizing) version of the M-form hypothesis seems preferable; and (3) the case for generalizing the objective function to include other goals is less compelling when consideration is given to the systems consequences of the M-form innovation.

This last is an essential point. It can be illustrated by tracing the effects of the U- to M-form transformation across a series of four stages. The first stage corresponds with that which the separation of ownership from control literature typically (or at least implicitly) postulates: the large U-form enterprise prevails in an environment where the product market is imperfect and the capital market is subject to nontrivial inference and takeover frictions. As a result, characteristic U-form discretionary behavior obtains. The M-form innovation occurs at stage two. Although devised mainly as a means of overcoming control loss problems of internal organization, it also, at least often, educes a profit preference at the top as well. The third stage involves the diffusion of the M-form innovation. Some firms imitate out of choice; for others, M-form rivalry makes reorganization necessary as a survival measure. Stage four involves the opportunistic takeover of unadapted U-form (or permissive M-form) firms by aggressive M-form enterprises. The policing powers of the capital market are mobilized in this way, with the result that neoclassical profit maximization, except for transitory deviations, tends generally to be restored.

Conceivably this description oversimplifies too greatly; possibly system frictions remain that make it necessary to give greater weight to volitional considerations. A way of characterizing management styles[10] and evaluating more precisely the efficacy of alternative control procedures may be needed. These, however, are empirical matters that can only be resolved by examining the data. For our purposes here it is sufficient to indicate that an examination of the systems consequences of the M-form innovation provides greater a priori confidence in the profit maximization hypothesis than would otherwise obtain.

FOOTNOTES

[1] A number of investigators have noted the importance of the small firm to invention—e.g., Jewkes, Sawers, and Stillerman [78], Hamberg [70], Nelson, Peck, and Kalachek [119], and Mansfield [103]—but none has developed the argument in a systems context. For a more complete exposition, see [156].

[2] There will, for example, occasionally be research projects for which the resources of large-sized enterprises are essential. Also, a few firms may regularly stand out as notable exceptions (again, the argument applies on the average). Finally, R & D comprehends more than high-risk activities; the disabilities of large size are not as great for well-specified research activities. (Process and improvement innovations may frequently be of this type.)

[3] For a more complete discussion of this and related varieties of market failure, see [156].

[4] Westinghouse Corporation has recently devised an M-form variant [81].

[5] The argument intendedly is an answer to the query put by Georgescu-Roegen: "Are there any laws that, just like the laws of matter in the case of the plant, would prevent the management unit from functioning beyond a certain size of plant complex?" [**66**, pp. 61–62]

[6] An exception is the executive displacement argument. The free-form management, like the M-form general office, is able to displace operating division managers much more easily than the unassisted capital market.

[7] For an elaboration of this aspect of the argument, see [**162**].

[8] For a field study of an M-form corporation in which this occurred, see [**160**, pp. 106–121]. At the time, I interpreted this as common behavior in the M-form enterprise. I now suspect that, while the behavior reported is not wholly unrepresentative, the firm in question represents a case where general office controls had broken down due perhaps to excessive diversification.

[9] This is not to say that a good deal of public relations energies will not go into representing the activities of the enterprise favorably, but this should not be mistaken for goal-seeking. The folklore of enterprise is doubtlessly replete with "examples" where enterprise prestige is alleged to have had a decisive effect on firm behavior. Even if occasionally this is true, its quantitative importance is hardly established.

[10] Relevant in this connection is Samuel Reid's recent study of conglomerate mergers in which he distinguishes between "offensive" and "defensive" styles [**128**].

11

concluding
remarks

Those who are familiar with the literature on the modern corporation will recognize immediately that, while the reliance on the research of others is extensive, this book is a somewhat idiosyncratic statement of the corporate control problem. I should nevertheless point out that, in addition to the citations in the text, my previously expressed indebtedness to the pre-1963 literature continues to hold [**160**, pp. 4–6, 10–17]. Also, there is a literature that relates somewhat more remotely, and hence has been cited neither here nor there, which bears on the issues examined and warrants acknowledgement. This includes studies of centralization (and decentralization),[1] economic natural selection and satisficing [**52**] [**167**] [**168**], the relation of rules of thumb to business behavior [**26**] [**53**], and the significance of technology for organization form [**39**] [**169**].

Directly or indirectly the analysis throughout has been concerned with the relations between organization form, size, managerial discretion, and efficiency. Although the firm has been the immediate object of analysis, the systems implications of the argument are often as important and sometimes more important than those that concern the firm itself. A capsule summary of the argument is that it is an attempt to consider "organizationally interesting" properties of the modern corporation at what might be regarded as an intermediate level of analysis—where by "intermediate" is meant that the firm itself, rather than the parts (as is characteristic of behavioral theory) or the industry (neoclassical theory), is the primary unit of study. A brief review of some of these organizationally interesting attributes is given in section 1. Some of the implications of the argument for economic policy beyond those examined in previous chapters are indicated in section 2.

1
ORGANIZATIONAL INPUTS

The reliance of the argument on organization theory inputs is at once extensive, selective, and rudimentary. Among the more important such inputs that have found their way into the text are the following: bounded rationality, control loss, threshold response, organization form, internal compliance processes, role playing, and discretionary behavior.

Nothing very novel has been added in our use of any of these concepts other, perhaps, than in the way they have been combined and in the effort to relate them, in a central tendency sense, to organization form differences. Organization theorists may nevertheless object that the argument, although possibly more sensitive to organizational considerations than the conventional theory of the firm, remains stilted and that still further extra-economic input is required if the theory of the firm is "adequately" to reflect organizational realities.

What constitutes adequacy, however, is not well defined. Richer organizational input might always be regarded as desirable, but this is rarely obtained without cost in modeling the relatively gross phenomena of primary interest to economics. Pushing much harder on this aspect of theory development may well require that the conventional maximizing apparatus be abandoned. Although some would regard this as no loss and others would count it a distinct gain, this can scarcely be judged until the alternative apparatus has been assembled. (Work on the "behavioral theory of the firm" [49] is the most ambitious commitment to a nonmaximizing framework to date.) My own feeling is that, while the invitation to introduce additional organizational input must always remain open, these efforts experience diminishing returns—at least within the conventional paradigm—and that, at present, an equally promising avenue is further to explore the systems implications of internal control, expressed as a function of organization form, in relation to product and capital market control processes.

1.1
Bounded Rationality

Simon expresses the significance of bounded rationality to the study of organizational behavior in the following terms [**140**, p. 199]:

> ... the theory of an organization, whose members are "perfectly rational" human beings (capable of unlimited adaptation) is a very nearly vacuous theory. It is only because individual human beings are limited in knowledge, foresight, skill, and time that organizations are useful instruments for the achievement of human purpose; and it is only because organized groups of human beings are limited in ability to agree on goals, to communicate, and to cooperate that organizing becomes for them a problem.

The concept has been important to us in explaining the need for hierarchy, which in turn contributes to an understanding of the control loss phenomenon. The latter is the organizational equivalent of transaction costs in market-mediated activities. *Ceteris paribus*, the boundaries of the firm will be expanded as these internal integrating costs decline in relation to those of the market.

Bounded rationality is perhaps so elementary as to be obvious, and being obvious requires no explicit treatment. Still, a self-conscious examination of behavioral assumptions is often useful. The dilemma faced by neoclassical theory in attempting to explain the limitations to firm size (see Chapter 2) illustrates the argument.

1.2
Control Loss

Simple control loss experience is, as indicated, a manifestation of bounded rationality and varies directly with the information transfer needs of the firm. These information transfer needs, in turn, are a function of how the firm is structured. Identification of natural or quasi-natural decision-making units—within which communications are rich but between which communication needs are lean—will permit a *ceteris paribus* reduction in simple control loss experience by comparison with that which will obtain in a nondecomposed (fully interconnected) system.

Compound control loss involves, in addition to simple control loss, calculated distortion in the transmission of data up and the operationalizing of instructions as they move down through the organization. In the degree to which organization structure influences role perceptions and the effectiveness with which the internal compliance processes can be exercised, this will also vary with organization form.

1.3
Threshold Responses

Bounded rationality prevents the organization from being continuously adapted to every change in the environment in a *mutatis mutandis* sense. One of the ways for reducing variety to manageable proportions is to employ thresholds. Ashby expresses this condition as follows: "Smallness of the amount of interaction [may be achieved] if . . . one part or variable affects another only under certain conditions. . . . One common cause of this is the existence of a threshold, so that the variable shows no change except when the disturbance coming to it exceeds some definite value" [16, p. 66].

The argument is illustrated by the step function adaptations of the firm to changes in the condition of the environment and in decisions to reorganize the enterprise. It was mainly on account of threshold sensitivities that it seemed plausible in the dynamic-stochastic model of the U-form organization to treat only two conditions of the environment: adversity and munificence. Likewise, internal organization was observed to remain constant over wide ranges of environmental variability. Only when adversity became relatively persistent and severe was organizational innovation called upon to transform the enterprise from U- to the M-form. It is also interesting to note that, among early imitators of the M-form structure, subsequent adoption was usually delayed until there was a change in the top command. A threshold change in perceptions was apparently needed.[2]

More recently, refinements in the tender offer technique, especially in conjunction with the quantitatively significant presence of the conglomerate form of organization, have had the effect of reducing the threshold sensitivities to takeover that established firms experience—although incumbent managements in some of these target firms have, by internal and political means (see the Northwest Industries— B. F. Goodrich chronology in Chapter 6, section 3), consciously attempted to restore threshold expenses to prohibitive levels. If, however, the attenuation of product and capital market competition often impairs least-cost performance and offers opportunities for discretion in other respects, the social interest in maintaining low threshold costs should be apparent.

1.4
Organization Form

Organization form is a relatively primitive concept in the lexicon of organization theory. Our use of it here is restricted to two general types, the U- and the M-form structures. Surprisingly, the organization theory literature has not been much concerned with the *differences* in the goal formation and internal efficiency attributes of these two organizational structures. Beer's observations, expressed mainly in a normative context, nevertheless have relevance in this regard [**29**, pp. 381–82]:

> Cybernetic insights show, in particular, that the totality of the organization ought to be made up of building-blocks that will be called *quasi-independent domains*. This is the compromise notion lying between actually independent domains (decentralization) and no domains at all (centralization). These domains have a certain local autonomy and may (in their own language) claim to be altogether autonomous. But they are not autonomous in the meta language of the whole system, which monitors their activity according to the laws of cybernetics. . . . The extent to which the domains are (meta linguistically) independent derives from the need for local fluctuation without which local homeostasis, still more local learning, is impossible. . . . On the other hand, it is vital that all these local controls be *mediated* centrally; otherwise they will suboptimize and destroy the total system by (as it were) internecine strife.

Given requisite size, one might conclude that this description corresponds roughly to what has been described previously as the M-form structure. The argument in the text, however, proceeds throughout in comparative terms. No attempt is made to express an abstract ideal and assess how closely the U- or M-form structures approach this condition. To do this would require an understanding of complex organizational behavior, including the sources and extent of system frictions, vastly more extensive than is presently available. An "evolutionary" approach is therefore taken instead. This focuses attention on the apparent problems that the large U-form organization experiences and regards the M-form innovation as an adaptive response intendedly designed to overcome these. Until our knowledge of complex organizations is further advanced, a biological approach to the question of organizational innovation would seem to have much to commend it.

1.5
Internal Compliance Processes

Of critical importance to an understanding of the corporate control issue is the distinction between external and internal control mechanisms. Within the external control class, it is further useful to distinguish between willful and system categories. The systems aspect is considered in 2.2 below. Here the comparison will be between internal compliance processes and willful external control agents.

The term "willfull external control agent" refers to any group outside of the firm that attempts self-consciously to enforce what it regards as legitimate expectations. Among such groups are the "public," duly constituted regulatory authorities, creditors, and the firm's stockholders. Intervention by the public or by creditors of the firm ordinarily takes the form of rules. Although these may have important behavioral consequences, they are strictly limited in scope. Many regard regulatory agencies as instruments for achieving much more comprehensive control, but in fact such authorities have limited information and are unable to act in the selective adjustment sense that is associated with fine-tuning controls [166]. The stockholders of the firm are similarly disadvantaged, as indeed is any external control agent that would attempt self-consciously to alter management's behavior. Willful external fine-tuning control is virtually a contradiction in terms [29, p. 263].

Once within the firm, however, a variety of additional internal compliance options become available; fine-tuning controls of an anticipatory as well as ex post adjustment sense are feasible. If, therefore, the effectiveness with which the internal compliance machinery can be exercised varies systematically with organization form, and assuming that managements ordinarily have the necessary fortitude to exercise the internal control machinery in ways that favor what they regard as desirable outcomes, changes in organization form can on this account alone be expected to have significant performance consequences.

It is relevant to note in this connection that as the firm assumes a progressively larger part of the integrating function traditionally imputed to the product market, the problems of capital market policing are apt to be made more severe. The extent to which the firm acts as a capital market substitute is thus also important to an overall judgment with respect to what the consequences of internal integration will be.

1.6
Role Playing

The analysis assumes that the behavior of managers is highly conditional on their environment. As Simon puts it, the "goals and constraints appropriate to the role become part of the decision-making program . . . that defines the manager's role behavior" [143, p. 13]. One of the problems of organizational design, therefore, is to provide a structure that elicits the desired role characteristics. Expressed in this way, one of the failures of the large U-form structure was that it solved the strategic decision-making problem with the assistance of managers whose natural (and indeed only viable) posture was one of partisanship. The M-form structure leads to different outcomes partly because the natural role for the general office to assume is enterprise-wide in character. (Executives in the M-form enterprise should not on this account have imputed to them any special stewardship superiority in relation to their U-form counterparts; both are simply responding to the role requirements of their respective assignments.) Vickers goes so far as to suggest that the *main* control to which management is subject is that of control by role [**158**, p. 94]. Although others may regard this as overstrong, it is sufficient for our purposes here if role design is given serious consideration in evaluating the properties of alternative organization forms.

1.7
Discretionary Behavior

That power is typically exercised in ways which redound to the benefit of those who possess it is a proposition which few would be inclined to dispute. Disraeli, in a typically irreverent passage, advocated the aggressive use of the patronage sysem in the following terms: "Patronage is the outward and visible sign of an inward and spiritual grace, and that is Power" [**34**, p. 372]. McGeorge Bundy, in referring to college professors, observed that "It is in the nature of power that most men use it to meet their own most urgent needs" [**38**, p. 43]. The assumption that managers will use opportunities for discretion to advance their individual and collective interests is intended to reflect neither a greater nor lesser inclination on their part to exercise power than is characteristic of politicians and faculty. This is not to deny the possibility of unfailing stewardship behavior, but only to suggest that such is not the general case.

Consideration of the limitations that external control agents typically experience in attempting to control the behavior of complex systems in any but a crude way makes all the more evident the importance of designing systems that, by the nature of the role assignments and incentives which are set up internally, tend to be self-regulating with respect to desired objectives. In many respects, the M-form structure can be regarded as an adaptive "solution" to the following assignment: design a control system that will achieve integrity of purpose by realizing effective, low-cost selection on profitability criteria. The large U-form structure, by contrast, does not so obviously favor this outcome and thus has come to be associated with more aggressive discretionary behavior.

Broadly, discretionary behavior is a function of discretionary opportunities and situational incentives. The M-form organization alters behavior by changing the situational (role) incentives at the top and by limiting the discretionary opportunities available to lower-level participants through the operation of a powerful internal compliance machinery.

2
TOWARD SOME NEW PERSPECTIVES

The argument has a number of implications for characterizing the competitive process, several of which have been examined in previous chapters. For purposes of perspective, it may be useful to pull some of this material together here and extend the argument in hitherto unexplored directions. Five interrelated aspects of the analysis will be considered: a dynamic characterization of the capitalist process; competition in the capital market; a broad characterization of efficiency; antitrust; and a program for empirical testing.

2.1
Dynamic Capitalism

The essence of capitalism, presumably, is its adaptive capacity to generate and select on viable alternatives. Given this emphasis on dynamics, it is surprising that more attention has not been given to the full range of variety that innovation can take. As Schumpeter emphasized, the kind of competition that is decisive is that which comes from "the new commodity, the new technology, the new source of supply, the new type of organization" [**133**, p. 84]. The interest of economists and others in product and process innovation in recent years has been considerable. Likewise the question of entry has received substantial attention. Innovation which takes the form of a new type of organization, by contrast, has been relatively slighted. If, however, the multidivision form has the properties which we have imputed to it, it seems not inconceivable that this has been American capitalism's most important single innovation of the 20th century. The conglomerate organization, regarded in these terms, becomes merely a modern variant on the original multidivisionalization concept.

One of the reasons for this neglect may be that the benefits of organizational innovation are more difficult to appropriate than for most technical innovations: patents are unavailable and imitation is relatively easy. Also, it may not be evident initially which organizational innovations will have more than transitory effects. Thus, whereas "reorganization" is a common response to crisis circumstances, not all such changes have lasting consequences. Distinguishing the successful from the aberrant responses may not at first be easy. (Although the same may be claimed for technical developments, the degree of objectivity with which these can be established is probably greater.) But difficulties of these types do not render organizational innovation any the less important. As Arthur Cole has observed, "If changes in business procedures and practices were patentable, the contributions of business change to the economic growth of the nation would be as widely recognized as the influence of mechanical inventions on the inflow of capital from abroad" [48, pp. 61–62].

Schumpeter himself may be partly responsible for this neglect. In his *Theory of Economic Development*, organizational innovation is discussed mainly in conventional monopoly terms: (thus organizational innovation is illustrated by reference to "the creation of a monopoly position (for example through trustification) or the breaking up of a monopoly position" [134, p. 66]). The treatment in *Capitalism, Socialism, and Democracy* uses as an illustration of organizational innovation "the largest scale unit of control" [133, p. 84]. Although this moves closer to organizational innovation in the structural sense employed here, it fails explicitly to call attention to the goal pursuit and internal efficiency considerations that would appear to be the essence of organization form comparisons. Also, for reasons given earlier, one might hope that institutional incentives might somehow be arranged which would induce now giant-sized firms to undergo mitosis—an innovation that could well have beneficial goal pursuit and efficiency consequences but would run quite at variance with Schumpeter's second example.

If, moreover, organizational innovation often does or can be made to have self-renewal properties, the decay of capitalism postulated by Schumpeter loses much of its inevitability. It is interesting to note in this regard that the M-form enterprise is, in relation to an equivalent U-form structure, much the less "bureaucratic." Mitosis of the giant M-form structure could also be expected to have antibureaucratic, enabling qualities. Although other organizational innovations even now in process may (as did the U-form structure) work in the opposite direction, extrapolating the experience of the first two-thirds of the 20th century does not seem to spell capitalism's early bureaucratic demise.

2.2
Competition in the Capital Market

Not only does the firm internalize integrating functions that would otherwise be provided through product market exchange; it also internalizes functions of the capital market. With but a few exceptions (notably Alchian [6]), this latter variety of internalization has generally been neglected.

Recall that the capital market has traditionally been expected to exercise controls of three types: funds metering, incentives, and displacement. The M-form organization partially supplants the capital market in each of these three respects. Indeed, the general management of an M-form enterprise may, for many purposes, be regarded as acting, in effect, as a miniature capital market. Although its investment opportunities are limited, its knowledge with respect to each is incredibly deep. Moreover, the repeated exposure aspect of the relationship of the general management to the operating division management makes it especially difficult for the division management successfully to "game" the general executive. Resources are allocated (funds are metered) across competing uses according to what plausibly can be represented as a profit maximization criterion. Pecuniary incentives can be awarded to division managers based on the separable (or nearly separable) performance results for which each can meaningfully be assigned responsibility. Incompetent, misguided, or discordant managers whose performance fails to meet expectations can, if more modest compliance measures are unsuccessful, easily be removed —which is to say that internal displacement incurs relatively low cost.

In addition, the M-form structure has the remarkable capacity of mobilizing traditional capital market forces with respect to displacement. Although it is necessary to achieve a critical mass before the threat of takeover by established M-form enterprises becomes sufficiently great to be credible, once this is achieved the potential of effecting organization form economies through takeover gives vitality to the competition in the capital market argument that was previously lacking. Managements of industries that would otherwise be content to maintain their sluggish ways (subject only to the condition that entry by potentially obstreperous and undisciplined rivals could be discouraged) have, by reason of the takeover impact of the M-form innovation, been placed in genuine jeopardy. A symbiotic equilibrium thus develops between internal organization and conventional competition in the capital market forces. A revitalizing of the enterprise system of no small degree may well have occurred (and be occurring) as a consequence.[3]

2.3
Efficiency

The theory of the firm has been of interest to economists mainly as a means of motivating industry behavior (hence the emphasis on perfect competition and representative firms) and as a source of com-

parative statics propostions. The question of efficiency is usually bypassed (least-cost conditions are assumed) or is treated in the simple
allocative efficiency sense of welfare distortions (externalities, dead-
weight losses, etc.). Organization form analysis, by contrast, directs
attention explicitly to the integrative and internal compliance properties of the firm, both of which raise quite different efficiency issues.

This is not, however, to suggest that internal efficiency has been
altogether neglected. Concern over internal efficiency conditions has
been expressed by others for some time [49] [69] [95] [127] [135] [148],
including Harvey Leibenstein's recent treatment of what he refers to
as "X-efficiency" [91]. Despite this interest, the relation of internal
efficiency to organization form has mainly gone undeveloped. Yet,
potentially, organization form would appear to provide a useful framework within which to conduct internal efficiency analysis.

Whether such an effort is warranted is another question. Although
difficult to answer in an absolute sense, in a comparative sense the
answer would appear unambiguously to be affirmative. Any showing
of systematic internal efficiency differences, even those which in percentage terms appear "small," is apt to swamp in welfare importance
the losses attributable to conventional distortions (which typically
take the form of Marshallian triangles).[4] Some may doubt whether the
latter are even worth estimating, but interest in welfare losses has
proven to be remarkably irrepressible. For those who regard the matter
as relevant, greater attention to internal efficiency conditions would
appear to promise (relatively) impressive returns.

2.4
Antitrust

Several antitrust implications were noted in the course of the
argument. With respect to technical progress, for example, antitrust
enforcement officials (as well as economists interested in the influences
of firm size and industry structure on the technical performance
dimension) may need to consider system as well as individual firm
effects. Different firms with different size and organizational properties
may excel at different stages of the technical innovation process. In
particular, small firms may be especially well suited to perform early
stage inventive activities, while the advantages of the large M-form
enterprise may emerge only at later stages and for more highly routinized activities. In this event, the problem of maintaining (in a
moving equilibrium sense) an optimum industry structure, especially
assuring the requisite ease of entry for new product innovators, would
need to be faced.

The potential managerial economies available under the multidivision form of organization suggest that mergers involving the transformation of a U- to an M-form structure may frequently permit the realization of greater economies than have previously been imputed to such mergers. This does not, of course, constitute an absolute defense for such mergers. There may be countervailing considerations. But the managerial economies aspect of the M-form organization would appear to warrant greater weight than has been accorded to it previously.

If, more generally, mergers are apt to be the least-cost way of achieving displacement, and if in a system where product market insularity is common credible threats of displacement are needed to maintain the vitality of capitalism, an active merger market may be essential. An already tough antitrust enforcement policy against horizontal mergers should therefore be extended to include conglomerates only with caution. Thus, although one might specify rules that limit the acquisitions open to giant-sized firms on account of possible diseconomies and undesirable social or political consequences (real or imagined), the line should not be extended uncritically.

Note in this connection that, but for the giant-size qualification, the social gains to be imputed to the M-form conglomeration process, *expressed in a systems sense*, can be expected to exceed the sum of the *real* efficiency gains experienced on individual instances of takeover. This is because the background threat of takeover induces self-regulatory behavior on the part of firms that would otherwise be content to run slack.[5]

If indeed one of the most remarkable attributes of American capitalism is its adaptive capacity to devise efficient and viable organization forms in pursuit of private gain, to characterize the system in static, historical, or traditional terms may be to miss much of what accounts for its most significant achievements. To be relevant, therefore, antitrust may need periodically an updated interpretation of that institution, the modern corporation, with which it is principally concerned. This counsels a policy of caution in evaluating new organization forms whose properties are imperfectly understood. These *may* represent an effort to achieve monopoly power under novel auspices; often, however, really fundamental organization form changes are apt to signal beneficial efficiency effects as well or instead.

2.5
Empirical Testing

Interesting though each is, none of the recent studies of discretionary behavior in the large corporation [68] [80] [90] [94] [118] [128] makes the organization form distinctions suggested here. Even differential product market conditions are generally neglected—Gordon's study of comparative airline efficiency being a notable exception [68]. Discretionary behavior is apt to be quantitatively significant, however, only when environmental conditions support a nontrivial opportunity set and either the strategic decision-making process favors such behavior or the internal compliance processes are weak (or both). Ordinarily (that is, on the average) neither the small U-form enterprise nor the aggressively constituted, large (but not necessarily giant-sized) M-form organization statisfies either of these last two conditions. Tests of discretionary behavior that fail to provide for size, organization form, and product market effects are, if the argument here is substantially correct, apt to discover weaker associations than the data would otherwise sustain.

Conventional industrial organization studies of market performance might similarly be extended to include, in addition to the usual market structure variables, measures of internal organization (including size) as explanatory variables. If, for the reasons advanced in the text, internal structure (organization form) has pervasive goal pursuit and internal efficiency consequences, and if market structure and internal organization are imperfectly correlated, one might expect that attempts to explain interfirm and interindustry differences in performance based only on differences in market structure would leave a large unexplained variance—even if refined market structure measures could be obtained. If business behavior is jointly a function of both market and internal organization, measures of both, ideally, will be used as explanatory variables. Although adequate measures of internal organization may prove difficult to work up, the preliminary evidence (mainly Chandler's historical survey [42] and casual observation) together with the a priori reasoning and the long-standing [111] but largely undeveloped interest of industrial organization specialists in this aspect of structure would seem to augur in favor of such an undertaking.

Note in these connections that the U- and M-form structures do not exhaust the range of corporate organization. In particular, distinguishing the M-form from the free-form structure would appear to be essential. Other distinctions may be suggested in the course of investigating the consequences of organization form more completely.[6]

Also note that the question of organization form *per se* is not concerned with such matters as specialized versus diversified firms or concentrated versus unconcentrated markets. Rather, given equivalence in product variety and market power respects, the question is: Does internal organization make a difference? Conglomeration, however, explicitly raises the diversification issue. Here the critical test is what are the *marginal* returns to ploughback. Thus, although a specialized M-form enterprise in a concentrated industry might experience both high average returns and a substantial cash flow, marginal returns can normally be expected to decline as the industry matures. It is by shifting resources at the margin to higher yield uses that the M-form conglomerate enjoys a potential advantage.

FOOTNOTES

[1] This is a rather extensive literature, with which the names Arrow, Hurwicz, the two Marschaks, and Radner are principally associated. It is, however, excessively abstract for our purposes here. For recent additions to this literature, including references to earlier work, see [75] [109].

[2] More than mental attitude, however, is apt to be involved in a change in the top command. Reorganization is an effective way of realigning power in the firm. The new executive team can be better assured of allegiance if it is able to make key appointments. Reorganization (of whatever sort) facilitates this result. But reorganization also involves uncertainty and hence risk. The "old" management, having worked out an accommodation, may frequently perceive these risks as outweighing the predictable gains. The "new" management, by contrast, recognizes the opportunity to work out a more favorable accommodation. A different estimate of gains (and possibly risks) thus makes the decision to reorganize more attractive to the new management.

[3] Even if the takeover threat to remiss or supine managements were attenuated by legislative or regulatory means—a possibility that seems not altogether remote [40] [88] —the efficiency consequences of this innovation will nevertheless tend to be transmitted through product market experience. Thus, although each industry might now require an innovator (possibly a new entrant), and for this reason diffusion of the M-form structure would be delayed, the effects of successful organizational innovation are apt to be pervasive. The principal exceptions to the argument are (1) mature industries in which the interfirm organization has reached an advanced degree of adherence to a mutually satisfactory result and for which the barriers to entry are substantial [124] [161], (2) regulated industries, and (3) nationalized industries. For these, organizational innovation and imitation (assuming that it is feasible) may sometimes have to be forced.

[4] See [91] [163] for some suggestive parametric results on this proposition.

[5] This assumes that the main response to a general background threat to takeover is not mainly dysfunctionally defensive—in the sense of constituting a drain on corporate energies and resources for narrow purposes of maintaining the incumbents—but is designed to correct conditions of internal inefficiency. Ordinarily, especially in the long run, this seems plausible.

[6] Inasmuch as the transformation of the large corporation from the U- to an M-form structure is in many industries now substantially complete, matched comparisons of these two structures may currently be difficult to obtain. It should nevertheless be possible to perform historical comparisons over the period during which large U- and M-form enterprises that were otherwise equivalent (or for which differences are partialed out) coexisted. Intraindustry studies are perhaps the easiest to perform in this regard, but interindustry comparisons should also be practicable.

bibliography

1. Adelman, M. A., "The Antimerger Act, 1950–60," *American Economic Review*, May, 1961, *51*, 236–44.

2. ———, "Efficiency of Resource Use in Crude Petroleum," *Southern Economic Journal*, October, 1964, *31*, 101–22.

3. Albrook, R. C., "Europe's Lush Market for Advice—American Preferred," *Fortune*, July, 1969, *80*, 128–31, 180–81.

4. Alchian, A. A., "Uncertainty, Evolution, and Economic Theory," *Journal of Political Economy*, June, 1950, *58*, 211–21.

5. ———, and R. A. Kessel, "Competition, Monopoly, and the Pursuit of Pecuniary Gain," in *Aspects of Labor Economics*. Princeton: National Bureau of Economic Research, 1962.

6. ———, "Corporate Management and Property Rights", in *Economic Policy and the Regulation of Corporate Securities*, ed. H. G. Manne. Washington, D.C.: American Enterprise Institute, 1969, pp. 337–60.

7. Anderson, Patrick, "Ralph Nader, Crusader; Or The Rise of a Self-Appointed Lobbyist," *New York Times Magazine*, October 29, 1967, p. 25 ff.

8. Andrews, P. W. S., *Manufacturing Business.* New York: The Macmillan Company, 1949.

9. Ansoff, H. I., and J. F. Weston, "Merger Objectives and Organization Structure," *Quarterly Review of Economics and Business*, August, 1962, *2*, 49–58.

10. Anthony, R. M., *Planning and Control Systems: A Framework for Analysis.* Boston: Graduate School of Business Administration, Harvard University, 1965.

11. Arrow, K. J., "Toward a Theory of Price Adjustment," in Abramovitz et al., *The Allocation of Resources.* Stanford, Calif.: Stanford University Press, 1959, pp. 41–51.

12. ———, "Economic Welfare and the Allocation of Resources for Invention," in *The Rate and Direction of Inventive Activity.* Princeton; 1962, Princeton University Press, pp. 609–25.

13. ———, "Control in Large Organization," *Management Science*, September, 1963, *10*, 397–408.

14. ———, "The Organization of Economic Activity: Issues Pertinent to the Choice of Market versus Nonmarket Allocation," in *The Analysis and Evaluation of Public Expenditures: The PPB System.* Washington, D.C.: Joint Economic Committee, 1969, I, 47–64.

15. ———, "Classificatory Notes on the Production and Transmission of Technological Knowledge," *American Economic Review*, May, 1969, *59*, 29–35.

16. Ashby, W. R., *An Introduction to Cybernetics.* New York: John Wiley & Sons, Inc., 1956.

17. ———, *Design for a Brain*, 2nd ed., New York: John Wiley & Sons, Inc., 1960.

18. Averch, H., and L. L. Johnson, "Behavior of the Firm Under Regulatory Constraint," *American Economic Review*, December, 1962, *52*, 1052–69.

19. Bain, J. S., *Barriers to New Competition.* Cambridge, Mass.: Harvard University Press, 1956.

20. ———, *Industrial Organization.* New York: John Wiley & Sons, Inc., 1959.

21. Barnard, C. I., *The Functions of the Executive.* Cambridge, Harvard University Press, 1962.

22. Bartlett, F. C., *Remembering.* New York: Cambridge University Press, 1932.

23. Baumol, W. J., *Business Behavior, Value, and Growth.* New York: The Macmillan Company, 1959.

24. ———, "The Theory of Expansion of the Firm," *American Economic Review*, December, 1962, *52*, 1078–87.

25. ———, and T. Fabian, "Decomposition, Pricing for Decentralization, and External Economies," *Management Science*, September, 1964, *11*, 1–32.

26. ———, and R. E. Quandt, "Rules of Thumb and Optimally Imperfect Decisions," *American Economic Review*, March, 1964, *54*, 23–46.

27. ———, *The Stock Market and Economic Efficiency*. New York: Fordham University Press, 1965.

28. Becker, G. S., "Irrational Behavior and Economic Theory," *Journal of Political Economy*, February, 1962, *70*, 1–13.

29. Beer, Stafford, *Decision and Control*. New York: John Wiley & Sons, Inc., 1966.

30. Berg, Norman, "Strategic Planning in Conglomerate Companies," *Harvard Business Review*, May–June 1965, 79–92.

31. Berle, A. A., and G. C. Means, *The Modern Corporation and Private Property*. New York: Commerce Clearing House, Inc., 1932.

32. Berle, A. A., *The Twentieth Century Capitalist Revolution*. New York: Harcourt, Brace & World, Inc., 1954.

33. Blair, J. M., "The Conglomerate Merger in Economics and Law," *Georgetown Law Review*, Summer, 1958, *43*, 79–92.

34. Blake, R., *Disraeli*. New York: Doubleday (Anchor Book edition), 1968.

35. Boulding, K. E., *Conflict and Defense*. New York; Doubleday & Company, Inc., 1962.

36. ———, "The Economics of Knowledge and the Knowledge of Economics," *American Economic Review*, May 1968, *58*, 1–13.

37. Brown, Donaldson, "Pricing Policy in Relation to Financial Control," *Management and Administration*, February, 1924, *1*, 195–98.

38. Bundy, McGeorge, "Faculty Power," *Atlantic*, September, 1968, *222*, 41–47.

39. Burns, T., and G. M. Stalker, *The Management of Innovation*. Chicago: Quadrangle Books, 1962.

40. Celler, Hon. Emanuel, "A Study of Conglomerates: Where Are They Leading Us?" address before the American Management Association, June 12, 1969.

41. Chamberlin, E. H., "Proportionality, Divisibility and Economies of Scale," *Quarterly Journal of Economics*, February, 1948, *62*, 229–62.

42. Chandler, A. D., Jr., *Strategy and Structure*. New York: Doubleday, Anchor Books edition, 1966.

43. ———, and F. Redlich, "Recent Developments in American Business Administration and Their Conceptualization," *Business History Review*, Spring, 1961, pp. 1–27.

44. Charnes, A., R. W. Clower, and K. O. Kortanek, "Effective Control through Coherent Decentralization with Preemptive Goals," *Econometrica*, April, 1967, *35*, 244–320.

45. Coase, R. H., "The Nature of the Firm," *Economica*, N. S., IV (1937), 386–405. Reprinted in George J. Stigler and Kenneth E. Boulding (eds.), *Readings in Price Theory*. Homewood, Ill.: Richard D. Irwin, Inc., 1952.

46. ———, "The Problem of Social Cost," *Journal of Law and Economics*, 1960, *3*, 1–44.

47. Churchill, N. C., W. W. Cooper, and T. Sainsbury, "Laboratory and Field Studies of the Behavioral Effects of Audits," in C. P. Bonini, et. al., eds., *Management Controls: New Direction in Basic Research.* New York: McGraw Hill, 1964, pp. 253–67.

48. Cole, A. H., "The Entrepreneur: Introductory Remarks," *American Economic Review,* May, 1968, *58,* 60–63.

49. Cyert, R. M., and J. G. March, *A Behavioral Theory of the Firm.* Englewood Cliffs, N.J.: Prentice-Hall, Inc., 1963.

50. Davis, H. T., *The Analysis of Economic Time Series.* Granville, Ohio: Principia Press, 1941.

51. Davis, O. A., and A. Whinston, "Externalities, Welfare, and the Theory of Games," *Journal of Political Economy,* June, 1962, *70,* 241–62.

52. Day, R. H., "Profits, Learning, and the Convergence of Satisficing to Marginalism," *Quarterly Journal of Economics,* May, 1967, *81,* 302–11.

53. ———, and E. H. Tinney, "How to Cooperate in Business without Really Trying: A Learning Model of Decentralized Decision Making," *Journal of Political Economy,* July–August, 1968, *76,* 583–600.

54. Demsetz, Harold, "Some Aspects of Property Rights," *Journal of Law and Economics,* October, 1966, *9,* 61–70.

55. Downs, Anthony, *Inside Bureaucracy.* New York: Little, Brown and Company, 1967.

56. Dworsky, D., "Fight Looms at Air Brake," *New York Times,* Financial section, December 31, 1967, p. 5.

57. Edwards, C. D., "Conglomerate Bigness as a Source of Power," in *Business Concentration and Price Policy.* Princeton: Princeton University Press, 1955.

58. ———, statement in *Economic Concentration, Part 1: Overall and Conglomerate Aspects,* Hearings Before the Subcommittee on Antitrust and Monopoly, 88th Cong., 1964, pp. 36–47. Washington, D.C.

59. Emery, J. C., *Organizational Planning and Control Systems: Theory and Technology.* New York: The Macmillan Company, 1969.

60. *Forbes,* "Softening the Harsh Words," June 1, 1969, *103,* 23–24.

61. Friedman, M., *Essays in Positive Economics.* Chicago: University of Chicago Press, 1953.

62. Fuchs, V. R., *The Service Economy,* New York: National Bureau of Economic Research, 1965.

63. Galbraith, J. K., "Market Structure and Stabilization Policy," *Review of Economics and Statistics,* May, 1957, *39,* 120–29.

64. ———, *The New Industrial State.* New York: Houghton Mifflin Company, 1967.

65. Geneen, H. T., "Management Must Manage," an address before the Investment Group of Hartford, Conn., February 15, 1968.

66. Georgescu-Roegen, N., "Chamberlin's New Economics and the Unit of Production," in R. E. Kuenne, ed., *Monopolistic Competition Theory: Studies in Impact.* New York: John Wiley & Sons, Inc., 1967, pp. 31–62.

67. Gordon, R. A., *Business Leadership in the Large Corporation*. Berkeley: University of California Press, 1961.

68. Gordon, R. J., "Airline Costs and Managerial Efficiency," in *Transportation Economics*. New York: Columbia University Press, 1965, pp. 61–91.

69. Hadley, A. T., "The Good and Evil of Industrial Combination," *Atlantic Monthly*, March, 1897, *79*, 375–86.

70. Hamberg, D., "Invention in the Industrial Laboratory," *Journal of Political Economy*, April, 1963, *71*, 95–115.

71. Harberger, A. C., "Monopoly and Resource Allocation," *American Economic Review*, May, 1954, *44*, 75–87.

72. Hayes, S. L., III, and R. A. Taussig, "Tactics of Cash Takeover Bids," *Harvard Business Review*, March–April, 1967, *45*, 136–47.

73. Heflebower, R. B., "Observations on Decentralization in Large Enterprises," *Journal of Industrial Economics*, November, 1960, *9*, 7-22.

74. Howard, R. A., *Dynamic Programming and Markov Processes*. Cambridge, Mass.: MIT Press, 1960.

75. Hurwicz, L., "Centralization and Decentralization in Economic Systems," *American Economic Review*, May, 1969, *59*, 513–24.

76. IBM, "A New Pattern for Progress," *IBM Business Machines*, December 28, 1956.

77. Ijiri, Yuji, and H. A. Simon, "Business Firm Growth and Size," *American Economic Review*, March, 1964, *54*, 77–89.

78. Jewkes, J., D. Sawers, and R. Stillerman, *The Sources of Invention*. London: Macmillan & Co., Ltd., 1958.

79. Kaldor, Nicholas, "The Equilibrium of the Firm," *Economic Journal*, March, 1934, *44*, 70–71.

80. Kamershen, D. R., "The Influence of Ownership and Control on Profit Rates," *American Economic Review*, June, 1968, *58*, 432–47.

81. Karr, A. R., "Westinghouse Revises Its Top Management to Prepare for Prompt, Continued Growth," *Wall Street Journal*, Jan. 8, 1969, p. 4.

82. Kaysen, C., "The Corporation: How Much Power? What Scope?" in *The Corporation in Modern Society*, ed. E. S. Mason. Cambridge: Harvard University Press, 1960.

83. ———, "Another View on Corporate Capitalism," *Quarterly Journal of Economics*, February, 1965, *99*, 41–51.

84. Keynes, J. M., *Essays in Persuasion*. London: Macmillan & Co., Ltd., 1931.

85. Klaw, Spencer, "The Soap Wars: A Strategic Analysis," *Fortune*, June, 1963, pp. 123 ff.

86. Knauth, O., *Managerial Enterprise: Its Growth and Methods of Operations*. New York: W. W. Norton & Company, Inc., 1948.

87. Knight, F. H., *Risk, Uncertainty and Profit*. New York: Harper & Row, 1965.

88. Kohlmeier, L.M., "U.S. Assails 'Super-Concentration'; May Move to Block Giant Mergers," *Wall Street Journal*, June 9, 1969, p. 4. For the text of Attorney General Mitchell's speech, see "Antitrust Policies," *BNA Antitrust and Trade Regulation Reporter*, June 10, 1969, x-9 to x-11.

89. Koontz, H. and C. O'Donnell, *Principles of Management*. New York: McGraw-Hill Book Company, 1955.

90. Larner, R. J., "Ownership and Control in the 200 Largest Nonfinancial Corporations, 1929 and 1963," *American Economic Review*, September, 1966, *56*, 777–87.

91. Leibenstein, H., "Allocative Efficiency versus 'X-Efficiency'," *American Economic Review*, September, 1966, *56*, 392–415.

92. Livingston, J. A., *The American Stockholder*. New York: Collier Books, 1963.

93. McDonald, John, "Westinghouse Invents a New Westinghouse," *Fortune*, October, 1967, *76*, 143–47 ff.

94. McGuire, J. S., J.S.Y. Chiu, and A. O. Elbing, "Executive Incomes, Sales, and Profits," *American Economic Review*, September, 1962, *52*, 753–61.

95. McNulty, P. J., "Economic Theory and the Meaning of Competition," *Quarterly Journal of Economics*, November, 1968, *82*, 639–56.

96. Machlup, F., "Theories of the Firm: Marginalist, Behavioral, Managerial," *American Economic Review*, March, 1967, *57*, 1–33.

97. Malkiel, B. G., Review of [**100**], *Journal of Business*, April, 1968, *41*, 263–65.

98. Manne, H. G., "Some Theoretical Aspects of Share Voting," *Columbia Law Review*, March, 1964, *64*, 1427–45.

99. ———, "Mergers and the Market for Corporate Control," *Journal of Political Economy*, April, 1965, *73*, 110–20.

100. ———, *Insider Trading and the Stock Market*. New York: Free Press, 1966.

101. ———, "Our Two Corporation Systems: Law and Economics," *Virginia Law Review*, March, 1967, *53*, 259–84.

102. Mansfield, Edwin, "Innovation and Technical Change in the Railroad Industry," in *Transportation Economics*. New York: National Bureau of Economic Research, 1965.

103. ———, *The Economics of Technological Change*. New York: W. W. Norton & Company, 1968.

104. March, J. G., and H. A. Simon, *Organizations*. New York: John Wiley & Sons, Inc., 1958.

105. Marris, R., "A Model of the 'Managerial' Enterprise," *Quarterly Journal of Economics*, May, 1965, *77*, 185–209.

106. ———, *The Economic Theory of 'Managerial' Capitalism*. New York: Free Press, 1964.

107. ———, Review of [**64**], *American Economic Review*, March, 1968, *58*, 240–47.

108. Marschak, J., "Efficient and Viable Organization Forms," in Mason Haire, ed., *Modern Organizational Research*. New York: John Wiley and Sons, 1954, pp. 307–20.

109. Marschak, T., "On The Comparison of Centralized and Decentralized Economies," *American Economic Review*, May, 1969, *59*, 525–32.

110. Marshall, A., *Industry and Trade*. London: The Macmillan Co., 1932.

111. Mason, E. S., "Price and Production Policies of Large Scale Enterprise," *American Economic Review*, Suppl. 1939, *29*, 61–74.

112. Mason, E. S. (ed.), *The Corporation in Modern Society*. Cambridge: Harvard University Press, 1960.

113. Mayer, Thomas, "The Distribution of Ability and Earnings," *Review of Economics and Statistics*, May, 1960, *42*, 189–98.

114. Meade, J. E., "Is 'The New Industrial State' Inevitable?," *Economic Journal*, June, 1968, pp. 372–92.

115. Mechanic, David, "Sources of Power of Lower Participants in Complex Organizations," in W. W. Cooper, H. J. Leavit, and M. W. Shelly, III (eds.), *New Perspectives in Organization Research*. New York: John Wiley & Sons, Inc., 1964, pp. 136–49.

116. Miller, A. D., *The Supreme Court and American Capitalism*. New York: Free Press, 1968.

117. Monsen, R. J., Jr., and Anthony Downs, "A Theory of Large Managerial Firms," *Journal of Political Economy*, June, 1965, *73*, 221–36.

118. ―――, J. S. Chiu, and D. E. Cooley, "The Effect of Separation of Ownership and Control on the Performance of the Large Firm," *Quarterly Journal of Economics*, August, 1968, *82*, 435–51.

119. Nelson, R. R., M. J. Peck and E. D. Kalachek, *Technology, Economic Growth, and Public Policy*. Washington, D.C.: Brookings Institution, 1967.

120. Nevins, A., And F. E. Hill, *Ford: Expansion and Challenge: 1915–1933*. New York: Charles Scribner's Sons, 1957.

121. Papandreou, A. G., "Some Basic Issues in the Theory of the Firm," in B. F. Haley (ed.), *A Survey of Contemporary Economics*. Homewood, Ill: Richard D. Irwin, Inc., 1952.

122. Penrose, Edith, *The Theory of the Growth of the Firm*. New York: John Wiley & Sons, Inc., 1959.

123. Peterson, S., "Corporate Control and Capitalism," *Quarterly Journal of Economics*, February, 1965, *79*, 1–19.

124. Phillips, Almarin, *Market Structure, Organization, and Performance*. Cambridge, Mass.: Harvard University Press 1962.

125. Ramstrom, D., *The Efficiency of Control Strategies*. Stockholm: Almquist and Wiksell, 1967.

126. Rayner, A. C., and I. M. D. Little, *Higgledy Piggledy Growth Again*. New York: A. M. Kelley, 1966.

127. Rees, A., *The Economics of Trade Unions*. Chicago: University of Chicago Press, 1962.

128. Reid, S. R., *Mergers, Managers and the Economy*. New York: McGraw-Hill, 1968.

129. Robinson, E. A. G., "The Problem of Management and the Size of Firms," *Economic Journal*, June, 1932, *44*, 240–54.

130. ―――, *The Structure of Competitive Industry*. Chicago: University of Chicago Press, 1962.

131. Ross, N. S., "Management and the Size of the Firm," *Review of Economic Studies*, 1952–53, *19*, 148–54.

132. Scherer, F. M., *Industrial Market Structure and Economic Performance* (forthcoming).

133. Schumpeter, J. A., *Capitalism, Socialism, and Democracy*. 3rd ed. New York: Harper & Row, Publishers, 1947.

134. ———, *The Theory of Economic Development*. New York: Oxford University Press, 1961.

135. Scitovsky, T., "Economic Theory and the Measurement of Concentration," in *Business Concentration and Price Policy*. Princeton: Princeton University Press, 1955.

136. Servan-Schreiber, J. J., *The American Challenge*. New York: Atheneum Publishers, 1968.

137. Sherman, H. J., *Profits in the United States*. Ithaca, New York: Cornell University Press, 1968.

138. Sherman, Roger, review of "Insider Trading and the Stock Market," *Papers on Non-Market Decision Making, II*, Charlottesville, Va., 1967, pp. 103–104.

139. Simon, H. A., *Administrative Behavior*, 2nd ed. New York: The Macmillan Company, 1957.

140. ———, *Models of Man*. New York: John Wiley & Sons, Inc., 1957.

141. ———, "The Compensation of Executives," *Sociometry*, March, 1957, pp. 32–35.

142. ———, "The Architecture of Complexity," *Proceedings of the American Philosophical Society*, December, 1962, *106*, 467–82.

143. ———, "On the Concept of Organizational Goal," *Administrative Science Quarterly*, June, 1964, *9*, 1–22.

144. ———, *The Shape of Automation for Men and Management*. New York: Harper & Row, Publishers, 1965.

145. Smith, R. A., *Corporations in Crisis*. New York: Doubleday, Anchor Books edition, 1966.

146. Solow, R. M., "The New Industrial State or Son of Affluence," *The Public Interest*, Fall, 1967, No. 9, pp. 99–108.

147. Starbuck, W. H., "Organizational Growth and Development," in J. G. March (ed.), *Handbook of Organizations*. Chicago: Rand McNally & Co., 1964.

148. Stedry, A. C., *Budget Control and Cost Behavior*. Englewood Cliffs, N. J.: Prentice-Hall, Inc., 1960.

150. Stigler, G. J., "Monopoly and Oligopoly by Merger," in R. B. Heflebower and G. W. Stocking (eds.), *Readings in Industrial Organization*. Homewood, Ill.: Richard D. Irwin, Inc., 1958., pp. 69–80.

151. ———, "Galbraith's New Book: A Few Problems," *Wall Street Journal*, June 26, 1967, p. 13.

152. Thompson, V. A., *Modern Organization*. New York: Alfred A. Knopf, Inc., 1961.

153. Townsend, H., *Scale, Innovation, Merger and Monopoly*. London: Macmillan & Co., Ltd., 1968.

154. Tullock, Gordon., *The Politics of Bureaucracy*. Washington: Public Affairs Press, 1965.

155. Turner, D. F., "Conglomerate Mergers and Section 7 of the Clayton Act," *Harvard Law Review*, May, 1965, *78*, 1313–95.

156. ———, and O. E. Williamson, "Market Structure in Relation to Technical and Organizational Innovation," forthcoming.

157. Veblen, Thorstein, *The Engineers and the Price System*, 1921 (reprinted by A. M. Kelley, New York, 1965).

158. Vickers, G., *Towards a Sociology of Management*, New York: Basic Books, 1967.

159. Williamson, John, "Profit, Growth and Sales Maximization," *Economica*, February, 1966, *33*, 1–16.

160. Williamson, O. E., *The Economics of Discretionary Behavior: Managerial Objectives in a Theory of the Firm*. Chicago: Markham Publishing Co., 1967.

161. ———, "A Dynamic Theory of Interfirm Behavior," *Quarterly Journal of Economics*, November, 1965, *79*, 579–607.

162. ———, "The Economics of Defense Contracting: Incentives and Performance," in *Issues in Defense Economics*. New York: Columbia University Press, 1967, pp. 218–56.

163. ———, "Economies as an Antitrust Defense: The Welfare Tradeoffs," *American Economic Review*, March, 1968, *58*, 18–36.

164. ———, "A Dynamic Stochastic Theory of Managerial Behavior," in *Prices: Issues in Theory, Practice, and Public Policy*, ed. A. Phillips and O. E. Williamson. Philadelphia: University of Pennsylvania Press, 1968, pp. 11–31.

165. ———, "Corporate Control and the Theory of the Firm," in *Economic Policy and the Regulation of Corporate Securities*, ed. H. G. Manne. Washington, D. C.: American Enterprise Institute, 1969, pp. 281–336.

166. ———, "Administrative Controls and Regulatory Behavior," forthcoming.

167. Winter, S., Jr., "Economic 'Natural Selection' and the Theory of the Firm," *Yale Economic Essays*, Spring, 1964, pp. 225–72.

168. ———, "Satisficing, Selection and the Saving Remnant," unpublished paper presented at the Econometric Society Meetings, December, 1968.

169. Woodward, J., *Industrial Organization: Theory and Practice*. London: Oxford University Press, 1965.

170. U. S. Department of Labor, *Salary Structure Characteristics in Large Firms* (1963). Bull. No. 1417. Washington, D. C., August, 1964.

171. U.S. Federal Trade Commission Staff Report, *Economic Report on Corporate Mergers*, Subcommittee on Antitrust and Monopoly, 91st Congress, U.S. Government Printing Office, Washington, D.C., 1969.

index

Actual potential opportunity sets, defined, 50
Adelman, Morris, 78, 142
Agents, willful external control, 173
Alchian, A. A., 64, 96–97, 177
Ansoff, Igor, 142
Amplification, 110
    described, 19
Anheuser-Busch, Inc., 146
Antitrust Division (Justice Department), 102
Arrow, Kenneth, 8, 17
Ashby, W. Ross, 42–44, 133, 171
Ashby model of strategic decision making, 42–46
Auditing, internal control through, 129–30, 132

Bartlett, F. C., 25, 26

Baumol, William, 68, 90, 92, 143, 166
Beer, Stafford, 43, 172
Behavior, see Discretion; Imitative behavior; Short-run behavior; Strictly functional behavior; Syndrome behavior
Berg, Norman, 158
Berle, Adolph A., 4, 138
Bonuses as executive compensation, 153
Boulding, Kenneth, 22
Bounded rationality
    defined, 20
    firm size and, 35
    importance of, 21
    organizational inputs and, 170
Brown, Donaldson, 116
Bundy, McGeorge, 174
Business receipts, percent of, by economic sector (1954, 1965), 6

Capacity-augmenting strategy,
   defined, 25
Capacity problem, strategic decision
   making and, 124–25
Capitalism
   attributes of, 179
   dynamics of, 175–76
Capitalism, Socialism and Democracy
   (Schumpeter), 176
Capital market, 89–104
   competition in, 112, 176–77
      analyzed, 103–4
      control through incentives and,
         91–96
      direct control and, 90–91
      displacement and, 96–103
      M-form structures and, 138–41
      profit maximization and, 8
   See also Control
Chandler, Alfred, Jr., 47, 49, 113,
   115–17, 126, 136
Chrysler Corporation, 117
Clayton Antitrust Act (1914), 102
Coase, Ronald, 15, 17, 23
Cole, Arthur, 176
Communications industries, percent of
   net national income from, 5
Compensated tax change in variable
   proportions model, 61
Compensation
   employment (1954, 1965), 5
      paid by General Motors
         Corporation, 35–37
   executive, 91–95, 151–52
Competition
   attenuation of, 9
   behavior influenced by, 11
   in capital market, 112, 176–77
      analyzed, 103–4
      control through incentives and,
         91–96
      direct control and, 90–91
      displacement and, 96–103
      M-form structures and, 138–41
      profit maximization and, 8
   See also Control
   impaired by conglomerates, 147, 148
Conglomerates, 141–50
   analyzed, 141–42
   control processes of, 143
   as M-form structures, 117–18
   need to limit, 179
   potential economies of, 11–12,
      142–45, 179
   small firms and, 144
   social costs of, 145–50
Control
   agents of, 173
   approaches to, 8–10
   by conglomerates, 143

   dilemma of, 4
   hierarchical, 3; *see also*
      Hierarchical structures
   internal
      external control and, 12–13
      in M-form structures, 128–33;
      see also Multidivision form
      structures
   Law of Diminishing, 26
   organizational inputs and, 170–71
   ownership separated from, 138–39
   span of
      compliance and interaction with,
         33–35
      firm size and, 26, 31–32, 37, 38
      variations in, 32–33
   through capital market, 112
   direct control, 90–91
   by displacement, 96–103
   by incentive, 91–96
Corporate control, *see* Control
Corporations, *see* Hierarchical structures; Modern corporations;
   Multidivision form structures;
   Unitary form structures
Costs
   of displacement, 102–3
   social, of conglomerates, 145–50
   transaction, 15–16
Cross-subsidization for conglomerates,
   146–47

Decision making
   hierarchical, 3
   strategic, 42–47
      basic model, 42–46
      firm growth and, 46–47
      in M-form innovation, 124–27
Decoupling, defined, 25
Defense industries, M-form structures
   and, 163
Discretion, 11, 49–86, 111–12
   dynamic stochastic model of, 75–83
      described, 75–76
      pricing implications of, 84–86
      solution to, 79–83
      syndrome behavior and, 76–79
   empirical testing of, 179–80
   fixed proportions model of, 66–69
   in M-form structures, 163–64
   objectives of, 50–52
   opportunity sets and, 49–50
   organizational inputs and, 174–75
   staff-slack model of, 69–71
   strategic decision making and,
      42–47
      basic model of, 42–46
      firm expansion and, 46–47

Discretion (*cont.*)
  in M-form innovation, 124–27
  subgoal pursuit and, 47–48
  variable proportions model and, 55–66
    applied to public utilities, 64–66
    profits model and, 68–69
Displacement, capital market control through, 96–103
Disraeli, Benjamin, 174
Downs, Anthony, 26
Du Pont de Nemours and Co., E. I. 113, 114
Dynamic stochastic model, 75–83
  described, 75–76
  pricing implications of, 84–86
  solution to, 79–83
  syndrome behavior and, 79–83

Efficiency
  conditions for, 117–78
  internal, 121–24
Elite staff in M-form structures, 125–26
Emery, James, 26
Employment
  compensation for (1954, 1965), 5
  paid by General Motors Corporation, 35–37
  in largest corporations, 7, 30–31
Entrepreneurs, defined, 16
Entrepreneurship, characteristics of, 16
Executive compensation in M-form structures, 151–52
Expansion, *see* Growth
External control, internal control and, 12–13

Federal Trade Commission (FTC), 145–46
Federated structures (free-form structures), 161–62
Firm size
  M-form structures and, 160–61
  of multifunction firms, 21–39
    analysis of, 22–27
    basic model, 22–27
    dynamics of, 37–39
Firms, *see* Multifunction firms
Fixed proportions model, 66–69
Forbes (magazine), 100, 142
Ford Motor Co., 114, 117
Fortune (magazine), 4, 7, 146

Free-form structures (federated structures), 161–62
FTC (Federal Trade Commission), 145–46

Galbraith, J. K., 84–86, 152
Gardner, John, 26
Geneen, Harold, 117–18
General Motors Corporation
  reorganization of, 113, 116
  salary data of (1934–42), 35–37
Goal pursuit
  in M-form structures, 125–27
  subgoal pursuit and, 47–48
Goodrich Co., B. F., attempts to displace, 100–103, 171
Goodyear Tire and Rubber Co., 117
Gordon, R. J., 65, 112, 180
Growth
  hierarchical structures and, 18–21
  in M-form structures, 165–66
  Rayner and Little on, 83–84
  in U-form structures, 110–11
  See also Firm size
Gulf Oil Corporation, 101

Hamberg, Daniel, 157
Hayes, S. L., 100
Heflebower, Richard, 118
Hierarchical structures
  advantages of, 20
  control in, 3; *see also* Control
  limitations of, 21–22
  strategic decision making and, 42–46
Hierarchy, defined, 19–20
Horizontal mergers, 142, 144
Howard, R. A., 79, 82

IBM (International Business Machines Corporation), 117
Ijiri, Yuji, 38
Imitative behavior, types of, 50
Incentives as executive compensation, 151–52
Income effects in variable proportions model, 61
Independents, U-form, 155–57
Information, transmission of
  decoupling and, 25
  firm size and, 25–27
  strategic decision making and, 45

Innovation
  organizational, 109–35
    characteristics of, 115
    internal control and, 128–33
    internal efficiency and, 121–24
    need for, 113–14
    properties of, 120–35, 138, 176
    spread of, 116–18, 151
    strategic decision making and,
      124–27
    U-form structures and, 127–28
    technical, 157–60
Inputs, see Labor input;
    Organizational inputs
Insecurity, sources of, 51
Insider trading model, capital market
    control and, 93–96
Interdependence, conglomerate, 147
Internal control
  external control and, 12–13
  in M-form structures, 128–33
International Business Machines
    Corporation (IBM), 117
International Harvester Co., 117
International Telephone and
    Telegraph Corporation (ITT),
    117

Kaldor, Nicholas, 23, 24
Kaysen, Carl, 9, 75, 83
Kessel, R. A., 64
Knauth, O., 98
Knight, Frank, 15–17, 22–23

Labor, Department of, 28
Labor input, direct and productive,
    27–28
Law of Diminishing Control, 26
Leibenstein, Harvey, 78, 178
Leisure, on-the-job, 52
Little, I. M. D., 74, 83–84, 91
Loew's Theatres, 100

Managerial discretion, see Discretion
Manne, Henry, 92–95, 97, 99, 145
Manufacturing industries, percent of
    net national income from, 5
  percent of sales, employment and
    assets in (1954, 1965), 7
Market, permissive, defined, 8–9; see
    also Capital market; Product
    market
Markov process, 76
Marris, Robin, 165

Marschak, Jacob, 123
Mason, Edward S., 4
Mathieson, Olin, 162
Maximal potential opportunity sets,
    defined, 49–50
Means, Gardiner, 4, 139
Mergers, displacement through, 98–99;
    see also Conglomerates
M-form innovation, see Innovation
M-form structures, see Multidivision
    form structures
Miller, A. S., 4, 5
Mining industries
  percent of net national income from,
    5
  percent of sales, employment and
    assets (1954, 1965), 7
Models, 12
  dynamic stochastic, 75–83
    described, 75–76
    pricing implications of, 84–86
    solution to, 79–83
    syndrome behavior and, 76–79
  fixed proportions, 66–69
  insider trading, 93–96
  Markov process, 76
  of multifunction firms 27–35
  profits, 68–69
  staff-slack, 69–71
  of strategic decision making,
    42–46
  variable proportions, 55–66
    application to public utilities,
      64–66
    described, 55–64
  wage, 35–37
Modern corporations, 3–13
  attributes of, 169
  problems of, 168
Monopoly, see Conglomerates; Mergers
Motor Freight Corporation, 101
Multidivision form structures
    (M-form structures), 133–67
  capital market competition and,
    138–41
  as challenge to Europe, 150–51
  conglomerates and, 141–50
    control processes of, 143
    as M-form structures, 117–18
    need to limit, 179
    potential economies of, 11–12
    small firms and, 144
    social costs of, 145–50
  discretion in, 163–64; see also
    Discretion
  executive compensation in, 151–52
  exempted industries and, 162–63
  free-form structures and, 161–62
  objective function of, 165–66

Multidivision form structures (*cont.*)
  principal operating parts of, 10
  product market competition and, 137–38
  technical development and, 157–60
  U-form independents and, 155–57
  See also Innovation; Unitary form structures
Multifunction firms, 15–39
  growth of
    hierarchical structures and, 18–21
    strategic decision making and, 46–47
  rationale for, 15–18
  size of, 21–35
    analyzed, 22–27
    basic model, 27–35
    dynamics of, 37–39

National Dairy Products, 146
National income, percent of, by economic sector (1954, 1965), 5
Net substitution effect in variable proportions model, 61
Nonfunctional activity, defined, 50
Northwest Industries, 171
  displacement attempts of, 100–103

Operating divisions in M-form structures, 126–27
Opportunity sets
  defined, 9
  discretion and, 49–50
Optimum size firms, 22–24
Organizational control, *see* Control
Organizational inputs, 169–75
  bounded rationality and, 170
  characteristics of, 3
  discretion and, 174–75
  internal compliance processes and, 172–73
  threshold responses in, 171
Ownership, control separated from, 138–39

Pay-off relations, table of, 80
Penrose, Mrs. Edith, 23, 38–39
Performance programs, defined, 43–44
Personnel policies, control through, 131
Peterson, Shorey, 97, 98
Power of conglomerates, 141; *see also* Conglomerates

Pricing, dynamic stochastic model and, 84–86
Product market
  competition in, 4; *see also* Competition
  displacement and, 97
  imperfections in, 32
Productive output, formula of, 32
Productivity losses through wealth concentration, 148, 149
Profit maximization
  capital market competition and, 8
  in public utilities, 64–65
Profits, discretion and, 50–51
Profits model, 68–69
Proxy contests, displacement and, 99, 100
Public as controlling agent, 173
Public utilities
  M-form structure and, 163
  percent of net national income from, 5
  percent of operating revenues (1965), 7
  variable proportions model applied to, 64–66

Rationality, bounded
  defined, 20
  firm size and, 35
  importance of, 21
Rayner, A. C., 83–84, 91
R & D (Research and Development), allocations for, 159–60
Receipts, percent of business, by economic sector (1954, 1965), 6
Redlich, F., 47, 49
Rees, Albert, 78
Research and Development (R & D), allocations for, 159–60
Resource allocation
  internal control through, 129–30, 132
  for R & D, 159–60
Responses, *see* Static responses
Robinson, E. A. G., 23, 24
Ross, N. S., 23 .

Safeway, 146
Salaries
  paid by General Motors Corporation (1934–42), 35–37
  structures of, in large firms, 28

Schumpeter, J. A., 175
Scitovsky, T., 62
Sears Roebuck and Co., 113
Servan-Schreiber, Jean-Jacques, 150
Sherman, Roger, 96
Short-run behavior, 135
Simon, Herbert, 20, 33, 38, 46, 95–96, 130, 170, 173
Smith, Richard Austin, 162
Social costs of conglomerates, 145–50
Social domination, defined, 5
Socio-political problems posed by conglomerates, 148, 149
Staff
  elite, 125–26
  expansion of, 51
Staff-slack model with fixed and variable proportions, 69–71
Standard Oil of New Jersey, 113
Starbuck, W. H., 23, 34
Static responses
  comparative, 34
  for staff model, 59
  for staff-slack models, 71
Step-function intervention, as means of internal control, 130–31
Stock options
  control through, 92–93
  as executive compensation, 152
Stockholders
  as controlling agents, 173
  displacement and, 98
Strategic decision making, 42–47
  basic model of, 42–46
  firm growth and, 46–47
  in M-form innovation, 124–27
Strategy, capacity-augmenting, 25
Strategy and Structure (Chandler), 113
Strictly functional behavior, defined, 50
Structures, see Hierarchical structures; Multidivision form structures; Unitary form structures
Subsidization, conglomerates and cross, 146–47
Syndrome behavior
  analyzed, 76–79
  defined, 75
  firm growth, 83–84

Taussig, R. A., 100
Theory of Economic Development (Schumpeter), 176
Threshold responses in organizational inputs, 171
Transaction costs, multifunction firms and, 15–16
Transition probabilities, table of, 80
Transportation industries
  percent of net national income from, 5
  percent of operating revenues in (1965), 7
Tullock, Gordon, 26
Turner, Donald, 142

U-form structures, see Unitary form structures
Ultrastable system, components of, 128
Uncertainty
  multifunction firms and, 16–17
  solutions to, 18
Unitary form structures (U-form structures)
  difficulties experienced by, 114–15
  growth of, 110–11
  internal control in, 130–33
  M-form innovation and, 127–28
  principal operating parts of, 10
  See also Multifunction firms

Variable proportions model, 55–66
  applied to public utilities, 64–66
  described, 55–64
Vertical mergers, 142
Vickers, G., 50, 174

Wage model, 35–37
Wealth, conglomerates and concentration of, 147–58
Weston, Fred, 142
Willful external control agents, defined, 173